"MOONIES" IN AMERICA

Volume 92, Sage Library of Social Research

Sage Library of Social Research

"Moonies" in America
Cult, Church, and Crusade

David G. Bromley and Anson D. Shupe, Jr.

Foreword by John Lofland

Volume 92
SAGE LIBRARY OF
SOCIAL RESEARCH

 SAGE PUBLICATIONS   Beverly Hills   London

For information address:

SAGE PUBLICATIONS, INC.
275 South Beverly Drive
Beverly Hills, California 90212

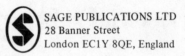

SAGE PUBLICATIONS LTD
28 Banner Street
London EC1Y 8QE, England

Printed in the United States of America

Library of Congress Cataloging in Publication Data
Bromley, David G
   "Moonies" in America: Cult, Church, and Crusade
   (Sage library of social research ; v. 92)
   Includes bibliographical references and index.
   1. Segye Kidokkyo T'ongil Sillyŏng Hyŏphoe.
2. Moon, Sun Myung. 3. Holy Spirit Association for the
Unification of World Christianity. I. Shupe, Anson D.,
joint author. II. Title.
BX9750.S4B76   301.5'8   79-16456
ISBN 0-8039-1060-6
ISBN 0-8039-1061-4 pbk.

FIRST PRINTING

CONTENTS

"If you regard our movement as just another denomination, you will be making a great mistake. This is not a denominational movement, this is not a sect, it is not just one religion."
The Master Speaks, 1965

"He who loves father or mother more than me is not worthy of me, and he who does not take up his cross and follow me is not worthy of me."
Matthew 10:37-38 (Rev. Standard Version)

PREFACE

The present monograph is the first of two volumes in the SAGE Library of Social Research series dealing with one of the major religious controversies of the twentieth century: the rapid proliferation of "cults" in the 1970s, and the subsequent reaction to these, commonly known as the "deprogramming" or anticult movement. Despite the drawbacks of attempting to place in a larger context events so recently transpired, the authors feel some imperative to shed whatever sociological light possible on this conflict since it continues up till the present time and promises to extend beyond the decade. As of the late 1970s, courts still consider such issues as the "free will" of religious "cult" members (many of them legal adults), legislatures still debate the merits of passing bills to distinguish "legitimate" from "illegitimate" religions, and occasionally young adults are still abducted and coercively detained by their exasperated parents until the former recant their new faiths.

In this brief volume we hope to accomplish two purposes. First, we seek to explain the organizational structure, development, and societal response to one particular movement within this proliferation of cults, i.e., the Unificationist Movement of Reverend Sun Myung Moon, in the sociohistorical contexts in which it emerged. As we shall show, the organizational features of the Unificationist Movement were primarily determined by two interacting sets of factors: (1) the internal process of mobilization to achieve the movement's goals, and (2) the societal reaction to the external consequences of that internal mobilization. Second, as in most prolonged, emotionally charged controversies, there was a discernable tendency in this social conflict for each side to create mythologies about the other and then use these myths to legitimate its own partisan activities. Thus, our second purpose in this volume was both to analyze the process of the social construction of motives by each side and to demythologize Moon's Unificationist Movement as well as its anticult movement opponents. As individuals and as citizens we also hope to translate the seemingly frightening or mysterious into more patterned, understandable terms.

A large number of persons assisted us in indispensable ways during the first two years of this project. First, we would like to express our appreciation to John Lofland who first encouraged us to undertake this project and who patiently reviewed earlier drafts of this volume. John McCarthy, Robert Balch, Frank Weed, Bruce Busching, David Taylor, Warren Lewis, Lonnie Kliever, and Joe Barnhart also provided constructive criticisms of our ideas. Thanks are also due to several (anonymous) members of the Unificationist Movement who kindly reviewed the theological portions of the manuscript for its internal consistency as well as consulted with us on our presentation of historical events.

While the bulk of our research went unsupported by any research grant, we are indebted to Eugene Ramsey, chairman of Sociology at the University of Texas, Arlington, and Dean Robert Perkins of UTA's Graduate School, for helping underwrite our more far-flung travels across the country. Without such support it is doubtful that certain types of data could ever have been gathered.

Donna Oliver and Cheryl Davis performed a number of often tedious but instructive surveys of popular and professional literatures. Beverly Wiest and Diana Nelson deserve great credit for their patience in helping us produce manuscripts on often sporadic and "crisis" schedules.

A multitude of respondents, informants, and others, both in Unificationist Movement and in the anticult movement, provided us with the data for our analysis. We have declined to name most either at their own request or out of genuine concern that they not be blamed or embarrassed by what may be unpopular or controversial interpretations, hence the persons whom we interviewed, observed, and learned from remain anonymous. In this conflict there has been a tendency for each side to impugn the motives and integrity of the other. We do not share this view of either side, and in fact as the project proceeded we developed relations of respect and even friendship within both camps. The fact that both the "Moonies" and the anticultists so freely and openly provided us with the ammunition to take our respective critical "shots" is testimony, we believe, to the sincerity of each.

Finally, our families, too, deserve mention for their patience and forbearance during our virtual exile from normal domestic patterns to finish the writing.

David G. Bromley
Anson D. Shupe, Jr.

Arlington, Texas

FOREWORD

BY JOHN LOFLAND

David Bromley and Anson Shupe's excellent study of the Unification Church is a work of professional social science. That fact ought to alert lay readers. Even though the book is the single most comprehensive, in-depth and objective source of facts on Sun Myung Moon and his movement, being such a source is not its main or final goal. That achievement merely provides the platform upon which to pursue the yet more arduous goal of advancing social analysis; more specifically, of advancing our understanding of social movements per se, using the particular data provided by the Unification Church as a vehicle for that quest.

The authors quite correctly devote themselves directly to the achievement of that goal and therefore leave aside or mute several aspects of the larger and more diffuse scholarly milieu in which they work and to which they are oriented. I think, though, that readers' appreciation of this study (and its subsequent companion, *The New Vigilantes*) will be enhanced by brief treatments of some of the more salient milieu aspects. In overview these are: one, an explanation of the phenomenon of the omnibus social movement monograph and how Bromley and Shupe have transcended it; two, a report on the current fashion in resource mobilization thinking among social movement scholars and how these authors creatively use it; three, a reflection of how such thinking has emerged from past social movement theory; four, a thought on the limits of the resource mobilization perspective; and five, an expression of appreciation for the unusual difficulties encountered by scholars of social movements.

(1) Book-length studies of social movements are typically written to a standard—I am tempted to say, stereotyped—format. A near-litany of movement features is commonly rehearsed, a litany that goes something like this: ideology, leadership, recruitment, conversion, commitment,

11

organization, hierarchy, social conditions of founding and growth, strategies of goal attainment, social reaction. The particular elements listed may vary somewhat as does the depth with which any one might be treated, but in the aggregate, a distinct genre of the *omnibus social movement monograph* is easily identifiable.

Many dozen of such social scientifically attuned books have appeared over the last three or so decades and the accumulating mass of them is beginning to stimulate a restiveness among their scholarly consumers. For, in reading, let us say, the one hundred thirtieth chapter on leadership, or whatever, at least a portion of the previous 129 are brought to mind and the chapter at hand is judged against it. Given that the accumulated mass of chapters teaches a great deal, the standard for judging each new one continues to rise. In order to say something new and interesting, any particular aspect of a given movement must be set in an informed and comparative context of what is already known about that aspect. That is an arduous task, the competent execution of which can itself require almost an entire book. But to write a near-book on every item in the litany of the omnibus monograph is to write a book that is vastly too long.

One obvious accommodation to this emerging impossibility is to construct more specialized monographs, to treat perhaps only one aspect or two or, at most, three, and to do so in a way that fully takes account of what is known, incorporates it and transcends it. Such, indeed, is one salient and recent trend among reports on social movements. For better or worse, that trend will likely become a dominant one in the future.

But the passing of the omnibus social movement monograph is a sad event. It has the vice mentioned but the virtue of being "holistic" and "rounded" in the picture it provides. Might there be some rehabilitated form in which the omnibus monograph can usefully survive? Yes, I think there is at least one form and a rationale for its productivity—a principle that allows treating the litany of movement aspects albeit in selective and disciplined fashion.

The principle is *selectivity* to treat each of the litany items in terms of a unifying and overarching theoretical concern. One among several fruitful unifying concerns is that of resource mobilization and it is, specifically, the one employed by David Bromley and Anson Shupe, Jr. in their outstanding study of the Unification Church. Their study is, indeed, among the first of a new generation of social movement monographs, a more sophisticated genre of studies, that treats the diverse aspects of a specific movement in terms of an abiding theoretical orientation. In sewing the litany together with a "conceptual thread," as it were, they exemplify and thereby help to establish a new and higher standard for judging the achievement of social movement monographs. The *selective* omnibus monograph they have produced, and the specialized monograph just mentioned, provide, likely, two of the main models of the future.

(2) The specific conceptual thread Bromley and Shupe employ, resource mobilization, has become almost disgustingly fashionable in the past few years, but it is nonetheless exquisitely appropriate to the specific movement materials at hand. Reacting against assorted deprivationalist explanations of the rise of social movements, mobilizationist thinkers have focused their attention, instead, on "how movements are done." Starting from the proposition that levels of objective or subjective deprivation in a population seem to have little or no relation to the level of social movement activity in that population, analysts look to organizational efforts and associated resource manipulations. Put baldly, the shift is from hearts and minds to money and labor.

Inspired but not captured by mobilizationist thought, Bromley and Shupe have taken a broader than usual view of what "resources" are and of the meaning of "mobilization" and have asked how a wide range of matters are acted toward for the purposes of a movement. That broadened view brings them back to something like the litany of movement aspects but it is a return with a directed rather than a mere inventory aim. The resulting analysis is the largest-scale effort thus far actually to apply the resource mobilization perspective in detail to a specific movement.

(3) I will not resist the "I told you so" temptation and will point out that even though resource mobilization is currently fashionable, its spirit and logic have long been known in the field, the historical amnesia of many scholars notwithstanding. While not labeled such or elevated to current levels of articulation and clarity, one school of social movement scholars has advocated and practiced it for several decades. Indeed, its rapid acceptance on the current scene is doubtless facilitated by the long-standing acceptance of very similar notions. I refer to the views of the prominent symbolic interactionist and collective behavior theorist, Herbert Blumer, and to the research of his numerous students. In a variety of publications over several decades, he and his associates have hammered away at resource mobilization imagery. For example, in a 1957 survey of movement studies appearing in Joseph Gittler's *Review of Sociology*, Blumer set an agenda that still serves well today:

[Most treatments of movements ignore] . . . what seems to be so essential . . . , namely, the intricate play of factors which must be skillfully employed to forge and direct a movement. . . . [A] *movement has to be constructed* and has to carve out a career in what is practically always an opposed, resistant, or at least indifferent world. . . . Movements have to depend on effective agitation, the skillful fomentation and exploitation of restlessness and discontent, an effective procedure for the recruitment of members and followers, the formation of a well-knit and powerful organization, the development and maintenance of enthusiasm, conviction and morale, the intelligent translation of ideology into homely and gripping form, the development of skillful strategy and tactics, and, finally, leadership which can size up situations effectively, time actions and act decisively. These are the ingredients of successful movements. To ignore them through preoccupation with the "causes" of movements leads to inadequate and distorted knowledge.

(4) The current enthusiasm for resource mobilization is surely appropriate but it, like all frameworks, is limited. Movements are only in part brought into focus through the lens it provides. It achieves "high resolution" of such matters as financing and organization but it does so by pushing other and equally important matters into the blurred background and beyond its "depth of field." It blurs, of course, the "hearts and minds" aspects that have not gone away simply because they have gone out of focus. The point can be seen clearly in Bromley and Shupe's documentation of the changed "climate" of American life from the sixties to the seventies. The Unification Church made large changes in its strategies of resource mobilization, but they made those changes at the same time that a significant portion of American youth were becoming more receptive to religious definitions of their situation. The spurting growth of the Unification Church was concurrent with the spurting growth of hundreds of new religions in the early seventies. The "climate" began again to shift in the late seventies, forcing membership stabilization or even decline among new religions, despite concerted efforts to compensate. Resource mobilization alone cannot account for such shifts.

There is, rather, something vaguer, broader and "deeper" at work— something more "collective behavior" than social movements, as sociologists are wont to speak of it. In the terms used by MIT sociologist, Gary Marx, in speaking of covert and ineffective federal efforts to disorganize protest movements of the sixties, there can be an "emotional energy" abroad in a population that can be harassed but not easily created, controlled, extinguished, or sustained. The crowds, momentum and turmoil of the Iranian revolution of 1979 provide, perhaps, a more recent and vivid illustration of such "emotional energy."

(5) I would like, finally, to call attention to a social relations aspect of the *serious* study of social movements in vivo that is not sufficiently

appreciated. Such study is much harder work than ordinary campus or institute-based scholarship and ordinary field work in natural settings. It is harder because, among other reasons, it is carried on under trying emotional circumstances. Social movements are, by definition, controversial and provoke strong feelings of love, hate, and fear among the variously involved. Social movements and their inevitable enemies form arenas of highly polarized and contending emotions and beliefs. Now comes the poor social scientific soul who wants "merely" to understand rather than to judge and join up. Such a figure finds himself or herself an object of proselytization, distrust, suspicion, and efforts to compromise. Cognitive polarization produces an outpouring of "atrocity tales" on all sides, as Bromley and Shupe amply document in this book and in their companion volume on the anticult movement, *The New Vigilantes.* Getting even the basic facts right, much less achieving sociological analysis, is for these reasons much more difficult in movement situations than in the less emotionally aroused scenes of more ordinary life. One tempting and oft used device for reducing the emotional and cognitive buffeting encountered is to join up with one or another side, thereby reducing the stress by at least half—even if at the cost of much information and balance.

We must count Bromley and Shupe heroes of empathy and data collection—perhaps also of masochism. For, despite the pain, they did not resort to a simplifying withdrawal to only one part of the social field involving the Unification Church. They persisted in learning as many "sides" as possible and have come out with the virtually unique distinction of studying both a movement and its prime enemies at the same time!

Even though very difficult, the gain seems clearly to have been worth the emotional and other cost. The pictures they provide of the Unification Church and the anticult movement are more probing, tempered, balanced, complicated, and, yes, more *true,* than if they had elected the greater safety of one side. Ironically, in taking seriously what each side had negative to say about the other, a necessary part of their task, it is likely that neither side will be especially pleased with their reports. Circumstances of polarization and conflict are not circumstances of "balanced" and "tempered" pictures but of pictures that are *useful in winning;* pictures that is, that are self-servingly selective. It is the rest of us—the less embroiled—who must act as the sympathetic and supportive audience for scholars such as Bromley and Shupe, scholars who undertake the hazardous mission of neutrality and objectivity in the vortex of warring doctrines. Their rewards are less than certain. But if we, the less immediately involved, are to act toward social movements in an informed and intelligent manner, then it is surely imperative that we have dispassionate accounts such as theirs and that we therefore support those who construct them. For that service and for being heroes of endurance and empathy, as well as pioneering social movement theorists, David Bromley and Anson Shupe, Jr. have earned our gratitude and thanks.

—J. L.

Davis, California

INTRODUCTION

This monograph deals with one of the most widely publicized religious groups in America during the past two or three decades, and one that has become the focal point of possibly *the* major religious controversy of this century: the Unification Church of America, founded by Korean evangelist Sun Myung Moon. This national Church was incorporated as a branch of the Unification Church International, and the latter in turn was one component of a larger international complex of various affiliated organizations. Of those Americans who were aware of the Unification Church many perceived the "Moonies" as either a cult, complete with charismatic leader and communal lifestyle, or a crusade of idealistic young people. Indeed, as we shall see, the broader network of groups including the Unification Church, which we shall refer to as the Unificationist Movement (hereafter the UM), has some elements of *cult, church,* and *crusade.*

At the same time, despite its variegated qualities as a group, the UM very closely fits sociological conceptions of a social movement, i.e., as "a conscious, collective organized attempt to bring about large-scale change in the social order by non-institutionalized means" (Wilson, 1973: 8). In this book we examine the UM through a relatively new approach in the sociology of social movements, the resource mobilization perspective. The strength of this perspective is its emphasis on the organizational (as opposed to the social psychological) aspects of social movements, and it is as a complex of interrelated organizations that we will analyze the American UM.

Contrasting Perspectives on Social Movements

MOTIVATIONAL MODEL

Sociologists traditionally have relied on what has variously been referred to as the "hearts and minds" approach, the motivational model or the predispositional approach in explaining the emergence and continuation of social movements. The dominant emphasis of this perspective is on the psychological states of those who are attracted to and participate in social movements, although macrosocial factors (e.g., rapid social change, structural discontinuities, culture conflict) often are considered as the cause of individuals' discontents. As Zygmunt (1972: 451) noted, the emphasis of the motivational approach is overwhelmingly on recruitment to social movements, in particular on the establishing of "psycho-functional connections between the properties of social movements (usually construed as 'appeals'), on the one hand, and the social-psychological characteristics of potential or actual recruits (generally construed as motivational predispositions), on the other." In essence the motivational model assumes a three-stage sequence in social movement affiliation: (1) predisposing conditions, such as needs and motives, of the individuals (sometimes supplemented with discussion of societal conditions), (2) an exposure to the new beliefs which appeal to those predisposing needs or motives (occasionally supplemented with discussion of that exposure's interaction context), and (3) resulting behavior as a committed member of the group.

The motivational perspective posits a "why" question: Why do individuals join social movements? The implication is that movements arise and persist because they provide coping mechanisms for individuals. Two unfortunate tendencies follow from this line of reasoning. One is that there has been a tendency to slide into a social pathology perspective and become preoccupied with "psychological analyses of maladjustments, pathologies, emotional inadequacies, or specific personality attributes which predispose an individual to seek collective solutions to private problems (Hine, 1974: 646)." Existing research generally has not provided support for this approach (Zygmunt, 1972; Hine, 1974; Bromley and Shupe, 1979). The other is that there has been a relative lack of concern with examining social movements from an organizational perspective.

Because it is taken for granted that social movement organizations merely constitute structures through which discontents can be reflected and expressed, a variety of assumptions are made about the functioning of social movements that have led to ignoring or distorting their organizational dynamics. First, it is assumed that individuals' motivations remain constant throughout their careers in social movements thus ignoring the possibility that, once recruited, an individual is socialized to meet the requisites of the social movement organization. Individuals' alienation or discontent may be created or intensified by, rather than being the product of, participation in the movement. Second, if individual discontents in themselves account for the emergence and continued existence of social movements, it becomes almost imperative to assume high levels of alienation, discontent, or tensions. It is at this point that it becomes relatively easy to gravitate toward a pathology orientation. There is correspondingly a downplaying of environmental conditions (e.g., segregation of populations) that facilitate or deter social movement formation, the effectiveness of social movement organizations in mobilizing whatever discontents do exist (which now becomes an empirical question), and the extent to which these organizations pursue their own organizational needs to ensure survival as opposed to those of their membership. Third, social movements are formed to produce social change and yet there is little emphasis on *how* this is accomplished *organizationally* when a motivational model is adopted. Fourth, the interaction between the movement and the larger society is deemphasized. Social movements not only mobilize resources internally, they also draw upon resources of the larger society and appropriate them for their own purposes. This use of the environment frequently produces a societal reaction to the movement which may significantly influence a movement's tactics, organization, or even its persistence in organized form. While this list of deficiencies of the motivational model could be extended, it is not our purpose to provide a detailed critique of that model because that has been done elsewhere (see Bromley and Shupe, 1979; Hine, 1974; Segger and Kuntz, 1972; Zygmunt, 1972; Neal, 1968). Rather, we simply wish to demonstrate the absence of an organizational perspective in the motivational model and to suggest that from a sociological standpoint it does not stimulate us to ask and answer numerous important questions.

RESOURCE MOBILIZATION PERSPECTIVE

The resource mobilization perspective offers a welcome corrective to traditional theorizing about social movements precisely because it facilitates an organizational analysis of social movements (see Zald and Berger, 1978; McCarthy and Zald, 1977, 1974, 1973; Gamson, 1975; Zald and Ash, 1973). Not assuming high levels of discontent allows discontent to become a variable, and the question of the link between individuals and social movements remains open. Analysis then turns to the balance of costs and rewards of participation for the individual member and the potential influence of participation on whatever discontents existed initially (i.e., were these amplified or reduced).

At an organizational level a variety of new questions can be posed. It becomes important, for example, to examine how various kinds of social movements aggregate resources relevant to the pursuit of their goals. This emphasis leads to a concern with how movements organize internally (to most effectively manage resources) and externally (to assemble resources from the larger society). For example, if high levels of discontent are not necessarily the basis of resource mobilization, then what is the process whereby vital resources are mobilized? It may be that certain forms of social movement organizations do not require large numbers of discontented individuals if other vital resources (e.g., money, visibility) can be generated without them. Potential sources of ideological or financial support which do not involve movement members then need to be explored. There are very different organizational implications if a movement mobilizes members, financial supporters, and ideological supporters separately (and each group relates differently to presumed beneficiaries) than when it is assumed that discontented members are the sole or primary resource base. Of course the question of the extent to which movement organization actions and policies follow vested interests of elites, organizational interests per se or interests of presumed beneficiaries also becomes salient in an organizational perspective.

The resource mobilization perspective also more fully incorporates a concern with the interaction between a social movement and the larger society. Rather than focusing exclusively on the movement's attempt to foster social change, the resource mobilization approach allows for the possibility that a variety of audiences, in addition to formal authorities, may have to be influenced in some fashion (e.g., neutralized, transformed into supporters) in order for the movement to continue to work toward its goals. Mobilization becomes very much an interactive process in which the societal response to movement activities and policies modifies future exchanges. Because many social movements create little visible, lasting change this concern with the interaction between movement and society is particularly important, for it lends perspective to organizational dynamics whether or not there is change.

Despite the numerous advantages of the resource mobilization approach in analyzing social movement organizations, there are some unresolved conceptual problems. Many of the basic terms such as "resource," "mobilization," and "success" lack clear definitions. For example, no encompassing definition or list of resources has been formulated, in part because any tangible or intangible asset which is scarce (i.e., there is competition for it) and which can serve as a basis for social exchange can constitute a resource. Some clarification of this concept can be achieved by determining what types of resources are mobilized by different types of social movements. In this sense the problem is not what could a priori be a resource but what types of resources empirically are vital to social movements with various goals and strategies. The concept mobilization is also vague. McCarthy and Zald (1977) define it as "gaining control" over resources. It is not clear, however, whether control is measured relative to the movement's goals, the total amount of the resource available, or the amount of resistance to be overcome. What would constitute "full mobilization?" At this point in the development of the perspective it would seem to emphasize the process by which resources are mobilized, that is, "gaining," rather than "control."

Related problems are evident with respect to the concept "success." A social movement may consist of a number of social movement organizations which may be variably "successful" (however that is defined). How is overall success to be measured? What is to be taken as the criterion by which success is measured—survival of the movement, generating widespread support relative to the size of the target group, or achievement of the movement's stated goals? If a movement, faced with resistance, scales down its aspirations, is the original or replacement goal the basis of determining success? If we assume that individuals use social movements for their own purposes as well as serving as movement adherents, to what extent can achievement of individual goals be incorporated into the concept of success? Is success an appropriate indicator of change if movements produce change other than that designated as a goal? Is greater insight gained by examining total change or success? What temporal limits should be set in evaluating the success of a movement? What is the meaning of achieving objectives after they have lost significance either to the movement or the society?

In light of these conceptual problems we would argue that it is important to examine the mobilization process for specific *types* of social movements. Success (according to whatever definition used) can be more accurately compared for movements having relatively similar goals, strategies and resource needs. Correspondingly, if the resources needed and utilized by various types of movements can be established empirically, a working definition of resources can be more readily formulated. We would conclude, then, that the various levels at which mobilization can occur— survival, continuance, and success—be distinguished and that comparisons be conducted for specific types of movements.

There have already been some attempts to explore the mobilization process for similar movements. Indeed, Oberschall (1973: 119) has argued for the limitation of the theory to particular types of groups. He stated:

It is assumed that a collectivity ... with common latent interests already exists and that members of the collectivity are dissatisfied and have grievances. . . . We also assume a collectivity that is at least fairly large and geographically concentrated so that communication between members exists or can be established. The theory is concerned with substantial opposition movements and other forms of collective behavior such as riots and rebellion and not with a sociology of sects, small deviant subcultures and similar phenomena.

If this limitation is intended to facilitate comparisons of similar types of movements, then we would agree with its logic. However, there is no a priori reason to assume that mobilization theory cannot be applied equally productively to other types of movements. In fact, we would argue it is precisely by examining the mobilization for the widest possible array of social movements that concepts can be clarified and meaningful generalizations formulated. In this book we shall attempt to apply resource mobilization theory to a relatively small social movement treated as a specific organizational type.

World-transforming Social Movements

TYPOLOGIES OF SOCIAL MOVEMENTS

In this book we shall analyze the UM as an illustrative case of what we refer to as a *world-transforming movement,* i.e., one which seeks total, permanent, structural change of societies across all institutions. The social movements literature offers several typologies that consider important dimensions relevant to such a movement. In particular those of Smelser (1962), Aberle (1966), Wallis (1978), and Robbins et al. (1978) converge in certain critical respects and identify important elements of social movement organization which, we shall argue, are extremely salient to the ways in which social movements mobilize resources. In reviewing these typologies, however, we emphasize that our interest lies not in defending or critiquing them but rather in highlighting certain common elements most useful in our analysis.

Smelser's major distinction among movements relevant to this discussion concerns whether they are *norm oriented* or *value oriented.* The basis of classification is the *extent* or *amount* of change to which a given movement aspires: *norm-oriented* movements aim at modification of specific rules whereas *value-oriented* movements seek more fundamental change aimed at radical transformation of basic values. Aberle's typology not only includes this dimension of *extent* or *amount* of change (using the dichotomy *partial* and *total*) but also distinguishes the level at which the *amount of change* is pitched, i.e., at either the *individual* or *social struc-*

tural levels. The two dimensions interact, yielding four possible change combinations:

> *Transformative* —aimed at total change in the social structure
> *Reformative* —aimed at partial change in the social structure
> *Redemptive* —aimed at total change in the individual
> *Alternative* —aimed at partial change in the individual

Two more recent typologies formulated with the 1970s proliferation of religious movements in mind isolate somewhat similar dimensions. Wallis classifies movements according to a *world-rejecting/world-affirming* dichotomy that implicitly but incompletely combines the *extent* and *level* dimensions of Aberle's typology. *World-rejecting* movements are similar to Smelser's *value-oriented* and Aberle's *transformative* types: they condemn the society as a whole, its institutional components, and its underlying values. Wallis' scheme does not provide for *partial* change aimed at the social structure (Aberle's *reformative* type). Likewise, *world-affirming* movements "claim to possess the means to enable people to unlock their physical, mental, and spiritual potential, without the need to withdraw from the world" (Wallis, 1978: 7-8) and view the social order "less contemptuously." Change is thus aimed at individuals and is *partial* (comparable in *level* of change to Aberle's *alternative,* and to some extent, Smelser's *norm-oriented* type). Wallis does not provide for *total* individual (Aberle's *redemptive*) change.

Robbins et al. ground their typology in the concept of value dissensus, interpreting separate religious movements as different responses to normative breakdown in society. They distinguish two basic types of movements, *dualistic* and *monistic. Dualistic* movements are responses to perceptions of profound moral breakdown in society, emphasizing traditional moral absolutism (albeit with novel sectarian twists) in "an exaggerated and strident manner" that puts them at odds with dominant "corrupt" social institutions. Conversely, *monistic* movements reaffirm relativistic and subjectivistic meaning systems. Although this typology does not divide as neatly along the two dimensions under discussion, the *dualistic* type seems to include movements oriented toward total structural change while the *monistic* type apparently refers to movements organized to produce *partial,* individual change.

Throughout this book we shall argue that *amount* and *level* of change sought by social movements significantly influence the resource mobilization process. The extent of change a movement seeks affects the range, amount, and mix of resources required to achieve movement goals. A

movement which calls for basic sweeping change must develop an elaborate critique of the current state of affairs as well as an alternative vision,
whereas more limited change can be justified in terms of lags, inconsistencies, and the like which do not challenge the basic values or priorities of
society. Sweeping change, by definition, confronts a movement with the
task of creating organizations capable of making contact with and promoting change in a range of institutions or gaining access to large numbers
of individuals and promoting change in their personalities. By contrast,
movements with narrower goals frequently seek to wield influence with
respect to a single institution and need only appeal to their interests.
Finally, movements which promote broad, fundamental change must
create organizations to utilize the total energies of their members while
movements with more limited objectives neither need nor want such a
total commitment.

Movements which seek to restructure institutions are distinguishable
from those whose goals are to transform individuals. In reality this distinction is often blurred by the fact that each type envisions both kinds of
change ultimately occurring. That is, the former type of movement sees
individuals' hearts and minds changing (e.g., becoming harmonious, loving,
healthy) if appropriate conducive structural conditions are created; the
latter type views structural change as the product of individual motivational or character/value changes. In general, then, one type of change is
seen as leading to the other rather than as occurring to the exclusion of the
other. Nevertheless, a concern with transforming social structure leads to
an emphasis on controlling key institutional power bases that determine
organizational goals, priorities, and rewards, while transforming individuals
leads to the creation of organizations designed to disseminate the message,
technique or commodity whereby such transformations can occur.

STRATEGIES FOR RESOURCE MOBILIZATION

While amount and level of change sought are important determinants of
social movement organization, they do not in themselves determine *how*
appropriate resources are mobilized. This latter is a question of strategy. It
concerns the means by which a movement will gain control over resources
vital to it and in that sense the basis of exchange between the movement
and the larger society (i.e., externally) and within the movement itself
(i.e., internally).

In contrast to much of the social movements literature that deals
primarily with the issue of movements mustering support for their goals
(and operationally defining success in terms of such support), Turner's
(1970) analysis of social movements stresses the strategies used by a

movement as it acts in pursuit of its goals. Turner presented a typology of three strategies, based on Etzioni's (1961) types of social control (coercive, utilitarian, normative), each an attempt by a movement to elicit changes in a "target group" that could serve the movement's aims. A *coercive* strategy manipulates the target group so that it pursues the course of action desired by the movement in order to avoid costs or punishments being levied by the movement. A *bargaining* strategy is used when the movement possesses something of exchangeable value that can make compliance rewarding to the target group. A *persuasive* strategy relies on symbolic manipulation—it can offer no substantial rewards or punishments; hence it must identify its future course(s) of action with values and interests already held by its target group. In all three cases the use of any given strategy is determined by both the latter's anticipated effectiveness as well as the strategy's compatibility with the values and the self-image which the movement wishes to project to members as well as publics.

World-transforming movements cannot adopt bargaining as a strategy for several reasons. Most such movements lack resources approaching the scale of change which they seek; assuming vested interests and resistance to change, it is unlikely that the movement could provide sufficient inducements to rely on bargaining as a primary strategy. More importantly, however, the ends which world-transforming movements pursue are collective, moral, and nondivisible, hence bargains cannot be struck because the specific items to be exchanged are difficult to specify and compromise (and partial success through bargaining is viewed as failure by members). World-transforming movements thus usually adopt a strategy of either coercion or persuasion. There is always a preference for voluntary exchange in human relationships (i.e., persuasion over coercion) for several reasons. Persuasion is less costly than coercion; the latter involves the constant expenditure of resources to maintain compliance. Voluntary relationships can be more readily cloaked with the symbols of legitimacy which themselves encourage compliance and the stability of exchanges. And while coercion can be effective in deterring unwanted behaviors, it is relatively ineffective in instituting new desired behaviors.

In addition to the general preference for voluntary exchanges, several other factors influence the choice between persuasion and coercion. First, coercion provokes severe social sanctions because the use of force within a society is closely regulated by the state. While groups utilizing persuasion as a strategy may face symbolic and legal repression, they are more likely to be able to avoid becoming the objects of arbitrary, uncontrolled violence. Second, the kind of links the movement has or desires to maintain with the larger society influences the choice of strategies. To the extent that those who provide support for the movement overlap with the movement's target group, the movement is likely to rely on persuasion; to do otherwise is to erode the source of basic resources such as members, money, and legitimacy. Finally, the movement's ideology imposes restrictions on strategic choices. A movement which defines fundamental human problems as emanating from power disparities or opposed class interests is more likely to rely on coercive means than a movement which sees mankind as having fallen away from ideals of love, humanity, or brotherhood, and that stresses these as requisite to all human relationships.

Research Objectives

In this book we utilize the resources mobilization perspective with its organizational-level emphasis in order to examine the specific type of social movement which we have termed *world-transformative,* i.e., one that aims at *total change* of the *social structure* through employing *persuasion* as its primary strategy. Ours is a *case study* intended to offer readers inductive, organizational statements about how mobilization takes place in such a movement at an *early stage* in its development. Thus, our focus is on early developmental problems rather than on the entire range of crises, dilemmas, and issues in a movement's "natural history."

There are, of course, limitations to such data. Though we will consider developmental issues through longitudinal consideration of the movement at different points in time, these observations are not strictly comparative and this study is in no sense able to generate the propositions and generalizations which might flow from a comparative analysis of a number of such movements. Indeed, this study of the Unificationist Movement is presented as a contribution toward establishing precisely the sort of data base upon which more ambitious comparative statements about world-transforming movements must be based. We would argue, however, that such a case study is of theoretical value, not only as an addition to our knowledge of world-transforming movements but also as an opportunity to utilize the resource mobilization approach in analyzing a category of movements which proponents of that approach have previously eschewed.

At the same time we have attempted to present the narrative detail in such a way that it would be useful to scholars with different theoretical perspectives. Thus, the format of each chapter in this book is to present an historical account of a separate aspect of the movement conceptualized sociologically but allowing the richness of narrative detail to reconstruct events and structures. Literally appended to such descriptions are sets of implications for resource mobilization in light of this case's empirical experiences. In this way presentation of our data per se is structured but not totally determined by our own theoretical concerns. These implications are grounded in our data but we believe they have more general relevance to the mobilization of social movements in general and world-transforming movements in particular.

Characteristics of World-transforming movements

The case study of the mobilization process of a world-transforming movement presented in this book is organized around the basic, perennial structural aspects of any social movement (ideology, leadership, organization, recruitment/socialization) and its relational patterns with the larger society (environmental context, public identity negotiation, normative compliance/social control). In the paragraphs that follow we shall delineate the unique attributes of world-transforming movements with respect to these structural-organizational and relational dimensions of social movements.

MOBILIZING ORGANIZATIONAL RESOURCES

Ideology. Ideology refers to "a set of beliefs about the social world and how it operates, containing statements about the rightness of certain arrangements and what action would be undertaken in light of those statements" (Wilson, 1973: 91-92). *What is unique to the ideology of a world-transforming movement is its forecast of total, imminent, cataclysmic structural change placed in the context of an interpretation of history that demonstrates its necessity and inevitability.* Thus, such an ideology typically locates the source of current social ills in some perennial human dilemma that has as a result of historical forces worked itself out in such a way that current times represent a period of critical but propitious opportunity. the world-transforming movement claims to offer new insight into these heretofore little understood problems and a vision of a world liberated from them. This vision of the (however unclearly formulated) new society incorporates a new set of values and priorities that stand in contrast to the corrupted values of the contemporary order. It also typically defines the movement's role and interests in the transformation process.

Leadership. World-transforming movements characteristically exhibit charismatic leadership. Such leaders have the ability "to exercise diffuse and intense influence over the normative orientations of other actions" (Etzioni, 1961: 203). In the early stage of such a movement's development the founder/leader usually is the dominant repository of charismatic authority. Because charisma is the source of legitimation for the exercise of authority, the leadership structure is pyramidal. The founder/leader and a few close disciples are clearly separate from the mass of movement members who stand in egalitarian relationships to one another. Because members acknowledge this unique authority, this founder/leader potentially and (in actuality) frequently exercises pervasive control over movement activities and even the daily lives of those individual members.

Organization. World-transforming movements typically display both bureaucratic and communal characteristics the combination of which constitutes a persistent source of organizational tension. Bureaucratic characteristics include a strict delineation of power among role occupants, a high degree of role specificity, a focus on the pursuit of certain specific common interests, deliberate purposeful cooperation, and compliance based on utilitarian involvement. By contrast, communal characteristics include egalitarian relationships among role occupants, role diffuseness, an emphasis on belongingness, participation based on common sentiments, and compliance based on moral/normative involvement. Over time there is mounting pressure toward bureaucratization as the size and complexity of the movement increases, yet at the same time there is also pressure to retain the communal style of organization which engenders the high levels of member commitment.

Recruitment/Socialization. World-transforming movements usually *must rely on intensive socialization of new recruits due to low selectivity.* Such movements often lack a clear conception of the type of individual who can be attracted to the movement and have a low recruitment success rate; as a result they are forced to rely on self-selection for new members. *Intensive socialization practices both substitute for selectivity in recruitment and help to foster and sustain a high level of commitment.* This intensive socialization can be conducted most effectively in communal groups where the novitiate can be insulated from the values and demands of conventional society and provided with a diffuse, encompassing role supported by a network of interdependent, affective relationships. In such an environment members rapidly attain a sense of involvement and commitment to the movement.

MANAGING MOVEMENT/SOCIETAL RELATIONS

Environmental Context. World-transforming movements emerge in environments where there is substantial discontent in at least some segment of the population. Environmental conduciveness refers to how readily discontents can be mobilized as well as the level or scope of the discontent itself. The size of a movement, for example, may be significantly affected by the extent to which the movement can recruit through preexisting collectivities (e.g., communities, regions, or social strata) and the personal cost for potential recruits of enlisting in the movement. Further social cooptation or repression may have the effect of limiting the expression of discontents; if existing institutions ignore grievances, the potential for noninstitutionalized adaptation may remain high. By and large these environmental factors are beyond the control of the movement, though it may attempt to capitalize on them or adapt, within limits, to new discontents if the movement is transplanted into a new sociocultural environment.

Public Identity. World-transforming movements, which begin as small anonymous groups with the goal of inaugurating massive structural change through a strategy of persuasion, are critically dependent on creating social visibility and legitimacy virtually simultaneously, if that strategy is to be employed successfully. Social visibility, which refers to collective recognition and some collective evaluation of the movement, is critical because of the massive scale of change that the movement envisions. Legitimacy, which refers to voluntary social support for the movement, is imperative if the movement is to rely on a strategy of persuasion. The dilemma the movement faces lies in trying to promote change in the status quo yet not engender hostility among those who must accommodate or participate in that change.

Normative Compliance/Social Control. A world-transforming movement, by challenging the status quo beliefs and institutional order, engages in ideological and organizational nonconformity. The former type of nonconformity involves innovation on culturally sacred symbols which may be defined as heresy; the latter type may range from simply culturally strange behavior to practices that actually violate legal codes. As a result, those threatened by this deviance may seek to initiate social control measures either through formal legal channels or through *ad hoc* vigilante-style countermovements. *Because world-transforming movements rely so heavily on a persuasion strategy, are subject to vigorous social control efforts, and cannot forcibly resist repression without abandoning their basic strategy, there is enormous pressure toward some measure of accommodation with the larger society.*

Methodology

Data to support the conclusions of this study were gathered over a two-year period by various methodologies and from a wide range of sources. Through a difficult, ongoing process of negotiation we were able to maintain sufficient rapport with leaders and component organizations of the Unificationist Movement and of its opponents, the American anticult movement, to interview many rank-and-file members as well as executives, to obtain documents, and to observe their organizational activities. For reasons of brevity we have omitted many methodological details that can be found elsewhere. For example, the problems of maintaining rapport between two groups in adamant opposition to one another (with the awareness by each of our study) are discussed in Shupe and Bromley (1979) and Bromley and Shupe (1980). In instances where we have previously analyzed specific topics considered in this study the reader is referred to our publications and papers which provide further information on methodology and discussions of findings. Otherwise general descriptions of methods and sources can be found in the prefaces to Parts I, II, and III, in the text, or in appropriate notes.

PART I

THE FOUNDATION OF THE MOVEMENT

PREFACE

The chapters in Part I examine the early history of the Unificationist Movement in Korea and the United States. Little reliable information exists in print on the UM's origin and initial development in Korea. What information does exist consists of the UM's own apologetic reconstruction of its history and a few scattered descriptive studies which interpret their data largely in terms of a deprivational perspective. Thus, any attempt to reconstruct the initial mobilization of the UM in terms of our own theoretical perspective is fraught with innumerable difficulties.

More systematic, sophisticated observation is available for the period immediately following the UM's transplantation to America. We begin Chapter 2 by describing the American cultural environment in which the UM found itself during the early 1960s. This information is intended as a backdrop to our own and sociologist John Lofland's (1966, 1977) accounts of the UM during this period. Lofland conducted participant observation research on one of the UM's early missions to this country in 1962-1963. However, much of his data were interpreted from a social psychological perspective. In our own summary of Lofland's research we have attempted to recast his findings in structural/organizational terms. We have also incorporated additional details on the UM's early American experiences as gleaned from our own interviews with early movement participants and leaders.

These two chapters are provided to lend perspective to the UM's apparently rapid mobilization during the 1970s. In fact the movement had been accruing experience and a variety of resources vital to its course of development in the 1970s for several decades. The initial organizational form in which the movement emerged in the United States and a significant portion of its early activity can best be understood in terms of its Korean cultural origins and subsequent struggles for survival. For this reason, the theoretical and organizational implications of the observations contained in these chapters will be reviewed in the appropriate chapters in Parts II and III.

Chapter 1

THE BIRTH OF THE UNIFICATIONIST MOVEMENT:

KOREA, 1930-1955

In this chapter we trace the early history of the UM from its founding in 1954 to its transplantation to the United States in 1959, and we outline the primary tenets of its ideology for restoration. As we shall see, the sociocultural environment in which the UM emerged, its initial organizational structure, and the subsequent sociopolitical response to the movement all had a direct bearing on its later organization and operation. Nor was the appeal of its ideology unrelated to the sentiments of many persons in post-World War II Korea. During its formative years the movement developed a unique compromise between the free-wheeling style of a charismatically inspired sect and the pressures for bureaucratization as it grew in sheer numbers, transferring this integrated character to the United States. Thus, contrary to many popular impressions that Moon's success in the United States came "overnight," the seeds of his movement's growth can be located in his Asian experiences. The latter in turn served as a prelude to the movement's ensuing mobilization in other parts of the world.

Support for UM Growth in Postwar Korea

Little is known about how the UM mobilized in the sociocultural context of postwar Korea. While there is some rudimentary information on the history of the Korean Church itself and some scholarly description of "new religions" of that era, these treatments provide us only the most meager base for understanding the UM's emergence and development. Further, the interpretation of available information through the "deprivational" model renders later reconstructions from alternative perspectives problematic. While the deprivational model emphasizes the historical context in which the movement emerged, it provides little insight into its organizational development. Thus, the following observations provide only a glimpse of the UM's relationship to that historical era.

The Unification Church began as one among a series of religiously based social movements in post-World War II Korea. Its founder, Sun Myung Moon, was born in 1920 in rural Pyungan Bukedo province of northwestern Korea and grew to young manhood in a family which converted to a Pentecostal brand of Presbyterianism when he was ten years old. At the age of sixteen, on Easter Sunday morning, 1936, Moon claimed to have received a vision in which Jesus Christ announced to him that he, Moon, had been chosen by God to attempt to complete restoration of the physical Kingdom of God on earth. However, Moon did not act publically on his revelation until he began preaching in 1946. In the intervening years between his vision and public ministry we know that he studied electrical engineering in Seoul and, after graduating from high school, continued these studies as a foreign student at Tokyo's prestigious Waseda University. Following the defeat of Japan in the war, Moon returned to Korea and initiated his ministry at Pyongyang. From 1946 until 1955 he alternately prayed, studied, and meditated. Out of these efforts, according to Moon, came his formulation of the spiritual "prime mover" in human history, eventually developed into the movement's scriptural text, *The Divine Principle.*

The beginnings of a number of new religious groups such as Moon's as well as the resurgence of many nationalistic movements coincided with several propitious changes in post-World War II Korean society. Prior to 1945, Korea had been occupied by Japanese military forces, and legally enforced emperor-worship had sharply curtailed diversity of religious expression. Immediately following Japan's surrender, however, religious liberty was restored. The combination of postwar chaos and the removal of these restrictions provided the context for a sudden spurt of religious innovation in terms of doctrines and organizations. During the late 1940s and early-to-mid 1950s, Korean society saw the rapid emergence of a number of groups that featured charismatic founders with messianic or prophetic claims and syncretic blends of Confucian, folk, and Christian traditions. Koreans referred to these as *Shinhung Jonggyo* (Newly Risen Religions) or *Sin Jonggyo* (New Religions), similar to their burgeoning counterparts in postwar Japan, the *Shinkō Shūkyō*, or New Religions (on Japan's 'New Religions,' see McFarland, 1967, and Thomsen, 1963).

That there were other similar movements flourishing at the same time indicates that, like these others, the Unification Church struck a responsive chord at the popular level.[1] The themes of many of these groups stressed a distinctly this-worldly orientation in their doctrines, emphasizing not only the hope of human perfectability and salvation but also of achievable prosperity. Many held millenarian expectations, cast in Biblical terms, and in fact what little Unification Church historiography exists explicitly mentions Moon's contact with several of these groups in his role as fulfiller of Biblical prophecy.[2]

Scholars who have researched the era contended that there existed a real, pervading sense of insecurity experienced by many persons. This widespread climate of uncertainty originated, first, in the country's political bifurcation into communist and noncommunist sectors (and in the ensuing military conflict), and second, in the economic depression following the war that was exacerbated by thousands of unemployed, homeless refugees from the north. The picture which emerges of this poor, preindustrialized country in the chaotic postwar years is one in which absolute deprivation was a daily problem facing many Koreans, and the implication follows that there would be a large pool of potential converts to millenarian movements promising eventual transformation of the world. For example, Moos (1967: 16) utilized this "cargo cult" perspective when he summarized the reasons for the New Religions' popularity:

These new religious cults in Korea have not only helped to fill the psychological vacuum resulting from the end of the Japanese occupation and the subsequent liberation of Korea in 1945 *but also have succeeded in providing a seemingly hopeful and more secure psychoeconomic future to many hitherto economically depressed and hopeless individuals* [Italics Ours].

It seems reasonable to conclude that Moon's ministry and the origins of the UM can be located in this milieu which has been characterized as one of instability, fear, competing ideologies, and rival religions. However, this milieu could not by itself account for the rise and successful expansion of the UM. It is entirely speculative as to what the link was between this characterization of postwar Korean society and the UM's origins. The questions of to whom the movement *did* appeal, how broadly based was *actual* support/interest, and precisely what were the appeals *as perceived* by postwar Koreans cannot be resolved by the existing post factum studies and the relative dearth of empirical studies of early UM members. However, there is somewhat more information available for the UM's theology/ ideology, organization, and reception by conventional Korean society, and it is to these data that we now turn.

Unificationist Ideology

During its earliest years in Korea, the UM possessed important resources that enabled it not only to survive and prosper at home but that also gave it sufficient stability to begin proselytizing abroad. One of the most important of these resources was a complex theology that synthesized Western Christianity and Eastern philosophy. While the elements of Unification theology are tightly interwoven and do not permit easy dissection, we will discuss them according to Killian's (1965: 434-437) four-part scheme as a means of sorting out their salient points. Killian has suggested that the ideology of a social movement can be understood in terms of four analytic parameters: (1) *the problem* to which the movement is oriented and toward which it has been mobilized; (2) *a detailed solution* to restore, amend, or eradicate some part of the problematic condition; (3) *a social philosophy* which legitimates the movement's concerns and goals in terms of larger society's own values; and (4) *a reinterpretation of history,* more or less unconventional, that permits the movement a sense of positive self-evaluation. In employing these parameters we caution that Killian's scheme is used mainly as a heuristic device and not for theoretical purposes.   \

In the paragraphs to follow we summarize Unification theology; in doing so we hasten to offer the caveat that this synopsis by outsiders to the faith provides no more than a cursory outline.

The theology is a complex system of historical parallels with a radical revision of orthodox Western Christology rich in numerology and neo-Confucian elements. Its essential tenets were established by the mid-1950s, although there have been ongoing refinements of it ever since. As we will eventually discover, the belief system constituted both an organizational asset and, paradoxically, an important liability.

THE PROBLEM: GOD'S INTENTIONS VERSUS HUMAN FRAILTY

Unification theology is preoccupied with "the Fall of Man" from an idyllic existence in the Biblical Eden and views history as a series of unsuccessful attempts to restore that original familial relationship between God and humanity.

God, an androgynous being, created mankind[3] and all aspects of reality according to the complementary principle of give and take, or the Universal Prime Force (otherwise familiar as the Taoist Yin/Yang dichotomy). God *gave* the gift of life and creation in order *to receive* the pleasure of seeing the seed of His own nature in mankind. Thus, as stated in *The Divine Principle* (HSA-UWC, 1977: 6): "God created men and the universe as His substantial objects so that He could feel His own original nature through His substantial objects."[4] Mankind was not intended to exist as a cluster of isolated individuals but rather to recapitulate God's basic nature of unity or completeness by joining together in loving relationships of reciprocity. Just as God Himself represents the totality that transcends "positive" and "negative" contradictions, such as possessing both feminine and masculine aspects, so a marriage of man and woman which was "God-centered" would express this completeness.

Adam and Eve might have achieved individual perfection by performing a proper give-and-take process of devotion to God, and in marrying they would have given birth to perfect children, thus realizing a God-centered sinless family. However, the archangel Lucifer became jealous of God's love for Adam and Eve and, turning his attention to Eve, developed an erotic attraction that resulted in her physical seduction. Conscience-stricken, Eve then copulated with Adam in an attempt to erase her sin but in fact only complicated the problem by transferring "the elements of evil and sin" to him. In this way, Satan became the spiritual ancestor of all humanity. This was the Fall of Man.

After a 1,600-year period of indemnity (termed an "age of providential time-identity") to atone for the Fall, the opportunity to once again achieve perfection in mankind and bring about restoration of the Kingdom of God repeated itself. Yet, as *The Divine Principle* chronicles with a succession of Old and New Testament luminaries that includes Noah, Abraham, Moses, King Solomon, and Jesus Christ, the opportunity was repeatedly offered by God and misused by man. In fact, Unification theology maintains that this cycle of opportunity for perfection/transgression/indemnity has reoccurred since the Fall of Eden up to the present time. Why has it been necessary? According to *The Divine Principle* (HSA-UWC, 1977: 9), "The fact that God's providence of salvation has been prolonged for so long is because the central figures in His providence of restoration have repeatedly failed to accomplish their portion of responsibility with which even God cannot interfere."[5]

Jesus Christ was the last of the Biblical figures to attempt complete restoration of man to God. After a laborious "foundation" for the coming of the messiah had been established by the Israelites, God dispatched His only Son to bring about the restoration. Events went awry, however. John the Baptist, appointed by God as "forerunner" to the messiah, failed to trust in Jesus as savior and did not recognize his special status. The Jewish people followed suit, accusing Jesus of blasphemy and "trumping up" criminal accusations that resulted in his premature crucifixion. Had Jesus lived to fulfill his mission, "the purpose of creation would have been accomplished and thereby the kingdom of Heaven on earth established" (HSA-UWC, 1977: 19). Israel would have fulfilled her messianic office to all nations, mankind would have been redeemed, and the wars, suffering, and hate of the past two millennia would not have occurred.

Yet Jesus' mission was not a total failure; he did achieve a "secondary course of salvation," i.e., spiritual salvation, for mankind. However, this partial victory still left human beings' physical bodies at the mercy of satanic invasions through temptation and ignorance.

The Divine Principle conceptualizes a spiritual aspect and a physical aspect of man, the former achieving perfection only through the latter. *Without physical restoration of the Kingdom, therefore, God's providence cannot be fully realized. Such a material achievement is the goal of the Messiah who takes up where Jesus left off.* Thus, in the 1970s the world arrived at the "last days" of the current cycle, when sufficient indemnity had been worked off to permit another magnanimous gesture towards restoration by God. Once again, mankind was to be offered the opportunity to undo the wrongs originally committed by Adam and Eve.

THE SOLUTION: UNITE, LOVE, FOLLOW

The Divine Principle states:

> The reason human history appears as nothing but a constant enact-
> ment of sinful history with the prospect of an ideal world seemingly
> so distant is not because God is impotent or not absolute, but
> because so few men accomplished their portion of responsibility to
> fulfill God's providence [HSA-UWC, 1977: 30].

In practical terms this responsibility of man entails being "born again" (i.e., receiving personal sanctification) through accepting the messiah when he appears on earth and then by performing strict obedience to his directives. In this way, each person can obtain God-intended perfection and contribute to restoring God's Kingdom.

In concrete terms this responsibility means harkening to the revealed doctrine of *The Divine Principle* and obeying God's current messenger,

Sun Myung Moon, through whom it was revealed. One question obsessing the UM's critics and observers concerned whether or not Moon considered himself the "Lord of the Second Advent," the messiah come-again, the person appointed to complete Jesus' mission, the "Third Adam" (to Jesus' role as "Second Adam") in this history of restoration attempts. Moon himself was cryptically evasive when publically asked. For example, in a *Newsweek International* interview (HSA-UWC, 1976) with Moon, the following exchange ensued:

Q: You are obviously saying that you are a prophet, but do you also consider yourself the New Messiah?
A: We are in a new Messianic age. But 2,000 years ago Jesus Christ never spoke of himself as a Messiah, knowing that would not serve his purpose. I am not saying, "I am the Messiah." I am faithfully fulfilling God's instructions.
Q: But you don't rule out the possibility that you are the Messiah?
A: Let God answer you, let God answer the world.

Ex-members of the UM, particularly those disgruntled with it, readily affirmed that Moon's messiahship was a staple of "insider" socialization. While no public statement that Moon was indeed the Lord of the Second Advent was ever issued by the movement, our own in-depth interviews with dozens of members and UM leaders drew mixed responses on this issue. Some seemed to have no doubt that Moon indeed was the new messiah; others expressed their uncertainty openly, preferring to let Moon's own cosmic agenda vindicate or disprove his spiritual status. From still others this question produced quizzical smiles, and they simply enjoined us to study *The Divine Principle* for our answer. Even a cursory study of its scriptures, however, would leave no doubt in the minds of any but the most ingenuous as to Moon's thinly veiled messiahship. In answer to the question, "When Will Christ Come Again?" *The Divine Principle,* after an elaborate juxtaposing of pre- and post-Christian historical parallels and numerological deductions, concluded that the birth of the messiah occurred approximately in the year 1930. Though Moon was born in 1920, a caveat to these mathematics indicated that "The year cannot be pin-pointed so exactly because a difference of up to plus or minus ten years was often observed throughout the providential history" (HSA-UWC, 1977: 46). Furthermore, *The Divine Principle* inferred from selected Biblical quotations that the messiah emerged out of the "third Israel"— Korea—and that he married at age forty in 1960 (as did Moon) to begin a perfect God-centered family as a model for the world. In addition, Moon commonly referred to his present wife as the "bride of Christ" and identified himself and her as the "True Parents" (as opposed to Satan and Eve) of mankind. In one edition of *The Master Speaks* (MS-1, Part 2, 1965: 4), Moon bluntly addressed his messianic role:

> I was destined for that mission. I was born for that mission. The Divine Principle does not yet reveal my personal history. Once my personal history is known as part of the Divine Principle, no one in the world can ever deny this truth. . . . I am here through the passage of 6,000 years of history, as the conclusion of the 6,000 years of history.

There is other evidence for Moon's messianic status within the movement. In his study of the Church's earliest mission to this country, Lofland (1977: 23-24) narrated the details of one of Moon's "journeys" into the spirit world where he appeared before God in heaven to be tested for messiahship potential.[6] Before an audience of both Jesus and Satan as well as the hosts of each, Moon was presented by God with the task of selecting "the secret sin of Satan" from seventy possible causes of the Fall from Eden. After eyeballing the reactions of respective partisans as he considered each cause, Moon finally chose copulation. Twice Moon presented his choice to God and was told that he was wrong. The third time God "embraced him and announced: 'You are My Son.' "[7]

Establishing Moon as the messiah from the perspective of believers, albeit through indirect evidence, has more than mere academic significance. The commitment of Moon's followers, and their willingness to undergo personal sacrifices for his goals, cannot be divorced from the role he played in his own cosmic scheme. While as of the late 1970s Moon had publically neither confirmed nor denied messianic status, there is no question that he fit perfectly the criteria of his own revealed doctrine and that, *functionally* at least, he performed that role in his movement.

Finally, God will not extend the opportunity for restoration indefinitely. Moon, according to Young Oon Kim (an early convert and UM theologian), originally forecast 1967 as the year in which complete restoration would occur. However, Moon later announced that the restoration would require three seven-year periods: 1960-1967, 1968-1974, and 1975-1981 (see Lofland, 1977: 281). While there were indications from conversations with UM informants during 1976-1978 that these periods might eventually be regarded as symbolic rather than as literal time periods, nevertheless they conveyed a certain urgency to believers. Even those interviewed members who dismissed 1981 as any significant "cut-off" date still believed that it would present an important benchmark for the movement. However, if one takes the time periods literally, as some apparently did, by the late 1970s time for realizing the millennium was running out.

THE SOCIAL PHILOSOPHY: THE WORLD MUST UNITE

A cornerstone theme in the Unificationist movement from its inception was the inability of mankind to be obedient to God as long as it was fragmented into a plurality of religions and denominations occasionally engaged in internecine competition. Moon never denied that all great religions were true. He did maintain, however, that their truths were only partial; none had ever fully grasped the nature and will of God nor understood His providence as did Moon. Without *The Divine Principle,* these things understandably had eluded them.

Of course, this conviction was not unique to Rev. Moon's philosophy. Similar sentiments had been espoused earlier by Bahaiism, Meher Baba's followers, and Vedanta, among other groups. Moreover, the arrival of Moon's message in America coincided with the 1960s wave of ecumenical hope in mainstream Christian groups. Still, no one claimed to be engaged in the crusade for religious rapprochement quite as vigorously as Moon. UM missionaries claimed that Moon had studied the world's great religions during his nine years of divinely inspired meditation and prayer, distilling the essential wisdom of these belief systems. Furthermore, Moon reportedly once held a banquet in heaven for the founders of the world's great religions at which they ceded to Moon superiority over their own particular truths (Personal Interviews, 1978).

In actuality Moon's expectations for the worldwide social order to emerge after universal acceptance of his message called for a "worldwide socialist theocracy." Church and state, theology and science, economy and religion: all were to become one in the ideal society to follow, united under the messiah and restored to God in His realized Kingdom on earth. Separate religions would have no further reason to exist. Nor would war, poverty, and a host of other problems plaguing humanity since the Fall from Eden. The world would in fact become one harmonious family under God the Father. As *The Divine Principle* had revealed, the illicit union between Eve and Satan had displaced God as the spiritual father of human families, and the coming messiah would restore God to that former position by first bringing to God loving, obedient sons and daughters. To this end the members of the UM were taught to regard themselves as models for the rest of mankind. Life in the UM was intended to instruct members how to live God-centered lives as individuals in God-centered families. This involved the uncompromising lifestyle of celibacy among members before marriage (thus avoiding the perils of Eve's carnal indiscretion) and having mankind's True Spiritual Parents—Rev. and Mrs. Moon—select mates and "bless" (i.e., perform marriage ceremonies for) couples. By absolute obedience to their Spiritual Parents, first at the local team or group level in the persons of those spiritual "mothers" or "fathers" who first brought members into the movement, and second at the movement level itself in the persons of Rev. and Mrs. Moon, members would not only appear righteous in the eyes of God but also inspire and guide the rest of the world. Thus, as we shall see, the Unificationist concept of the family, however much it departed from conventional images of that unit, was an extremely seminal part of the movement's overall philosophy.

REINTERPRETATION OF HISTORY: THE COMING MILLENNIUM

Historical justification for the UM's establishment and mission was extremely important to Unification theology. An elaborate numerological interpretation of Biblical and post-Biblical events, organized into parallel lines of development for the past 6,000 years, concerned much of *The Divine Principle*. In this way, God's love for humanity and His reciprocal need for human love, mankind's past inability to reciprocate this love, and the consequent indemnity which humanity must pay were seen as the prime movers in world history.

We have seen how history was regarded by Unification theology as the chronicle of man's uphill struggle to regain his original harmony with God. Contained within this perspective were several other major reinterpretations of traditional Christian belief. Among these was the reduction of Jesus Christ to simply one among a succession of unsuccessful agents of God who strove but failed to restore humanity to God (albeit as the Son of God who acheived a limited but nonetheless incomplete spiritual salvation for man). There was one slight twist in that the previous Old Testament attempts failed due to some inadequacy on the part of each agent, whereas Jesus was deserted and betrayed by his followers. Nevertheless, this interpretation of the stature of Jesus represented a radical departure from that of orthodox Christianity. In the set of notes and speeches on doctrinal points entitled *The Master Speaks* (later abbreviated to simply *Master Speaks*), transcribed from tape-recordings of Moon and intended to be circulated only among members, Moon specifically claimed superiority over Jesus due to his own concrete fulfillment of merging truth and love. Moon's self-claimed success "is greatly different from Jesus. When you read the Bible, it appears as if Jesus knew everything. But he didn't. He did not know how the fall of man took place as clearly as we do. He did not comprehend the history of restoration" (MS-1, Part I,

1965). As a result, Jesus' stature was reduced considerably. "Jesus stands in the position of a son to be Lord of the Second Advent, and calls him 'Father.' Jesus ranks among us as our elder brother. Those who receive revelations in prayer call him 'Brother' " (MS-1, Part I, 1965).

Moreover, the Bible was regarded as an inadequate and incomplete expression of divine revelation. *The Master Speaks* (MS-7, Part 2, 1965) stated: "Unless you truly know the meaning behind it, the Bible can reveal very little. . . . The Divine Principle gives the true meaning of the secret behind the verse." The conclusion followed that mankind could have been spared millennia of spiritual confusion and physical suffering if only the prophets and saints had been able to articulate *The Divine Principle* as Sun Myung Moon had done. This was the superiority Moon claimed over past agents of God and constituted his "edge" in this contemporary attempt to realize the restoration of God's Kingdom on earth. In this sense, Unification theology resembled many of the gnostic off-shoots of early Christianity during its first three centuries. If anything, the Bible was regarded as a cryptogram, and a special *gnosis*, or revealed wisdom, was considered necessary to "correctly" understand scriptures and ascertain God's will (e.g., Jonas, 1963).

In sum, the *problem* addressed in Unification ideology was mankind's initial irresponsibility manifested through sexual impropriety which severed its divinely intended relationship to God. Based on this definition of the problem, Moon *reinterpreted* all of human history as a series of unremitting but unsuccessful attempts to restore man to God. Moon's analysis also provided the *solution:* to establish realtionships of pure love and to submit, with genuine filial piety, to Moon the True Parent and founder of the "Perfect Family" on which all future God-centered relationships would be based. Finally, building from the individual to the family, social institutions would gradually come to reflect this revealed truth and unity between man and God.

The theology was to become a two-edged sword in America. In certain respects it would transplant rather easily. In others it would evoke enormous controversy. Finally, in its initial form UM ideology is reported to have lacked references to Western philosophy, to a specific role for America in the restoration process, and to a perspective that would appeal to American youth. All of these were developed following the UM's diffusion to the United States in the 1950s and 1960s.

Leadership, Organization, and Recruitment

Certain distinctive elements of the UM emerged very early. The movement soon moved from merely religious activity to also include economic and political enterprises. The scope of activity necessitated the formation of some minimum bureaucracy and separation of religious from administrative functions. At the same time the local churches and affiliated organizations demonstrated a strong commitment and familial style by which individual members were linked to the movement. Thus, from the beginning the UM manifested broad organizational activity and, simultaneously, both bureaucratic and primary group styles of organization.

Moon fled south to Pusan, escaping the conflict in northern Korea in 1953, and in 1954 at Seoul, with a small group of disciples, formally established the *Tong-il Kyo,* otherwise known as the Holy Spirit Association for the Unification of World Christianity. By the mid-1960s, Rev. Moon and his followers had built a denomination of substantial size and well-developed organizational structure. Some evidence that bureaucratization and the establishment of church hierarchy had occurred can be found in Korean scholar Syn-duk's description of the Seoul Church circa 1965, in which he described men's, women's, and youth *divisions* (each made up of 108 persons) that were further broken down into *areas* (thirty-six persons each) and *groups* (twelve persons each). In addition, Syn-duk (1967: 170-171) mentioned a multilevel pyramid of authority extending downward from a national headquarters through provinces to district-subdistrict heads and then to the village and individual levels. A further idea of the emerging Church structure can be gained from mention of the offices of the Church's national headquarters, described by Syn-duk (1967). Besides an executive head (separate from Moon), there was an Administrative section which had separate offices concerned with General Affairs, Cultural Affairs, Rural Districts, and Business Affairs, and a Students' Section which had separate offices overseeing middle school students, high school students, young children, and Sunday school students.

These findings adumbrate certain features later to be found in the American Unificationist movement. For example, the clear separation of the sexes and the centrality of youth in the movement were two early characteristics to be encountered later. The Korean administrative structure clearly provided for control of business enterprises. Perhaps most significant, very early Moon chose to separate his charismatic, prophetic function from the more mundane administrative role as bureaucratic executive, as he was to do later in the United States.

Like other social movements, the UM early in its history established symbolic occasions that demarcated the boundaries of membership with a distinctive subculture and fostered solidarity. For example, Syn-duk (1967: 13) reported the instituting of a number of holidays exclusive to the UM, such as Moon's birthday, his wedding day to the present Mrs. Moon (the bride of Christ), the date of his release from communist prison, and the Day of the Universe, referring to the date of Moon's proclaimed "redemption" of the Universe. Several of these were later transferred to the United States and became part of that country's UM subculture.

As in the later American experience, the UM's proselytization efforts were largely restricted to youth. As Syn-duk (1967: 171) observed:

> Special emphasis is put on youth in the Tong-Il Church. They don't expect much from those above forty. Old people over forty, they think, should regard themselves as the sacrifices offered on the altar to bring the kingdom of heaven on earth through Mr. Moon.

The youthful Peace Corps-like character of the UM could be seen in the semiannual evangelistic campaigns in impoverished rural areas where young members worked at no charge with farmers and administrators and taught village children a mixture of mathematics, reading and writing skills, and UM principles. Such projects resembled the American UM's occasional community-oriented activities (e.g., providing care to the elderly, aid to the poor).

Likewise, the broad outlines of socialization procedures (arduous training sessions, study groups, paramilitary drills, and so forth) that were later reported in the United States during the early 1970s also existed during this Korea period (Syn-duk, 1967: 172). There was heavy emphasis on study of *The Divine Principle* (a Korean version, compiled by a bed-ridden disciple of Moon, was available to members circa 1957) and, indeed, there were numerous examinations required of the membership at different organizational levels. Indoctrination included both theological studies and vigorous physical exercise. Resources to underwrite the expense of these recruitment and socialization activities appear to have come from UM members' voluntary efforts and from the diverse business interests (including ginseng tea production, armaments assembling, and stoneware) which Moon and the UM oversaw.

Finally, the organization of the early UM also possessed a strong familial emphasis. Moon, as head of the UM, was regarded as titular father of the church family, and he and his second wife (married in 1960) were literally referred to as members' spiritual parents. In this patriarchal role, Moon personally selected church-approved mates for members and conducted mass weddings in which newly "blessed" members swore to be "the nucleus of the Church and to fulfill their obligations to the Church" (Syn-duk, 1967: 173).

In sum, the UM developed an organizational style that incorporated elements of sect-like charismatic leadership as well as the outlines of bureaucracy. Both this fundamental duality and many specific organizational features (e.g., familial emphasis, youth recruits, sexual asceticism, and so forth) persisted in each of the cultural environments into which the UM later diffused.

Conflict and Social Control

It was not long after Moon began proclaiming his divine revelation that he and his followers were the objects of social repression. His militant anticommunism, heretical reformulations of Christian theology, and rapidly growing popularity (along with that of other new religions) created mistrust among communists, Korean Christians, and South Korean governmental leaders, respectively. Yet the movement survived this early persecution. Indeed, while the repression was insufficient to destroy the movement, it was severe enough to increase UM solidarity, provide confirmatory evidence for theological predictions, and supply raw material for apocryphal tales of the movement's early triumphs over evil and of Moon's personal sacrifice and dedication. Moon was opposed almost immediately by an unlikely coalition of conventional Christian leaders and communist officials.

Indeed, it appears that Christian church leaders were instrumental in mobilizing social control against the Unification Church even before its formal establishment. While details are sparse, it is known that in 1946 and again in 1948 Moon was imprisoned by the communists in Pyongyang and in a Hung-nam labor camp, respectively, "because of the agitation his preaching caused" (Sontag, 1977: 79). Syn-duk (1967: 168-9) noted that the second imprisonment of two years resulted from 64 letters sent to the authorities by orthodox Christian ministers complaining about Moon, but he simply mentions "disturbing the social order" as Moon's offense. Understandably, UM members later could look back and regard this period as one of martyrdom for Moon and one that aptly demonstrated the extremes of factionalism into which modern Christianity had fallen.

Later, in 1955, Moon's alleged recruitment practices generated considerable controversy. A brief three-month period of imprisonment for Moon and several UM officials occurred while they awaited trial for "injuring public morals" and alleged "draft evasion." Since 1955 there has been an ongoing, acrimonious debate between Moon's detractors and supporters over these accusations. The frequent charge of anti-UM spokesmen has been that Moon was repeatedly in trouble for sexual hijinks, specifically for his alleged ritual of *pikarume* ("cleansing of the blood") in which Moon purportedly performed intercourse with each female initiate to purify her of the pollution she had inherited from Eve. The Korean

National Council of Churches, representing various mainline Christian denominations, condemned the movement and refused it membership. UM members, however, countered by accusing other Christian missionaries in Seoul of being envious of Moon's success, of trumping up immorality charges against him, and of backing down in their anticommunism. Sontag (1977: 199), in a review of the most frequently repeated criticisms of Moon, acknowledged the rumor of sexual misconduct but concluded that there was insufficient evidence to support such accusations. Mentioning similar attacks on Jesus' reputation, he claimed: "We need a super-Freud to tell us why it is that religious leaders immediately draw stories of sexual impropriety." Sontag chalked this sort of charge up to intermural invidiousness among rival Christian mission groups. Almost a quarter of a century later, the truth or falsity of the charges still seems beyond demonstration. While there has been to our knowledge no concrete substance to these charges forthcoming, we do not raise the red-letter issue of sexual impropriety to promote sensational innuendo or merely as an historical anecdote. As we shall see, the repetition of such charges two decades later in the United States became one basis for impugning Moon as an insincere charlatan and a possible threat to individuals' liberties. In any event, a Seoul District court ordered Moon and several UM leaders released after three months, and shortly thereafter the Korean Unification Church obtained the necessary official government certification to exist as a legal entity.

The rise of new religious movements in Korea was a matter of concern to governmental as well as religious leaders. Several large movements with messianic leaders arose by comparison with which the UM was of relatively modest size (see footnote one). Indeed available evidence indicates that the UM never approached one million members. Because these movements commanded large devoted followings, lived communally, utilized their followers and funds as resources to establish commercial and industrial enterprises, and espoused theologies with clear political implications, they harbored considerable potential for exerting both economic and political influence in what was at the time a relatively small, poor war-ravaged country. Moon apparently was able to overcome his initial persecution by forging a strong relationship with the South Korean government during the ensuing years. His staunch anticommunism proved to be an invaluable resource in this regard, and he ultimately operated an anticommunist training school to which political leaders were sent as well as a small arms and munitions industry supported by government contracts. Neither of these enterprises could have been undertaken without the blessing of the ruling Park regime. Much later evidence of his continued political favor was provided by the fact that Moon and his wife were invited to sit with other national dignitaries on the reviewing stand during Military Day festivities in Seoul during the fall of 1978 (Personal Interviews, 1978).

Conclusions

SUMMARY

In this chapter we have chronicled the growth of the Unificationist Movement in post-World War II South Korea. The movement can actually trace its origin to the teenager Sun Myung Moon's alleged vision of Jesus Christ in 1936 in which Jesus charged Moon with undertaking the full restoration of God's kingdom on earth. In 1946 Moon began his public preaching, one among many competing charismatic religious figures in a tumultuous social context of heightened personal and nationalistic aspirations.

Reacting both to contemporary events and to culture conflict produced by the spread of Western Christianity within an Asian society, Moon ambitiously formulated a syncretic theology that blended these two traditions in a way that was relevant to many Koreans. According to this theology, the major problem confronting human beings was their alienation from God the True Parent (and, as a consequence, from one another as God's children) due to the original sin of fornication and the subsequent Fall of Man in Biblical Eden. The solution for restoring mankind to God and establishing His kingdom on earth involved a complex process of paying indemnity to Satan and earning back the original relationship with God. Moon's social philosophy to achieve this end called for the formation of God-centered families founded on ethical principles revealed by God through Moon. Finally, Moon's theology, which came to be embodied in a separate scripture entitled *The Divine Principle,* presented a reinterpretation of history that located the events and characters of both the Old and New Testaments, including Jesus of Nazareth, in a series of arduous but unsuccessful attempts to realize this world-transforming restoration. Thus, this theology radically redefined Christhood as a yet-to-be-fulfilled role as well as reshaped the meaning of Jesus' mission and crucifixion, and its emphasis on accumulation of wealth and power as means to this world transformation also represented a considerable departure from orthodox Christian tradition.

By the mid-1960s, after the UM had been formally in existence a decade and had weathered both political persecution and opposition from Korean Christian leaders, it had attracted several tens of thousands of members and was earnestly in pursuit of secular transformation on an international scale. Along the way it had developed a distinctive organizational style, merging charismatic leadership with bureaucratic structures so as to make the two forms of authority compatible yet preserve Moon's prophetic role apart from more mundane administrative leadership in the movement. This then was the aggressive, growing millennial movement which in 1959 sent the first two missionaries to the west coast of the United States.

IMPLICATIONS

World-transforming movements typically emerge in environments where the level of discontent in some segment of the population is high. Available evidence indicates that the citizens of post-World War II South Korea experienced considerable relative deprivation. The occupation of Korea by Japan, the postwar depression, the political bifurcation of the country and the invasion of South Korea by North Korea combined to produce extreme physical and social dislocation for a large number of South Koreans. Indeed, it was in the refugee camps, where it might reasonably be expected that loss of possessions, status, and power were greatest, and in the rural areas, which benefited least from urbanization and industrialization, that Moon centered much of his early missionary activity. Refugees and many other South Koreans not only faced personal and collective problems of enormous magnitude but also lacked empirical means by which to redress their discontents and deprivations. It is not surprising that under these circumstances a number of religious movements arose, of which the UM was characteristic, which promised immediate transformation, attainable prosperity and a central role for Korea (i.e., "the new Israel") in the dawning new order.

As they emerge, world-transforming movements develop more or less comprehensive explanations of the world they seek to change. There is a crucial difference between the way that a world-transforming movement's ideology "presents itself" as a belief system and is regarded by believers and its organizational implications. As a belief system, such an ideology represents a unique body of thought that reinterprets history and offers a vision of the future based on the insights derived from that reinterpretation. At this prima facie level the ideology's significant feature is its content. From an organizational perspective, however, the specific content of the ideology is less revealing of the movement's organizational structure than are its characteristics of *mandating total, imminent cataclysmic change*. Assuming minimum acceptance of the ideology, these qualities largely determine a structural situation that produces certain organizational requisites.

Internally four relational patterns emerge:

(1) Sacrifice (of conventional lifestyles and their accompanying rewards). The importance and imminence of change require complete, full-time involvement in pursuing the movement role to actualize this change.

(2) Insulation (of members from the corrupting influence of the contemporary social order). If the transformation of society is to be total and if members are to play roles (e.g., as the "faithful remnant" or the "elect vanguard") in ushering in the new era, then they must preserve their purity by limiting contacts with outsiders.

(3) Fraternity. Equality among members (as signified through terms such as "brother," "sister," or "comrade") is fostered by the magnitude of the transformation to be achieved. On the one hand, the complete discrediting of former bases for making status distinctions yields individuals who stand on equal terms relative to the new "dispensation." On the other hand, only collective efforts can suffice to produce the imminent change, and the qualitative nature of that change undermines attempts to establish rankings of individual inputs.

(4) Authority. Members' deep commitment and acknowledgement of authority in the person of the movement leader flow out of the totality of the anticipated change. Because the movement's leader is the discoverer (or repository) of the elements of this new reality and is the only person who has "seen" or "known" it, he or she alone has the gnosis to direct the movement's course. In addition, of course, the leader-disciples model is reinforced by the need for fraternity among members as it eliminates or inhibits the development of intermediate leadership positions.

Externally two relational patterns between movement and society become manifest:

(1) Normative violations. The imminence and totality of anticipated change lend oblique legitimation to mundane normative violations as the latter become relatively insignificant and even encumbering when contrasted with the critical importance of ushering in the new order.

(2) Outreach. All such movements are committed to at least forewarning populaces of the impending transformation. To the extent that the transformation is dependent upon human effort, rather than any magical/suprahuman agency, attempts are made to mobilize support for and neutralize opposition to the movement. At this point the content of the ideology becomes significant as such movements usually attempt to couch their appeals in terms of familiar, valued cultural traditions.

World-transforming movement ideologies contain metaphoric statements linking past and present with future states. In diagnosing the source of humankind's problems the ideology juxtaposes the world as it is and has been with the way it can and will be. In the UM's case the central metaphors were "family" (i.e., referring to both the original relationship between God and humankind and the fictive kinship system created by UM members in communal groups); the "fall" (and the reciprocal concept of "restoration"); and "love" (the natural relationship between God and His creation and among humans). It was in terms of these concepts that the ills of humankind were diagnosed by the UM and the potential for a new world were predicated. The metaphoric basis of the ideology in part explains its structure. There is usually a detailed historical description of the course of human events to the present along with an elaboration of the multifaceted consequences of the basic problem confronting humanity. There is, by contrast, relatively little detail on the nature of the new order. Indeed, world-transforming movements frequently are criticized for being more articulate in their condemnation of society than in depicting the new social order with which it is to be replaced. The sketchiness of detail on the latter is partially attributable to the fact that in diagnosing human problems a world-transforming movement has the whole corpus of recorded history on which to draw for evidence while the future is still to be unfolded. However, *we would argue that the structure of the ideology is not explainable simply in terms of ignorance of the future but is important in itself organizationally as a means of building commitment.* The metaphor is stated so as to depict a perfect world, a world that literally flies in the face of reality as contemporary individuals experience it. It is, therefore, critical to assert that such a world can exist, but because the postulated world is beyond the limits of direct experience, it can be most effectively communicated through metaphor. At the same time, while it is imperative to create a *vision* of the future it is also important not to despoil that vision through intrusion of the mundane. *For it is precisely the contrast between the mundane present and the visionary future, captured by the metaphor, that lends the drama and adventure to the movement.* Thus, the lack of specification on the nature of utopia is not a flaw of any particular ideology but rather is a generic characteristic of world-transforming movement ideologies.

NOTES

1. In fact, though Moon's church is usually the only such group known to Americans, his movement has never achieved the size and popularity in Korea of a

parallel group, the *Park Chang-no-Kyo,* or the "Olive Tree Movement" (for a description, see Moos, 1967). Founded around the same time as the Unification Church by an ex-Presbyterian named Tae Sun Park, this rival group established several industrial complexes for its multivarious economic ventures that housed and employed members and literally independent cities. By 1967 this religion officially claimed approximately two million members in South Korea (as compared to Moon's official 1964 total of 32,391 – see Syn-duk, 1967). Park's doctrines were a mixture of shamanistic folk religion and Christianity, and his Biblically based claims for his own historical role and revelations closely paralleled Moon's. Park's religion was especially noted for one conspicuous practice that outraged nonbelievers: because followers attributed efficacious healing results to Park's mere touch, they regularly retained his bathwater and drank it to cure all types of illnesses. Likewise, it was considered a great privilege to wash Park's feet and save the rinse water for similar purposes.

2. Many members seemed little concerned with recording the church's early history, but on more than one occasion Moon and some of his closest and earliest disciples, such as David S. C. Kim, gave lectures on the significance of early events in Korea. A start toward the building of such an historical literature, including the expected apocryphal elements, can be found in the church's in-house publication *Master Speaks* (1971).

3. We use the term "mankind" in the generic sense with which we heard UM members use it, i.e., to refer specifically to neither sex.

4. *The Divine Principle* received ongoing study and elaboration by Church theologians since its earliest formulations by Moon. Currently, several editions exist for reference. Abbreviated paperbound versions have been issued in order to present in more concise form the main points of Unification theology for persons not undertaking lengthy study of the full doctrine. Because it is likely that many readers would obtain and read the most recent 1977 (based on the famous 1973 "black book" edition which was itself a revised form of the 1966 translation from the Korean) edition, quotations used here are taken from it. For other detailed theological summaries and elaborations, see Hodges and Bryant, 1978; Sontag, 1977; HSA-UWC, 1977, 1973; Lofland, 1977: 14-28; and Kim, 1975.

5. The respective reasons for each luminary's failure to restore the Kingdom of God on earth seem, from the perspective of an outsider to the faith, somewhat arbitrary on God's part. For example, Noah's son Ham, in reacting negatively to his father's nakedness and drunken condition after the Ark voyage, showed that he was not of one heart with his father. Thus, another period of indemnity to be worked out over 1,600 years occurred. Abraham drew the task of symbolically distinguishing good from evil to restore the foundation of faith and the conditions for mankind's restoration. However, at the sacrificial moment he cut ram and heifer, but not a pair of doves (as instructed by God) into two pieces. As a result, his descendents spent 400 years of slavery in Egypt. Moses was then God's choice to be the restoration prophet following the Egyptian indemnity. The travails and wanderings of the Jewish people under Moses were adumbrations of Jesus' own trials. However, the faithlessness of the Israelites was matched by Moses' inability to strike a rock once instead of twice upon God's command in order to obtain water in the desert. One blow would have brought back Adam, but two called forth the coming appearance of Jesus (the second Adam). This mistake cancelled out the indemnity paid through the suffering incurred during Egyptian slavery. Finally, Solomon's reign, though beginning with promise with construction of the Temple, proved to waste another opportunity as Solomon engaged in idolatry and polytheism with his pagan wives.

6. It is now common knowledge among sociologists that John Lofland's *Doomsday Cult,* first published in 1966 and republished in 1977, is a study of conversion and commitment among the first members of Moon's pioneer mission to the United States in the early 1960s. While Lofland has staunchly resisted the recent pressure to abandon his "belabored" use of pseudonyms in discussing the Unification Church, the evidence that he was in fact analyzing that organization in embryonic form is overwhelming. For a discussion of the ethical implications and dilemmas posed by such a situation, see Lynch (1977).

7. There are a number of striking parallels between Moon's doctrines/revelations and those of Hung Hsiu-Ch'uan, founder of the Tai-ping Rebellion in mid-nineteenth century China. The similarity in fusions of neo-Confucian thinking with Biblical Protestantism deserves a separate analysis, not because of any possible connection between these two syntheses of Eastern and Western ideas but rather because this syncretic tendency appears often in the religious encounters between the two religious traditions.

Chapter 2

THE TRANSPLANTATION OF THE

UNIFICATIONIST MOVEMENT

That modern societies continuously spawn social movements is reflective of their complex, dynamic character. Most of these movements are quickly lost in history. They fail in the sense that they do not become part of the ongoing institutional structure of the society although they may well initiate or add impetus to social change. The first years of the Unificationist Movement in the United States following its transplantation from Korea in 1959 revealed the characteristic vulnerability of fledgling social movements. It would not be an exaggeration to assume that had even a few of the handful of early faithful become disenchanted or weary of the constant struggle simply to survive that the movement in the United States might have quietly disappeared. As it was, the UM appears to have survived in the early 1960s only as a result of the dogged determination of its few members.

As we shall document in the following pages, the UM's arrival in the United States was greeted by overwhelming indifference from its new host culture. Except for a tiny number of devotees, Americans were unaware and unconcerned that a new millenarian movement had landed on its shores, and for more than a decade the movement languished in relative obscurity. Why was the UM so unsuccessful in gaining visibility and recruits in the 1960s when only a decade later it registered an exponential growth rate and "Moonie" became a household word? It is our contention that the answer to this question has two parts. First, we shall argue, American youth, the major recruitment source for the UM, were drawn to and involved in secularly based movements during the early 1960s. The UM's recruitment potential was simply much more limited in the 1960s than it was in the 1970s. Second, and more important, the mobilization of a variety of crucial resources by the UM lacked the effectiveness that the movement was to demonstrate a decade later. For a variety of reasons the UM was unable to generate public visibility, accumulate substantial financial strength, effectively socialize potential recruits, or develop coherent strategies for implementing the cosmic timetable contained in *The Divine Principle*. The early 1960s, then, constituted a time of struggle for sheer survival and growth by accretion, a pattern which was an unlikely harbinger of the transformation which was to occur a decade later.

Lack of Societal Support for the UM in the Sixties

THE HISTORICAL CONTEXT OF THE YOUTH COUNTER CULTURE

Many of those who have sought to explain the rise of the 1960s youth movements have concluded that their emergence was rooted in macroscopic, long-term sociocultural forces. In a quasi-Marxian analysis Flacks (1971: 6) stated that the revolt of youth is a symptom of a "fundamental sociocultural crisis . . . which . . . involves a substantial conflict between the emergent technological potentialities of a society and the established social order and cultural system." Reich (1970), in a more polemical treatment, contended that the rebellion emanated from the rise of the corporate state which has dominated, exploited, and ultimately would destroy man and nature. He perceived a newly emerging consciousness among youth of what it means to be human which involved a rejection of the premises on which the corporate state was based and which ultimately would transform the structure of American society.

Glock and Bellah (1976) also both analyzed events of the 1960s in terms of an erosion of traditional American cultural values. Glock (1976: 354) portrayed the counter culture as "a highly visible sign of fundamental changes already underway" in which a new way of viewing the world, inspired by science, denied either man or God (the two components of the traditional world view) as the locus of control for human destiny. The counter culture thus constituted a "unique crisis of consciousness." Bellah (1976: 334, 337) interpreted the 1960s as "the repudiation of utilitarianism . . . and the biblical tradition" . . . those . . . "interpretations of reality that had been most successful in providing meaning and generating loyalty up until the sixties."

The contention that the underlying values and world view of American culture (and Western civilization generally) were eroding for some time has been linked to countercultural movements of the 1960s through the concept of "youth." At least two major aspects of youth as a social grouping in American society bore on the development of a youth counter culture. First, the time period between adolescence and the assumption of full adult status steadily lengthened, and for an increasing proportion of youth these intervening years were spent acquiring advanced formal education (Friedenberg, 1965; Goodman, 1960). This pattern itself had several important implications. Youth were concentrated on college campuses where their numbers combined with a substantial amount of discretionary time and inexpensive lifestyle yielded a large reservoir of individuals relatively free to participate in social movements (McCarthy and Zald, 1973: 10). As a larger cross-section of youth were exposed to a critical/ analytic perspective on their society, a variety of social conditions were more likely to be viewed as solvable problems rather than inherent conditions of life. Second, the macroscopic social changes which were occurring in American society bore disproportionately on youth who were socialized to accept and made initial efforts to assume traditional adult roles that were at odds with emerging sociocultural realities. As Flacks (1971: 6) put it:

> Young people are among the first to experience this crisis because they have yet to form stable vocational and social attachments, because they receive most fully and directly the socialization efforts of established institutions, and because they are future oriented. For many youths this situation is experienced as a crisis of identity.

In discussing the emergence of the youth counter culture it is important to emphasize that it was a select group which led the political/intellectual movement. As Matza (1961) had observed, youthful unrest sometimes has manifested a variety of forms simultaneously within different social strata. The 1960s counter culture clearly was initiated and led by upper middle-class, intellectually oriented college students (Flacks, 1971: 58; Kenniston, 1965, 1971). It should be stressed on the one hand that those actively involved in the protest movements constituted a distinct minority of youth and even of collegiate youth. Public opinion surveys consistently indicated strong conservative leaning particularly among noncollege youth even at the height of protest activities (Yankelovich, 1974: 22-37). On the other hand, the number of individuals who actively participated in some of the protest activity was considerably larger than this core and even larger if those adopting many of the counterculture concommitants—music, hair and dress styles, drug use—were included.

THE TRANSITION TO PROTEST

The latter part of the 1950s and the first few years of the 1960s both witnessed the last confident expression of what has been termed American civil religion (Mead, 1975: 30; Bellah, 1967). Leaders could still optimistically and credibly speak of America's goals, values, achievements, and unique role in world affairs with a sense, shared by most Americans, that the country had a special transcendental mandate. Politicians, clergymen, and business leaders alike could draw on revered ideals and symbols that functioned, according to Wilson (1978: 177-178),

> to promote national solidarity and sustain commitment of a religious intensity toward national goals. . . . Civil religion means, then, that the ultimate dimension of American life is sacralized.

President John F. Kennedy's inaugural address has been presented by many observers as the classic illustration of this civil religion:

> Man holds in his mortal hands the power to abolish all forms of human poverty and to abolish all forms of human life. And yet the same revolutionary beliefs for which our forebears fought are still at issue around the globe—the belief that the rights of man come not from the generosity of the state but from the hand of God. . . . Let us go forth to lead the land we love, asking His blessing and His help, but knowing that here on earth God's work must truly be our own [Sorenson, 1966: 275, 277].

Kennedy spoke charismatically of the challenge of the "New Frontier," a struggle on a worldwide scale for human rights and dignity, which was implicit in the values of the American civil religion. His successor, Lyndon B. Johnson, promised a "Great Society," an ongoing "battle" for equality and peace and against poverty, in no less inspiring and sweeping rhetoric.

When some significant discrepancies between American ideals and social realities were "discovered" early in the 1960s, the solutions were cast in secular terms and reflected continuing confidence in the civil religion. Because the civil religion "is not the celebration of society as it was but as it ought to be," it legitimated redress when current realities and ideals were not in accord (Wilson, 1978: 177-180). Among the issues in the forefront of public attention were peace, poverty, racial justice and equality, and the rise of "third world" nations. At the time there was still a reservoir of confidence that the challenges confronting America and the world, although formidable, were not intractable. The "call to arms" was supported and in some cases even sounded by leaders of established institutions. In short, youthful energy and idealism were rather successfully channelled into movements and organizations more or less compatible with the interests of established institutions.

Two social movements that captured the imagination of youth and for which they provided much of the rank-and-file membership were the Peace Corps-related organizations (symbolized through organizations such as the Peace Corps, VISTA, Job Corps) and the civil rights movement (symbolized through organizations such as NAACP, SCLC, SNCC, CORE). By contrast to the youth protest later in the 1960s American youth's involvement in the Peace Corps and civil rights movements enjoyed considerable public support and official encouragement, and initially there was official acknowledgement of and leadership in attacking the problems. Equally important, poverty and racism were viewed as somehow external to the American way of life; hence, participation in those movements did not place participants in conflict with traditional American cultural and institutional arrangements.

The Peace Corps is probably the best single illustration in the 1960s of a governmentally sponsored organization that successfully harnessed the enthusiasm and idealism of young Americans. The whole concept of the Peace Corps represented a vision of how the world could and ought to be, and it offered youth the opportunity and responsibility for transforming that vision into reality. For the individual volunteer service was an act of faith in the American *credo*—the same hard work, dedication, and sacrifice that had built America could be turned to solving world problems. The effort would not only lift other nations from their destitution but in the process make Americans stronger collectively and individually. American youth were praised for their commitment to ideals and urged to the task.

The civil rights movement too was at first viewed as an unfulfilled chapter in the American dream. Racism was a peculiar holdover from an antiquated southern culture. The youth who first went south to attack the remnants of the caste system seemed convinced that the majority of right thinking Americans would share their horror and indignation at racial discrimination and brutality. There was reason to believe that the established institutions would support a movement to abolish racism. Indeed, the Supreme Court had declared public school segregation unconstitutional in 1954 and a year later ordered an end to segregated seating on buses. Two years later President Dwight Eisenhower signed the first civil rights bill since reconstruction and sent federal troops to Arkansas to enforce a federal court decision ordering the admission of black students to classes in Little Rock High School.

Early in the 1960s a succession of protest activities in which youthful members played a leading role culminated in the day-long rally at Lincoln Memorial in Washington, D.C. in August, 1963 attended by nearly a quarter of a million Americans. This striking display of interracial solidarity was followed by the Mississippi Summer Project in which over a thousand northern white students volunteered to conduct a summer-long black voter registration drive aimed at counties in which blacks had been effectively disenfranchised.

THE EROSION OF LEGITIMACY

Early in the 1960s there was only a small group of college youth engaged in "radical" protest activity over such issues as deployment of Polaris submarines, the testing of nuclear weapons, and civil defense buildups. What happened through the remainder of the 1960s was the continuous erosion of established institutions' legitimacy. In the most general sense the counter culture gained momentum because social reform of the kind that might have allayed the sense of crisis which youth were experiencing was not forthcoming. As Flacks (1971: 90) put it, "hostility toward the older generation becomes fully manifest when substantial segments of the adult generation do not use available opportunities to oppose the existing regime and to promote social reform." In a more immediate sense the movement grew out "a conjuncture of dissatisfactions that did not all have the same meaning" (Bellah, 1976: 339). As the number of relatively distinct sources of dissatisfaction increased, they began to have an interactive effect particularly as they impacted on youth through the university environment. Idealistic fervor and efforts to realize the American dream through positive action or nonviolent protest turned gradually to embittered confrontation and rebellion.

By 1965 the university protest, antiwar, and black power/civil rights movements had become visible and the protest quickly broadened thereafter. Protest began in the civil rights movement. Despite a continuing flow of federal support for civil rights legislation, it became apparent that federal officials were not prepared for a massive crackdown on the South and that they frequently were goaded into action only by either blatant defiance of executive and court orders or confrontation provoking initiatives by civil rights workers. The antiwar movement also began to generate momentum in 1964 after the Gulf of Tonkin incident led rapidly to the bombing of North Vietnam and the deployment of combat troops in South Vietnam. By 1965 the university protest movement began to spread as the Free Speech Movement at Berkeley spawned demands on college campuses across the country for change in university governance.

Militancy steadily increased as nonviolent civil rights protest gave way to more student demands for black power, involvement in Vietnam continued to increase, universities resisted major reform, and key figures associated with the protest movements (e.g., Robert Kennedy, Martin Luther King) were assassinated. By the late 1960s it appeared that the levels of violence would increase as blacks rioted in hundreds of cities in 1967, students began seizing buildings and destroying property on college campuses and the Cambodian invasion sparked new fury in the antiwar movement.

THE DECLINE OF THE PROTEST MOVEMENTS

As the protest mounted through the 1960s it had become broader in scope and more militant, encompassing major movements surrounding the civil rights/black power movement, the antiwar movement, and the campus protest movement. It was somewhat surprising, then, that by 1970 the fury of the protest began to subside. This dissipation of active protest and confrontation occurred for several reasons. First, and importantly, certain of the overlapping issues which had fanned the flames of protest gradually moved toward resolution. Enforcement of drug laws was loosened, the draft was rescinded, the war was slowly winding down, some concessions were made with respect to student involvement in university governance, minority students and faculty were more actively recruited. Second, many of the issues seemed intractable—meaningful equality for minorities continued to be elusive, the War on Poverty had not dramatically reduced social inequality, universities proved to be ineffective vehicles for promoting social change, and public apathy continued toward radical change. Third, the various elements of the counter culture had begun to factionalize as their common opposition to existing policy failed to yield agreement on alternatives and neither nonviolence nor violence proved effective in promoting change. Fourth, political repression of the counter culture mounted. A number of leaders of each movement were jailed, went underground, fled the country or were killed.

RELIGION AND SECULAR PROTEST

During the 1960s not all hope was abandoned that contemporary American religion could respond in a meaningful way to social problems.

Many liberal clergymen and nonparish denominational leaders attempted to infuse concerns over social issues with more traditional moral commitment. Rev. Martin Luther King made the transition from the ministry to activism against racial segregation to opposition to the war. The Berrigan brothers were active leaders of the antiwar movement. Many other religious leaders found that their new self-defined activist roles involved them in a broad spectrum of challenges to the political and economic institutions, drawing them into marches and demonstrations alongside students and minorities.

Of course, not all such secular involvement was so dramatically radical. Much occurred in a more conventional fashion as churches sought to be "relevant" to their members in new ways. Sunday school classes began to discuss racial understanding and civil disobedience alongside original sin. Adult classes dabbled in encounter therapy. Special "youth ministers" were hired in some of the larger churches. Some popular folk and protest songs achieved the status of hymns. Many urban churches offered their facilities to such causes as day care centers, birth control and drug counseling clinics, and ministers became involved in marital as well as spiritual counseling.

Although many churches contributed to the solution of the decade's major social problems through activist leadership, they did so by abdicating religious authority and promoting secularization within the churches themselves. As Bellah (1976: 340) has noted, these reform-related activities did not improve the churches legitimacy as the counterculture "movements as a whole remained indifferent if not hostile to religion." As disillusionment spread during the 1960s the protest became more and more political; religion seemed less and less relevant. "By the end of the 1960s those conventional churchmen who had given everything to the political struggle found themselves without influence and without a following" (Bellah, 1976: 340).

UM Mobilization in the Sixties:
The Emerging Mainstream Tradition

Two rather distinctive theological and organizational orientations developed quite early within the American UM. The mainstream "East Coast" tradition closely followed the theological orthodoxy of *The Divine Principle*; what eventually became the West Coast's "Oakland Family" was much more humanistic and less theological in its orientation. These two traditions are distinguished in the following discussion since their continued divergence into the late 1970s raised the possibility of schism but at the same time each contributed to the movement's expansion and development.

SUBSTANTIVE AND STYLISTIC THEOLOGICAL DEVELOPMENTS

By the time the UM reached the United States in the persons of three missionaries—Young Oon Kim in California, David S. C. Kim in Oregon, and Bo Hi Pak in Washington, D.C.—the complex body of theology referred to as *The Divine Principle* had been developed and elaborated for some time. However, Moon himself had never written his own interpretation of the Principle; instead various Korean followers had recorded their own understanding of the principles, all in the Korean language. Prior to immigrating to the United States, Young Oon Kim in 1956 assumed the task of producing an English translation. Ms. Kim revised both the style and content of her first English draft of *The Divine Principle* soon after arriving in America in order to adapt the message to a new audience and to changing events. Stylistic revisions were quickly undertaken because the original version was "manifestly Korean and written in imperfect English" (Lofland, 1966: 138).

Because the theology was the center piece of the movement's proselytization activities, considerable effort was directed toward putting *The Divine Principle* into a form useful for recruitment and socialization. First, in an attempt to increase the salience of the theology to Americans, Ms. Kim elaborated the Principle so as to link it more closely to western thought, provided a detailed interpretation of western history since the death of Jesus (which Moon himself had not worked out according to Young Oon Kim), and found appropriate English translations for Korean concepts. Second, during 1960 and 1961 her translation went through several revisions in an attempt to produce grammatically correct, error-free copy so that it could be distributed to potential converts. Ms. Kim spent countless hours making these revisions and other movement members provided editorial assistance. Once acceptable copy was achieved in 1963 several small printings of a few hundred volumes each were produced and used for the study by members and in recruitment "workshops."

Even after an acceptable written version of *The Divine Principle* had been produced, the problem of motivating the only moderately curious to digest its contents remained. The "final" early edition ran more than 200 pages in length and contained philosophical and theological excursions and exegeses. Because the formidable nature of the theology deterred all but the most intrepid seekers, members began searching for a more manageable format. They experimented with the idea of producing tape-recorded summaries of the Principle to which potential recruits could listen as an introduction. The first recording ran four-and-one-half hours; subsequent editings produced versions of two-and-one-half hours, one hour and twenty minutes, and, finally, thirty-four minutes.

In the process of recording abstracted versions of *The Divine Principle* UM members also experimented with a variety of script readers. They discovered that the combination of a male and female reading alternately evoked greater listener interest, and this format was utilized in the final recording. However, even the voice recordings proved too tedious for most potential recruits. By the fall of 1963 these were abandoned in favor of a set of lectures followed by individual and small group tutoring of those who evidenced continued interest in *The Divine Principle.* The preparation of introductory lectures also forced members to produce a more simplified and manageable summary of *The Divine Principle.* This basic format for communicating *The Divine Principle* to prospective members remained intact through the 1970s.

The major substantive change in UM theology during the early 1960s involved a retreat from previous predictions regarding the beginning of the millenium. Lofland (1966: 267) stated, "During my observation in 1962-1963, [UM's] expected to rule the world, or a significant part of it, by 1967. By 1964 the total transformation predicted for 1967 had been reduced to an expectation 'that the international foundation of perfected couples would be laid in America by or before 1967.' " Once the process of restoration had begun, "The actual work of making the entire world perfect would take until about the year 2000." During the 1970s there was a further movement away from providing precise dates for the restoration process; rather these dates were viewed as "symbolic" and subject to the unfolding of world events and to the amount of effort and dedication given by members to fulfilling their spiritual role.

LEADERSHIP AND ORGANIZATION

The small size of the UM at the time of Lofland's participant observation precluded the development of any complex leadership hierarchy within the UM or the organizational complexity which emerged in the 1970s. The movement's acknowledged leader, Reverend Sun Myung Moon, did not even visit America until 1965 although plans for his imminent arrival were announced for four years running. Following his brief visit in 1965 he did not return to the United States until 1969 and then, again, for only a short stay. It was not until 1971 that Moon settled in the United States on a semipermanent basis, a move which had a dramatic impact on the American UM.

Without its charismatic leader each of the three missions of the American UM developed its own leadership structure. Among the cohort of UM members which Lofland studied there was relatively little leadership talent. Young Oon Kim was the sole and dominant leader of that mission. She possessed a certain degree of charisma; one recruit reported that Kim had a "beatific and glowing countenance" and said "I knew that woman had something I wanted" (Lofland, 1966: 97).

Her ability to generate feelings of attachment derived from her relationship to Moon and her spiritual status attained by a thorough understanding of *The Divine Principle.* Lofland (1966: 216) observed that converts believed she was far more advanced than they in her spiritual growth toward perfection. She stood, indeed, only slightly below [Moon] and God himself in the spiritual hierarchy. Because of this and because she was responsible for their conversion, she was their "mother in faith," with the responsibility of raising her spiritual children. Without her help they could not attain perfection or be worthy in the sight of God. Because members viewed her spiritual insight and development to be much greater than their own, they attributed what would appear to outsiders as her erratic, authoritarian tendencies to their own lack of understanding.

Given the UM's small size, limited resources, and the lack of social and leadership skills it was not surprising that the movement manifested little of the organizational complexity and division of labor characteristic of the movement in the 1970s. Few developments in organization were registered as the movement sought simply to survive. The major objectives of the movement—to increase membership, to gain visibility and legitimacy, and to establish the foundation for restoring man to God—were as prominent in the 1960s as in the 1970s. What was lacking were organizational forms and strategies for accomplishing these goals. Lofland commented on these problems with respect to their promotional activities. He (1966: 120) noted that while they:

> engaged in considerable promotional activities their procedures were not systematized. Promotion was in many respects haphazard and dependent upon inclination of adherents at any given moment. This variableness is most acutely indicated by [their] extremely limited vocabulary for referring to differential prospects, alignments and promotion activities. Thus almost all prospects were lumped together as either "interested people," "new people," "students," "material" or sometimes even "prospects."

In short the UM had not as yet even clearly defined the conceptual categories in terms of which organizational strategies and tactics might be formulated.

Only a few simply organizational innovations were recorded during the early 1960s. The UM's symbolic, ceremonial holidays were "progressively elaborated" (1966: 239) to serve more adequately as mechanisms for promotion of solidarity. A newsletter to share insider news and interpretations of current events was initiated as a monthly publication and later printed on a biweekly basis. There was considerable experimentation with recruitment tactics. Finally, in 1963, the communal group was dissolved in favor of individual "pioneering" witnessing missions to a number of cities in the hope of increasing the rate of conversions.

One of the most important reasons for the lethargic development of the UM during the 1960s and one of its most serious ongoing problems was the lack of a resource base sufficient for aggressively pursuing its goals. Virtually all of the movement's operating expenses were funded through the incomes earned by individual members employed in conventional occupational pursuits. Another more minor source of financing was the donation of cash and possessions to the movement by some individuals upon conversion. Because the movement initially had few members, none of their occupations commanded high salaries, and some members were periodically unemployed, the group's resource base was extremely limited.

Members contributed most of their modest salaries to UM coffers. Each member was allowed one hundred dollars per month for living expenses; all other funds were utilized for UM expenses and projects. Members subsisted on cheap bulk food; accumulated few personal possessions; and shared worn, second-hand clothes. The UM center was furnished in spartan fashion. By sacrificing personal amenities and pooling individual resources, the UM was able to purchase some of the equipment and space (e.g., an electric typewriter, multilith press, photocopier, house, and bus) used for proselytization and promotional activities. Despite such a determined accretion of wealth, however, the UM was in no position to launch the kind of nationwide campaign which it undertook a decade later.

The inadequate financial base had serious adverse effects across a wide spectrum of the movement's pursuits. For example, the flats, houses, and rented meeting halls used as residences and/or meeting centers were poorly situated to gain visibility, were extremely spartan in appearance, and, in several cases, were not even sufficiently private to ensure uninterrupted recruitment and socialization sessions. The movement's ability to package and convey its theological message also was significantly affected. The cost of newspaper and radio advertisements was prohibitively high, and so the movement was forced to utilize media with small or less appropriate audiences, rely on brief classified or personal advertisement columns, or advertise on only an occasional basis through the more desirable and expensive media outlets. Partly in response to the inaccessibility of radio and television media the movement turned to less desirable (and more impersonal) means of conveying its message such as handbills and sound truck broadcasts. As one might expect these tactics were ineffective in evoking public interest.

VISIBILITY, RECRUITMENT, AND SOCIALIZATION

One major problem confronting a variety of social movements and organizations is identifying the nature of the target population to which it can most effectively direct their recruitment activities. Like many other organizations the UM had a hazy and vacillating view of its most likely pool of potential recruits. In addition, the movement's confidence in the dramatic revelations of its doctrine and the augur of an impending apocalypse led naturally to an effort to gain the widest possible public hearing. The result was a succession of recruitment efforts which were directed at a broad range of audiences and which utilized a variety of techniques for making contact with those audiences.

The movement at various times directed its appeal to religious audiences in general, individuals disenchanted with other religions, coworkers of UM members, veteran seekers, and students. Other groups, notably Korean and Japanese Americans, married individuals and Catholics were regarded as poor prospects and not actively solicited. The former two groups were thought likely to have heard the "atrocity stories" circulated about the movement in several far eastern countries. Married and Catholic individuals were felt to be nonconvertible; this assumption was particularly ironic in light of the disproportionate representation of Catholics in UM ranks by the mid-1970s. Over time UM members began to recognize that their limited successes were greatest with youth and young adults. As a result, the movement gradually shifted its recruitment efforts to college campuses, and Ms. Kim began discouraging members from approaching individuals of middle age or older. It should be noted, however, that despite the fact that the UM began directing its recruitment efforts toward younger age groups, many of the initial cohorts of American UM's were between their midtwenties and early thirties at the time of their own conversion. This age structure was in sharp contrast to the much more youthful appearance of the UM by the early 1970s.

From the outset personal proselytization techniques proved most successful. As Lofland (1966: 53) commented, "It is particularly important to note that conversions frequently moved through pre-existing friendship pairs or nets." Indeed, the UM's success in recruiting increased perceptibly once the original family had been broken up by Ms. Kim and members "pioneered" their own missions in other cities. The probability of individual members forming or tapping into such networks appeared to have been greater working independently than it was when Ms. Kim's small group had resided communally. While personal relationships were more successful than impersonal appeals in producing conversions, the success rate was low enough and the UM's size small enough that the kind of explosive growth members hoped for was not forthcoming.

The UM's problems in producing new members involved more than its inability to attract initial interest of those whose attention it caught. The movement also was not successful in converting to membership those who responded to its recruitment appeals. The UM's low rate of success was not in general attributable to negative pressure from friends and family as outsiders knew little about the movement. Lofland (1966: 109) recorded that potential members were attracted to the UM center "at the rate of less than one a day." He (1966: 129) further observed that "computations based upon the guest books suggest that between January, 1959 and June, 1963, the [UM] induced more than 700 people into the briefing session. Something less than half that number probably attended a study group at least once, and a very small fraction of those went on to become converts." These figures suggested that, on the average, about seven persons per week attended briefings and only two or three participated in a study group. In another recruitment campaign Lofland (1966: 87) reported a UM member sent 1,900 letters to university foreign students, 150 (7.9%) responded with a phone call and 36 (1.9%) attended a briefing session. Lofland's (1966: 257) estimate of the UM's national membership as only 35 by 1963, 120 in 1964 and around 500 as late as 1971 underscores the seriousness of the problem.

Once potential recruits had been attracted to the UM center, members faced the problem of how to build their involvement in and commitment to the movement. UM possessed an overly intellectual conception of the affiliative process which actually inhibited the conversions they sought. From their perspective *The Divine Principle* contained a literally "mind-blowing" message which, if truly understood, would be wholeheartedly accepted. Thus, members expected potential recruits once confronted with this message "to enter, on their own volition, a period of struggle and then accept the [*Divine Principle*]" (Lofland, 1966: 185). If those participating in the initial lectures or study sessions failed to continue their study it was assumed that "they lacked the knowledge that would make them do so" (Lofland, 1966: 128).

The preponderant emphasis on the content of the message meant that most of the UM's socialization activities were directed toward the packaging and presentation of the theology. "Briefing sessions" were conducted to introduce the prospective recruit to *The Divine Principle.* It would then be suggested that a fuller understanding of the Principle could be gained by attending study groups which covered the entire volume, chapter by chapter, over a six-week period. The intellectual/theological thrust of socialization efforts was underscored by the fact that attempts to devise a more effective socialization process involved only rather mechanical changes in the format of these study sessions—the presentation was shortened or lengthened, the message was presented in a single session or spread over several sessions, and various voices were tried on the taped reading of *The Divine Principle* at briefing sessions. These innovations all were predicated on assumptions about the conversion process that were unrealistic from a sociological and psychological perspective. As Lofland (1966: 130) observed, the convert was perceived as a "person who will suspend his judgement for six weeks while attending study groups. He will not get ahead of the presentation or find stumbling blocks on any of the stairs to the Advent. And . . . he is a person who will not argue or ask for conclusions."

Given its emphasis on the content of the message itself, the UM also faced a major recruitment/socialization problem in deciding how quickly to unveil it to potential recruits. This constituted something of a dilemma in that, on the one hand, the theology contained some startling and revolutionary themes that might well alienate novitiates if presented out of context. On the other hand, without these more controversial elements the doctrine could easily be taken for a somewhat unorthodox version of traditional Christianity. The UM quite early adopted the practice of separating the insider and "public" portions of the theology and only gradually revealing the entire content and implications of the theology as the novitiate was "ready" to receive it. The insider portions of the theology included revelations that Moon was himself either the Messiah or a prophet who immediately foreshadowed his coming, that Korea was the new Israel, and a relatively precise timetable by which the restoration of man to God could proceed if mankind seized the opportunity.

The UM's overly intellectual conception of the conversion process led to a corresponding underplaying of personal ties and emotional involvement. UM members were not, of course, completely ignorant of the importance of affective ties. As Lofland (1966: 58) noted:

> Without this close association with those already committed, such an appreciation of the need for one's total transformation into a total convert failed to develop. In recognition of this fact, the [UM] gave greatest priority to attempting to get verbal converts (and even the merely interested) to move into the cult's communal dwellings.

Despite the failure of the movement's recruitment/socialization techniques to foster affective ties, individuals were affiliating with the UM on the basis of emotional or spiritual experiences. For example, Ms. Kim herself recalled that in her own conversion, "Although I could not agree with the message intellectually, I found myself one with it spiritually. I reserved my conclusions and waited for guidance from God" (1966: 52). Lofland (1966: 52) added that, "Other converts were observed to experience similar [intellectual] reservations, while at the same time building strong emotional bonds with members of the group. Particularly when there were no pre-existing friendship networks to serve as a basis of emotional attachment, new members were recruited as a result of an "instant and powerful rapport with a believer." Many converts, then, began involving themselves in the movement or even assumed full-time membership prior to intellectual acceptance of the theology. What the UM lacked, then, was a systematic, organizational strategy for moving potential recruits into role behavior designed to stimulate effective ties.

One indication of the movement's failure to build affective ties with prospective members could be found in the relatively long period of time (i.e., weeks or months) which elapsed between first contact with the UM and assumption of full-time membership. This situation contrasted sharply with the recruitment/socialization results produced by the UM in the 1970s when the majority of individuals became full-time members within a few days or weeks of their initial encounter with the UM. On the other hand Lofland (1966: 220) also observed that there were few, if any, defections from the UM during the period of his participant observation. The early 1960s, then, were characterized by a relatively long "conversion" time and low rate of apostasy while the 1970s saw rapid "conversions" but high rates of defection after a year or two of involvement.

The lack of a systematic strategy for generating a sense of involvement with the UM and a well-defined role for novitiates to play left UM members with little more than fraternity "rush" promotion tactics—insincere flattery and personal interest, exaggerated friendliness and outgoingness, and inappropriate warmth. Lofland (1966: 175) reported:

Despite distain for false friendliness, the DP's consistently engaged in self-conscious affectation of affability. They pretended warm and friendly interest in a peculiar and faltering Carnegie-Peale effort to "win friends and influence people." Thus, on one occasion, after having watched Elmer perform a spate of affectation, I commented: "You're certainly a friendly person." He replied: "You have to be if you are going to win people. You grit your teeth and smile anyway."

In describing Ms. Kim, Lofland described her style as particularly warm, often inappropriately so.

> She greeted prospects with broad smiles and gentle bows and continually initiated conversations with them. While inquiring into matters of background and current well-being, she projected an impression of genuine personal concern. This elaborate warmth and inquisitiveness was, at times, not only inappropriate but embarrassing, for prospects were at best mere acquaintances. Thus, Lee felt it proper to greet one male prospect who had attended a few meetings by holding his hand and warmly asking how he was. Later in the meeting she sat beside him, placed her hand on his knees, and stroked it while she again inquired into his intimate life situation.

CONFLICT AND SOCIAL CONTROL

During the 1960s little overt, formal social control was necessary to contain the Unificationist movement. Given the lack of environmental support, ineffective internal organization, and the apathetic response of the larger society, the movement could hardly mount a serious challenge to established institutions. Nevertheless, early in the decade the movement did encounter three distinguishable types of social control responses: public indifference, institutional impermeability, and overt constraint.

Probably the most frustrating fact that the Unificationist movement was forced to confront was the overwhelming disinterest in its message. Particularly because members viewed the theology as mind blowing, general unresponsiveness was disheartening. Given the limited resources available to the movement, members made herculean efforts to gain visibility, spread their message, and recruit new members. Yet, as the review of the movement's proselytization activities revealed, virtually all of their direct witnessing and media publicity was greeted with deafening silence. General apathy was, of course, extremely effective in containing the movement. Short of provoking a confrontation with established institutions (which in fact was avoided) or constructing or financing its own media events (which it lacked the resources to conduct) there was little way to arouse outsiders' curiosity and interest.

Fledgling social movements of all types are confronted by an institutional network which is less permeable than the democratic pluralist model would suggest. One major barrier which the movement encountered was lack of visibility. In light of the apocalyptic, millenarian nature of the theology, recruitment of new members who would establish the basis for full restoration of man to God was of paramount importance. One important step in recruitment was achieving visibility which the movement sought through the media as well as direct proselytization. Because the movement lacked financial resources, it was highly dependent on free publicity to achieve visibility. However, the movement was engaged in neither public service activity that might garner favorable coverage nor protest activities that would bring notoriety. As a result, despite considerable effort the movement was unable to interest the media in airing its views. Lofland (1977: 80-81) described one of the few such cases in which a talk show host conducted a brief, live phone interview with an UM member after reading one of the many classified ads placed by the movement in local newspapers. The interviewer's closing comment, "And that's another of the savory aspects of life I encountered as *I Called the Classified*." indicated the nonchalance and levity with which the interview was conducted. Unable to control image presentation, the movement was treated as yet another instance of the exotic, if innocuous, underlife of American society.

Other means of gaining visibility were equally inaccessible. For example, newspaper coverage of routine religious activity hinged on financial resources. Feature stories on church activities in the religion section of the local newspaper appeared in direct proportion to the church's prominence in the community and/or the amount of advertisement space purchased in that section. Similarly, the largest radio stations would sell air time only to members of the National Council of Churches. The less expensive stations, such as the small religiously oriented station with a predominently black audience over which the movement finally broadcast its message, lacked the more "desirable" type and size of listenership.

Other institutions resisted the movement's direct proselytization activities. Americans generally accepted the notion that one's religious beliefs were a private matter, separate from other aspects of public life and thus to varying degrees resented unrequested intrusion by those seeking religious converts. For example, when members of the movement approached local ministers and faculty members of a seminary with their message they met polite disinterest. More aggressive activities were greeted with stern rebuff. In one case a movement member managed to become a Sunday school teacher in a local church. For a while he confined discussions to uncontroversial religious themes, but as he gradually began to introduce Unification theology, the church elders quickly sensed something was amiss and removed him from his position. Similarly, when a male member of the movement began engaging patients in a hospital where he was employed as an orderly in conversation about *The Divine Principle* and two female members working as waitresses in a cafeteria began placing

Church business cards on customers' trays, complaints quickly surfaced and superiors made it clear that no further incidents would be tolerated (Lofland, 1966: 113-114). If little organized, formal social control was necessary to contain the movement, it was more a function of the movement's impotence than the lack of perceived violations.

Several cases were recorded in which those attending study groups described the movement as a "plot," "anti-Christ," or "subversive," (Lofland, 1966: 168ff) and one woman went so far as to report her suspicions to the F.B.I. The most detailed statement, and one which was strikingly similar to the atrocity stories constructed about the movement a decade later, charged:

> I think its a subversive movement, definitely. There's too many signs in the way they operate, their methods of living and doing things. It's not in their [book or in] anything that could be detected, but it's in what they are doing and what they tell that's not written down.
>
> You know the more I think about it the more I think the F.B.I. should be called in on this.
>
> They don't tell much to anyone following until they've been thoroughly brainwashed and they think they have them thoroughly caught in their snare, and then they tell them about the curses and dreadful things that will happen to their souls if they don't continue on, and if friend or husband won't come, then he's the devil and an evil spirit.
>
> They intend to take over and destroy our family, community, and governmental way of life, and they say so and [are] ruthless in their tactics, too. [They are] plenty tough [and] instill such fear. [Brackets are ours.]

The same charges made in the mid-1970s—deception, brainwashing, use of fear, destruction of family and governmental institutions, and ruthlessness—were evident. The major difference between the 1960s and 1970s was simply that the movement was having virtually no success in recruiting new members (irrespective of its alleged tactics) and hence such cries of alarm made little if any impact.

Continuing Diversity Within the UM: The "Oakland Family"

Because Lofland's treatment of the UM's first American mission provides detailed information on only one of its several factions, there is little known about the other UM groups scattered across the country. As we mentioned, David S.C. Kim continued a mission in Portland, Oregon while Bo Hi Pak conducted his mission in Washington, D.C. We do know, however, that the American UM in the 1960s had already begun to exhibit the diversity of outreach style and doctrinal emphasis that, by the time of Moon's arrival in 1971, had developed into a unmistakable factionalism. And by the mid-to-late 1970s, despite the unifying charismatic presence of Rev. Moon, the American UM was still bifurcated into two distinct "wings." Their initial differences were predictably a function of the movement's dependency on its earliest missionaries to the United States, each with his or her own temperament and perspectives: Young Oon Kim in San Francisco (initially), David S. C. Kim in Portland, Oregon, Bo Hi Pak in Washington, D.C., and, in 1965, a small party of Asiatics led by a man named Sang Ik Choi. Given the controversy surrounding the Oakland Family in the 1970s and its unique success in recruiting new UM members, it is worth briefly describing this wing's development.

In 1966 when Young Oon Kim transferred her activities to Washington, D.C., Mr. Sang Ik Choi, along with a handful of Korean and Japanese UM members (only one of whom spoke English), arrived in San Francisco to continue the missionary work. Clearly, less theologically oriented than Young Oon Kim, Choi's group "experimented" with various tactics, such as a deemphasized theological "pitch," to better attract college-age Americans. The 1960s were, as we have argued, not a period of widespread interest in religious (much less millenarian) solutions to social problems. Choi apparently recognized this fact and realized the need to depart from Kim's strictly theological approach to proselytization. Choi was, in the words of one member who joined in the late 1960s, much more "humanistically" oriented and concerned more to translate the core revelations of Moon into whatever terms were relevant to young Americans than was Kim, restrained as she was by her theological emphasis. This deemphasis of theology and greater stress on the educational/humanistic psychological aspects of *The Divine Principle* was an approach more in tune with the college-age subculture of the 1960s and later was to become a significant earmark of the Oakland Family. This minority tradition, once established, was both a major asset in promoting the UM's growth and a continuing source of potential schism.

In 1971, before Moon's arrival, Choi's first American converts (many of whom went on, a decade later, to become important state and national leaders in the national Unification Church) incorporated the International Reeducation Foundation and set up headquarters on Page Street in San Francisco. Its format stressed ethical education and lectures on the subject at area college campuses, with the intention of establishing a communally run "Ideal City" in the future to actualize its principles. However, unlike its organizational descendents in the mid-1970s, for whom it made good public relations sense to downplay any relation to Moon and his movement, the IRF openly acknowledged its strong ties to the Unification Church. Indeed, in the IRF's 1969 "Prospectus" (IRF, 1969) it explicitly traced its roots to the Unification Church International. Its annual report to California's Registry of Charitable Trusts for 1973 (California, 1973) put this relationship succinctly:

> The International Reeducation Foundation is a religious organization, the members of which are also members of the Unification Church International. All members live in community houses across the nation; this is an integral part of the religion and such facilities cannot be construed as compensation.

Its relatively rapid growth portended its later importance and potential for semiautonomy. For example, after one year of existence, its assets were valued (by the IRF) at $170,000 (California, 1972). When Moon arrived in 1971 the IRF became functionally inoperative for a temporary period as the majority of its members were ordered elsewhere by Moon for purposes to be discussed later. However, the Oakland Family did not completely merge into the Unification Church, nor as we shall see did it relinquish its integral identity with the Church.

Conclusions

SUMMARY

American society has been in the throes of a long-term cultural crisis. Youth, who experienced the incongruities between traditional cultural values and emerging social realities, were disproportionately affected by this crisis and were in a structural position conducive to participation in protest movements. Early in the 1960s there still was a reservoir of support for American "civil religion," and even when significant discrepancies were discovered between ideals and realities, the youth-based social movements that arose were linked to established instructions. The solutions that were accepted were secular, pragmatic, and reflective of continuing faith in the efficacy and legitimacy of the established social order. As the decade wore on, however, the civil rights, antiwar, and university reform movements became increasingly more radical and combined to challenge

the legitimacy of established institutions. Many liberal clergy sought relevance for the religious institution by accommodating to secularization and
allying with reform movements, but, as protest became more stridently
political, religion became less and less relevant to the countercultural
protest movements.

When the UM arrived in America in 1959 it was comprised of several
small, relatively autonomous groups scattered across the country of which
the West Coast group led by Ms. Kim was the only one for which
systematic ethnographic description exists. This group immediately set
about revising and extending the ideology and developing an organizational structure. The recently translated English version of *The Divine
Principle* incorporated elements of western philosophy and history, underwent numerous revisions to improve its readability, and was packaged in a
variety of formats to increase its appeal to potential American converts.
The early west coast family was headed by Ms. Kim, who was regarded as a
charismatic leader by her small band of followers but who lacked the
administrative skills to formulate and carry out a consistent strategy for
the group. The major organizational objectives of the UM during this
period were the recruiting of new members and achieving visibility/legiti-
macy for the movement. A wide variety of recruitment tactics were
employed to attract a diverse array of individuals the UM regarded as
potential recruits, and the group experimented with a number of socialization techniques all of which centered on fostering an intellectual acceptance of the theology. Similarly, the movement attempted to gain public
visibility through tactics as varied as renting soundtrucks and making
church visitations. The UM was largely unsuccessful in generating recruits
or publicity and remained a small, anonymous group through the 1960s.
Only rudimentary organizational elaboration occurred as a result of the
UM's lack of a membership base, economic resources, and visibility. The
most notable developments were establishment of communal residence
supported by member contributions, gradual focusing of recruitment
efforts on the young, designation of ceremonial holidays, and initiation of
a newsletter. Despite these limited developments the UM lacked national
unity and resources which kept the movement's expansion at an incremental rate until Moon's arrival in 1971.

IMPLICATIONS

In Chapter 1 we argued that the amount of support for various types of
social movements varies over time within a society. The actual amount of
support a movement gains is a function of (1) the nature, location, and
amount of discontent within the environment; (2) the effectiveness of the

movement in organizing and channelling that discontent; and (3) the impact of social control exerted by the larger society. Environmental support may facilitate or retard movement development, but it is not in itself a determinative factor. Youth constituted a major source for social movement recruitment because of the disproportionate impact of cultural change on individuals undergoing socialization, their concentration in increasingly larger numbers on college campuses, the relatively large amount of discretionary time available to them, and their freedom from commitment to families and careers.

For several reasons the United States in the 1960s did not provide an auspicious context in which to launch a world-transforming movement based on a religious ideology. First, world-transforming movements tend to emerge in response to diffuse, broad discontents. During the early 1960s problems were seen as limited and solvable; it was toward the end of the decade that transformative rather than reformative movements emerged. Second, social movements typically do not readily shift types of ideologies (e.g., political or economic to religious). The initial protest activities were aimed at specific grievances defined in political terms (e.g., poverty and racial inequality). Therefore, as initial reform efforts were not sufficiently responsive and additional issues divided along the same lines of cleavage, discontent broadened and deepened but remained political. Third, movements of any particular type (e.g., economic, political, religious) can incorporate protests which might otherwise be expressed in a different type of movement. The civil rights movement, for example, although explicitly political in its goals, manifested quasi-religious characteristics as well (e.g., prayer vigils, hymns as protest songs, and calls for God-given rights). The effects of this is to funnel discontents, which might be based on any of several types of imagery, into already established social movements. Finally, social movements require visibility to build support and membership. Once initial definitions of problems have been established (e.g., as political) and movements have emerged which mobilize that discontent, those movements tend to be equated with the protest and solution of problems. The visibility achieved by these movements reduces the ability of other types of movements (e.g., religious) to gain public visibility and recruits.

The UM's problems were, of course, more organizational than environmental. The description of the UM's early history in America presented in this chapter suggests that movements proceed by trial and error to discover the most effective means of mobilizing resources critical to their development, frequently make discoveries serendipitously, and gradually find ways of creating integration and consistency among these emerging structures. Of course, some crucial discoveries may never be made and some organization developments may prove to be unproductive and even counterproductive. Lofland's data lead to the conclusion that the UM lacked the organizational mechanisms to mobilize key resources effectively during this period. In succeeding chapters as we trace the movement's development after Moon's arrival in 1971 the contrast between the UM in the early 1960s and in the early-to-mid 1970s becomes strikingly apparent. Among the organizational problems which the UM did not satisfactorily resolve in the 1960s were the following:

(1) Unity. One persistent problem confronting world-transforming movements that impedes effective mobilization of resources is the strain toward factionalism. In the 1960s no national UM existed; rather, several small, autonomous local groups coexisted in relative isolation from one another. To some extent these groups might be regarded as competitive with one another because they developed independent leadership structures and even different versions of the ideology. As a result, maximum efficiency could not be achieved from the limited resources available to the movement.

(2) Leadership. In world-transforming movements the charismatic founder and leader of the movement plays a unique role and commands a special authority which is beyond the reach of any other individual. Without Moon's charismatic presence as a symbolic rallying point in the 1960s, national leadership could not have been created. In each of the local groups charismatic leaders emerged who served as a basis for unity but perpetuated competing loyalties within the movement as a whole.

(3) Ideology. The inherently radical ideology of a world-transforming movement must hold relevance for whatever environment into which it is transplanted and must be presented in a way that demonstrates that relevance. Certain of the revisions and extensions of the original UM ideology made during the early 1960s probably enhanced its appeal to Americans (e.g., incorporation of Western philosophy and history), but no specific linkages into America or American youth were formulated. Thus, the ideology remained relatively distant from the experience of those whom the UM most assiduously sought to attract. Further, there was no resolution of the problem of how to present the ideology. The movement vacillated between revealing its entire message and holding back the most controversial portions. Lacking a consistent strategy, the UM did not develop consistent means of dealing with the problems of audience hostility and boredom, respectively.

(4) Economic Resources. It is imperative for world-transforming movements to mobilize economic resources in such a way as to maintain total

involvement in and commitment to the movement. The UM's means of accruing economic resources during the 1960s were ineffective in several respects. First, relying on outside employment precluded full-time involvement in UM activities. Second, because members lacked highly valued skills, economic resources were not accrued at a rapid rate. Third, economic activity was not integrated with other movement activity (e.g., as in the case of a communally based enterprise).

(5) Recruitment. If world-transforming movements are unable to recruit members in preexisting groups (e.g., whole families, through communities), recruitment means vary with the clarity with which the target population is identified and access to that population is achieved. There were several major problems with the UM's recruitment techniques in the sixties' decade. First, the movement lacked a clear conception of the segments of the American population for which it would be most attractive (although a consensus did emerge to concentrate on youth), and, in light of later recruitment practices, appears to have been incorrect in certain assumptions it did make (e.g., nonrecruitability of Catholics). Second, recruitment campaigns were conducted only in the UM's immediate environs. Because only a tiny proportion of individuals contacted responded favorably to proselytization, failure to conduct regional or national recruitment campaigns severely limited the movement's growth potential. Third, recruitment activities were not closely integrated with other movement activities, the ideology, and the member role.

(6) Socialization. Because a world-transforming movement involves a major discontinuity with the lifestyles of conventional society, socialization is most effective when members are immediately provided with a well-defined and encompassing role and effective support for that role. The primary problem with UM socialization techniques in the early 1960s derived from members' overly intellectual conceptions of the affiliative process. Emphasis was placed on understanding and acceptance of the theology. As a result, no clear role existed which could immediately integrate a novitiate into the movement on a behavioral level (although moving into the communal setting was stressed) and affective attachments were not reinforced. Further, the relatively long time between first contact and assumption of full-time membership meant that the group had to expend a substantial amount of scarce resources in socialization efforts.

(7) Visibility/Legitimacy. World-transforming movements are highly dependent on gaining both visibility and legitimacy from the society they seek to transform in order to maximize support and minimize opposition. The techniques used by the UM to gain visibility did not produce any collective response, and thus no public definition of the movement

emerged. For the most part the UM sought to reach individuals singly and not in a form which fostered interaction among them, which would have produced public definitions. Thus, the movement did not achieve a definition as either a legitimate or deviant group which could have served to facilitate developing clear strategies for recruitment, creating internal solidarity, or moving toward either confrontation or accommodation.

PART II

**THE MOVEMENT CATAPULTS FROM
OBSCURITY TO LIMELIGHT**

PREFACE

Part II is concerned with the American Unificationist Movement's rapid transformation from relative stagnation in the 1960s to dynamic expansion in the early 1970s. What had been transplanted as relatively small, obscure, and ineffectual groups became, under certain conditions of mobilization, a growing, integrated, and well-publicized movement that aggressively pursued its millenarian goals on a nationwide basis.

Three significant factors in this transformation are identified. First, the sociocultural climate of the 1970s was more propitious to religious orientations, particularly as responses to pressing social conditions, than was the same climate of the decade before. Thus, the UM's initial years of rapid membership and financial growth (1972-1974) coincided with a period of general cultural receptivity to religious perspectives in which the "Moonies" (among other groups) thrived. Second, when Moon shifted his active personal ministry from the Republic of Korea to the United States in late 1971 he brought with him or later developed innovations in the UM's ideology that could not only be related to his Biblically based theology but which represented important extentions of it. Moon provided a new, divinely mandated role for the United States and its UM branch members to play in the restoration of the Kingdom of God on earth. Third, there occurred soon after Moon's arrival a number of changes in the formulation and administration of UM organization and leadership, finances, and membership recruitment as well as in its attempts to spread its world-transforming message to the American public. These changes, when combined with a supportive ideology and conducive sociocultural conditions, underlay the movement's "take-off" in the early 1970s and accounted for its subsequent growth and institutionalization.

The analysis in Part II employs data from a variety of sources. During 1976-1978 we travelled to various UM centers across the country and to the UM's headquarters in New York City, its Barrytown, New York seminary, and the main center of the Creative Community Projects, Inc., in San Francisco. At these locations we interviewed UM leaders at all levels as well as rank-and-file members and observed organizational activities. The UM's public relations office courteously gave us access to its extensive files of press accounts from newspapers across the country covering every aspect of the movement's relations with larger society and permitted us to utilize certain "insider" documents and publications of the UM. Notably among the latter was the UM's limited edition two-volume *Day of Hope* that meticuously chronicled the UM's first two years of active ministry from Moon's arrival in this country to his embroilment in the Watergate controversy. In some instances we also obtained innerorganizational correspondence and other documents from the UM's opponents, i.e., informants and organizations of the anticult movement. Finally, we relied to a limited extent on the relevant published and unpublished research of other social scientists who had studied the UM. Our interpretation of the emerging versions of American UM ideology in Chapter 4 as well as our account of the movement's organizational growth and public activities in Chapters 5 and 6 are based on these interviews, documents, and literally hundreds of newspaper articles. Much of the analysis of UM socialization and recruitment in Chapter 7 is based on our previous research with a sample of UM members (see Bromley and Shupe, 1979), supplemented with available material of other reliable observers.

Chapter 3

AMERICA'S RETURN TO RELIGION

IN THE 1970s

During the 1970s visible political protest activity waned, although a substantial reservoir of discontent and disillusionment remained among youth. Beginning late in the 1960s a resurgence of religiosity began which became highly visible by the early 1970s. This religious revival was broadly based, cutting across age groups and social classes, and took a variety of different forms. The new religions, and particularly those of oriental origin, attracted many youthful devotees although, like the political movements of the previous decade, the visibility and notoriety of these new religious movements far outstripped their numerical size.

The emergence of these movements and the larger religious revival with which they coincided have been traced to the continuing crisis of meaning and the erosion of traditional legitimating values and beliefs within American society. The discrediting of secular solutions and the failure of the scientific revolution to provide a metaphoric system of meanings to replace those it had weakened produced new interest in religious meaning systems. Among youth both Eastern religious groups which critiqued many traditional values and new versions of Western Christian religion which sought to reaffirm traditional cultural values were enthusiastically received. The Unificationist theology contained a unique blend of Eastern and Western philosophy and theology but in its lifestyle incorporated a set of highly traditional American values. The UM's appeal to some youth in the 1970s, then, was linked to a profusion of experiments of a religious and quasi-religious nature to construct meanings and lifestyles in response to the emerging sociocultural realities within American society. The transfer of this search from the political to the religious realm substantially increased the attractiveness of the UM to American youth in the 1970s.

PROTEST AND COUNTERCULTURE IN THE SEVENTIES

As Chapter 2 documented, by 1970 the protest movements which only a short time earlier had been growing in size and militancy began to dissipate and fragment. The extent of this turnaround was reflected in a Gallup poll which showed that in 1970 67% of college students sampled saw "campus radicalism as continuing to grow" while just a year later only 53% of those polled agreed with that statement (Wattenberg, 1976: 266). The dissolution of overt protest did not mean that all the participants in the political movements of the 1960s deserted their political orientation. As inquiries into the whereabouts of movement leaders in the mid-1970s revealed (U.S. News and World Report, January 13, 1975: 34-37; Time, August 15, 1977: 67-68; U.S. News and World Report, March 27, 1978: 38-39), many were still involved in political activity albeit in a much more conventional context.

Sam Brown, an antiwar leader, served a term as State Treasurer of Colorado and later was appointed national director of ACTION. John Froines of the Chicago Seven served as the director of the Occupational, Health and Safety Agency in Vermont. Former Black Panther leader Bobby Seale ran for the office of mayor in Oakland, California, but was defeated. Tom Hayden, a leader of SDS, was a candidate for the U.S. Senate from California. Jesse Jackson was promoting his own campaign, People United to Save Humanity (PUSH), to instill middle-class values in black school children—avoidance of drugs, better grooming, greater emphasis on academic achievement, and respect for parental authority.

Others appeared to be setting the stage for conventional careers. Bobby Rush, Illinois Black Panther leader, enrolled as a graduate student at the University of Illinois. Mario Savio, a major figure in the Free Speech Movement at Berkeley, was employed as a teacher at an alternative school. Even those involved in more radical activities began to "come in from the cold." Phoebe Hirsch, Robert Roth, and Mark Rudd of the Weather Underground all had surrendered to authorities by 1977, and no bombings had been claimed by the group since 1975. Many less known participants continued to play an active role in local or national organizations created during the previous decade by foundations, the federal government, or local communities to deal with social issues which had arisen during that period. Still others found viable means of support in occupations (e.g., artists, musicians, craftsmen, community workers, teachers) that allowed them to maintain some personal distance from conventional lifestyles.

The decline of overt political protest also did not signal the end of the counter culture. Yankelovich (1974: 56) observed that two overlapping but distinguishable movements had taken place simultaneously during the 1960s: the "social values movement" and the "political revolution." Through the 1960s these two movements had coexisted with many participants in common, but the demise of the political revolution was not accompanied by a parallel trend in the social values movement. His comparative survey data on young adults for 1969 and 1973 showed that a variety of values associated with the emergence of the counter culture (tolerance or acceptance of sexual freedom, marijuana use, homosexuality, unconventional lifestyles) increased while numerous traditional values (materialism, patriotism, duty before pleasure, economically motivated careers) decreased in importance, particularly for college youth. Self-fulfillment, love, and friendship became more important personal values. The decline of the political revolution also was evident. Few young adults were willing to characterize American society as sick or racist, identify themselves as politically radical, or espouse changing society as an important personal value.

The complex, amorphous problems confronting American society in the 1970s also served to frustrate the formation of political movements. There seemed to be few easy answers to issues such as the need for new energy sources versus dangers of pollution, the quest for lower unemployment rates versus risks of rising inflation, and maintaining military strength versus limiting the arms race. The political scandal surrounding the presidency, the CIA and the FBI continued to sap the legitimacy of the political institution. America's position as the foremost economic and military power appeared to be eroding, and many Americans sensed the country was reacting to events rather than controlling its destiny. Those graduating from college faced a more uncertain job market, and the growing number of individuals earning college degrees sharply increased the competition for available jobs. Students appeared less ready to involve themselves in political activity and more concerned with occupationally oriented education. The mood of youth, which had been rebellious a few years before, seemed more tentative and conservative.

RESURGENCE OF RELIGIOSITY

Even as the protest movements began to fade from public view there appeared to be a major upswing in religiosity. While the new religions have captured the greatest attention, they arose in the context of a more broadly based resurgence of interest in religion. For example, the percentage of adults reporting that they had attended church in the last week, which had declined to a low point of 40% in 1971, had climbed to 42% by 1976 and 44% by 1977 (Christian Science Monitor, January 19, 1977). Similarly, the perception of the churches' influence in American life showed a turnabout. In 1970 only 14% of adults polled saw the church as gaining influence; 31% of the survey sampled were willing to agree with that statement in 1975 and just two years later the figure stood at 44%.

Although there was an upswing in standard indices of religiosity, the trend did not materialize in mainstream denominations. The Methodist, Presbyterian, Church of Christ, and Episcopal denominations all continued to lose members. It was the evangelical (believers in making a personal commitment to Christ and through such a spiritual encounter being born again) and fundamentalist groups that experienced the most rapid growth. By the mid-1970s it was estimated that as many as fifty million Americans had had a born again experience. The religious upsurge was strongly based in the middle classes, and church attendance increased most rapidly in young adult age groups. In certain respects the quest for more direct, personal religious experiences might be underestimated as several million charismatics (i.e., individuals sharing a belief in baptism by the Holy Spirit) remained less visible by staying within their own churches rather than joining one of the neopentacostal groups.

The religious revival gained visibility too as many public notables lent their names and support to evangelical activities. President Jimmy Carter, Senator Mark Hatfield, Representative John Anderson, Governor Julian Carroll, athletic stars Archie Griffin and Stan Smith, entertainers Pat Boone and Paul Stookey, and billionnaire Nelson Hunt all were prominently associated with the evangelistic movement. A number of notorious public figures were swept up in the religious fervor and dedicated their lives to Christ. These included former Black Panther Eldridge Cleaver; Charles Colson, former Watergate defendant; Tex Watson, one time member of the Manson family; and Larry Flynt, editor of *Hustler*. In addition, several prominent political activists joined new religious groups. For example, Jerry Rubin, ex-Yippie, became a member of the human potential movement and Rennie Davis, a Chicago Seven defendant, became a disciple of Master Maharaj Ji.

At the same time it would be a mistake to overestimate the impact of these trends. The reaffirmation of faith by millions of Americans should not be confused with major changes in behavior. This point was illustrated by a follow-up survey (Time, January 23, 1978: 78) of those attending a Billy Graham crusade in 1976 which revealed that 54% of those who "came forward" to witness their faith in Christ were simply rededicating themselves and that of 8,400 pledge cards filled out by those attending only 15% ended up as church members several months later. A similar evaluation of Bill Brights' evangelical campaign concluded that only 3% of those who made a "decision for Christ" over the phone subsequently joined a church.

SOURCES OF THE RELIGIOUS RESURGENCE

Bellah (1976: 339) has convincingly argued that what occurred in the 1960s was a "crisis of meaning" in which "the inability of utilitarian individualism to provide a meaningful pattern of personal and social existence" became increasingly apparent. Concurring that Americans faced a crisis of meaning, Bell (1976: 28-30) observed that this was precisely the set of structural circumstances in which a reemergence of religiosity might be expected:

What holds one to reality, if one's secular system of meanings proves to be an illusion? I will risk an unfashionable answer—the return in Western society of some conception of religion.

If Bell was correct, then the religious revival occurred on schedule, at the nadir of secular institutions' legitimacy and at a time when faith in secular solutions to contemporary problems was fast receding. The most basic interpretive metaphors by which individuals understood themselves, their relationships to one another, and the meaning of life itself were at issue. Because religion traditionally has been the source of such meanings, a revival of religious interest was not at all incongruous.

The resurgence of religious interest and activity, then, constituted a broadly based reaction to secularity. As Heenan (1973: 1) observed:

Protestantism rejected mysterious, magical, and miraculous phenomena that had been endemic to the Catholic tradition. The effect was to place ecstasy, charismatic gifts, mysticism and emotionalism outside the mainstream Protestantism and into the sphere of religious minority groups.

It was precisely this earlier tradition that was reasserted as millions of Americans became evangelicals and neopentacostals.

Among youth who had experienced the full brunt of this crisis, there also was a resurgence of interest in religion principally outside the established churches. The political movements of the 1960s had changed certain cultural values and domestic and foreign policy but had never produced viable long-term lifestyle alternatives for their members. As the cultural crisis continued, established institutions were discredited, and political solutions were not forthcoming, many youth sought solutions in religious movements which offered thoroughgoing critiques of traditional cultural value systems. The same kind of experimentation that had characterized the counterculture movements of the 1960s assumed a religious flavor in the 1970s. As Bellah (1976: 341) put it:

> In many ways Asian spirituality provided a more thorough contrast to the rejected utilitarian individualism than did biblical religion. To external achievement it posed inner experience, to the exploitation of nature, harmony with nature, to impersonal organization an intense relation to a guru.

Needleman (1972: 1-22) concurred that Eastern religion offered a "corrective" to Western religion.

THE RISE OF NEW RELIGIOUS MOVEMENTS

Not all of American youths' revival of interest in religious and quasi-religious groups was directed at new religions; there was a substantial attraction to the Jesus movement as well (Heenan, 1973; Richardson, 1974). However, the new religions attracted the greatest attention and symbolized the variety of experimentation. All of these groups became visible and began to grow rapidly in the four- or five-year period bridging the 1960s and 1970s. The Jesus Movement first appeared in California in 1968 as did the Children of God. Hare Krishna was established in New York in 1965. Transcendental Meditation had attracted some attention early in the 1960s as a result of the Beatles' trips to India for instruction; however, it was not until the late 1960s that TM arrived in the United States and began to flourish. Scientology had been popular in the United States during the 1950s under the name Dianetics but it declined during the 1960s before experiencing a major resurgence toward the end of the decade. Divine Light Mission did not appear in America until 1971, and experienced rapid growth thereafter. The Unification Church had been in the United States since 1959 but grew slowly until 1971 when its rate of growth suddenly accelerated. Healthy, Happy, Holy, a variation of Sikhism, first arrived in America in 1968.

DIVERSITY AND IMPACT OF NEW RELIGIONS

Like the protest movements of the 1960s the proportion of American youth who were active participants in the new religious movements of the

1970s was small. Accurate membership figures are difficult to obtain for most of these groups due to the nature of many of the groups and the rapid turnover in membership. Most of the movements which have been regarded as "extreme" (e.g., Hare Krishna, Children of God, Divine Light Mission, Unification Church) never exceeded a few thousand active members. Other groups such as Transcendental Meditation and Scientology which have been regarded as less extreme have also grown much larger. Of course all of these groups have become part of the cultural landscape and have had some social impact. Wuthnow's (1976: 274) poll of 1,000 persons sixteen or older in the San Francisco Bay Area revealed that:

> Nearly four out of every five persons claim to know a little about at least one of these (thirteen) movements, over half claim to know something about at least three of them. . . . More than half of the population is currently attracted to at least one of them and about a third is attracted to at least two of them. . . . One out of every five persons claims to have taken part in at least one of these groups. Eleven percent . . . said they had taken part in other groups similar to these.

As Cox (1977) observed, participants in general were middle or upper middle-class individuals in their late teens or early twenties. Many were from liberal Protestant and reform Jewish backgrounds and were college drop-outs. However, there also were significant differences among the participants in these groups. Wuthnow (1976: 285) reported that movements such as Hare Krishna and Children of God attracted relatively young individuals (i.e., ages 16 to 20) whereas Transcendental Meditation and Scientology attracted young adults. A few groups such as Jews for Jesus even attracted older (i.e., over 50) adults. The movements also differed in the extent to which they attracted individuals interested in radical political change; movements such as Transcendental Meditation, Hare Krishna, and Scientology ranked relatively high, Jews for Jesus and Children of God ranked low. Similar patterns emerged with respect to support for unconventional values and lifestyles (Wuthnow, 1976: 279-280). All of the movements included in Wuthnow's survey attracted individuals who were among the better educated, but again there was considerable variation with groups such as Transcendental Meditation and Hare Krishna ranking relatively high and Children of God ranking quite low.

THE UM IN THE RELIGIOUS REVIVAL

Among the new religions the UM was clearly one of the more conservative, particularly as it vociferously reaffirmed America's traditional civil religion (albeit with a sectarian twist). In the 1960s, a decade characterized by liberal, political solutions to problems, the UM had been relatively unsuccessful in attracting youth. Suddenly in the 1970s it found that the traditional values which it extolled, such as patriotism, hard work, individual responsibility, diligence, monogamous relationships, sanctity of the family, and opposition to promiscuity and drugs were in much greater favor. At the same time the UM flirted with aspects of the counter culture: Eastern philosophy, communal lifestyles, an emphasis on self-actualization, and rejection of materialism. It thus competed with a variety of other new religions, but available evidence suggests that there was a rather systematic self-sorting of potential recruits into the various groups along several basic socioeconomic dimensions. Our own data from participant observation (Bromley and Shupe, 1979) and from interviews with national UM leaders indicate that among American UM members there was a high ratio of males to females, an average age of 23 years, and that about four-fifths were Caucasian. Their backgrounds included a disproportionately high percentage of Catholics, and members' families were heavily representative of the mid-to-lower strata of the middle class.

Conclusions

SUMMARY

By 1970 the political movements which had so dominated the American scene even a year earlier began to wane visibly although many of the counterculture values associated with those movements continued to gain acceptance. However, the decline of the political protests did not signal either the end of the cultural crisis or a resolution of the problems of youth vis-à-vis that crisis. Toward the end of the 1960s faith declined in political/secular solutions to the problems confronting America as they were offered either by the political institution or by the protest movements. The new problems that emerged in the 1970s seemed more amorphous and complex and did not offer a clear target for political protest movements. It was in this context of declining political efficacy and legitimacy that religious movements emerged. Most of this broadly based resurgence of religiosity took place outside of the established denominations. While for middle-aged adults who were born again this religious revival usually did not involve major lifestyle changes, many youthful members of the new religions made more total, if temporary, commitments. The ideologies and organizations of these movements suggested a continuation of youthful protest movements in different form and an ongoing search for viable alternatives to conventional lifestyles that the political protest movement had been unable to create. Like the political movements of the 1960s the religious movements of the 1970s stratified along a number of social dimensions such as age, class, and liberalism-conservatism. The UM could be located in this period as a relatively youthful, solidly middle-class, conservative movement that sought to reaffirm American civil religion while at the same time appealing to and seeking to integrate certain countercultural values of the 1960s.

IMPLICATIONS

This chapter's brief review of events in the 1970s reveals a sharp contrast with the preceding decade in the propitiousness of the sociocultural environment for religiously based world-transforming movements. We would argue that American society was conducive to the growth of religious movements in the 1970s for several reasons. First, the viability of forming a social movement around religious metaphors increased. *The basic metaphors around which social movements develop are most likely to change when a key symbolic system and supporting institutional systems have lost legitimacy and efficacy.* This occurred in the United States when both the political institution and the political protest movements which challenged it failed to redress discontents adequately. In modern, secular societies religiously based world-transforming movements become less numerous and influential. Such movements typically occur when empirical solutions to problems are ineffective. Second, *when a variety of different types of movements arise in response to the same set of sociocultural conditions, their presence is mutually reinforcing.* In contrast to the UM, for example, a number of religious and quasi-religious groups emerged seeking individual rather than structural change (e.g., Transcendental Meditation, Meher Baba, Scientology), and, further the new religious movements manifested distinctive socioeconomic membership bases. Although such individual movements may compete to a very limited extent, their mutual presence increases the visibility and impact of religious movements taken as a whole. Finally, *The proliferation and visibility of religious movements draw off potential support for political movements.* Many of the 1970s religious movements incorporated political as well as religious values (e.g., the UM's strong anticommunist stance), and a number of individuals who had been participants or leaders of political movements in the preceding decade became associated with these religious movements.

Chapter 4

AMERICA'S ROLE IN MOON'S MILLENNIUM

Once in the United States the UM gradually developed and extended its ideology to fit the cultural milieu. The major ideological innovations occurred after 1971 within the two principal wings of the movement: the mainstream, theologically orthodox East Coast Church, and the more humanistic, revisionist Oakland Family (i.e., Oakland, California). While the former was still the predominant worldview of most UM members as of 1978, the Oakland Family's interpretation and innovative application of *The Divine Principle* had significant implications for larger society's reaction to the UM as well as for the movement's mobilization of new recruits.

The Mainstream Ideology of the East Coast Church

Sun Myung Moon's arrival in the United States in 1971 coincided with a dramatically increased emphasis on the role that America was to play in establishing God's Kingdom on earth. Prior to that time the United States had played a relatively limited part in the international UM. While Moon had dispatched Young Oon Kim and David S. C. Kim to this country in 1959 as its first missionaries, and twice during the next decade (in 1965 and again in 1969) he personally visited centers in the United States, the American UM's small size and paltry resources had not enabled it to have more than a minor impact on the worldwide organization. There were even indications, based on the authors' discussions with one informant familiar with the early American Church, that Moon might never have come to this country to conduct his massive campaigns had not Young Oon Kim convinced him that the USA, rather than England, offered the most fertile ground for proselytization (Personal Interviews, 1978). Clearly, the American UM leaders whom Moon criticized for their lack of success upon his arrival possessed little inkling of how the international UM's efforts would shift to the United States.

Moon began this shift with what appears to have been a revision of *The Divine Principle*'s timetable for restoration. Lofland (1966) originally reported that Young Oon Kim had forecast 1967 as the target date to begin the millenium, a date which members later contended was simply her misinterpretation. As Lofland mentioned in his update on the UM (1977: 781-782), in the early seventies Moon expanded the 1967 date into three seven-year "courses": 1960-1967 was the course devoted to "restoring" the ideal family institution and consolidating the Korean Church; 1968-1974 was the "national" course during which spiritual and physical foundations were to be established in the "archangel" nation (i.e., the United States); and 1975-1981 was the "international" course in which the UM would take on its global mission.

Such "modifications" of prophecy posed no major problem for UM members whose faith was in a man they believed to be the medium of ongoing, evolving Divine revelations. It should be stressed that in the eyes of many believers Moon's historical parallels were much less sacrosanct than more fundamental "core" ideas surrounding *The Divine Principle*. The timing of various stages of the restoration process was *not* precise, they would have acknowledged, and moreover the actual length of "course" periods could be affected by members' concentrated efforts and suffering. If the cosmos did operate as Moon said it did, then the restoration process could manifest its apparent shifts and vicissitudes.

But for whatever reasons Moon reformulated the restoration timetable, postponement of the millenium was unquestionably critical for recruiting idealistic American youth. After all, the inducement to enlist in a world-saving movement would be greater if potential converts could be told that they were, for a short time, still able to join in on the "ground floor" of an enterprise that would soon become enormous and important, rather than that the movement's pioneer days were over. Sudo (1975: 184) expressed this idea in a lecture to leader-trainees when he exclaimed:

> Father's mission will finish in seven years. If you join Father's seven year course, this means that this is the most glorious time in your

life. At the end of the course, people will go to Father, but he will say that he has finished . . . afterwards even the President or Rockefeller may come but Father will say, My mission is finished.

THE MEANING OF RESTORATION: UNIFYING A DIVIDED WORLD

America's entry into the restoration process was fundamentally linked by Moon to the Fall of Man. Because God's basic nature was to love, Moon maintained, God created mankind to enjoy a true love relationship premised on a reciprocity of give and take. Moreover, because God created men and women in His image, all were meant to exist in a mutually loving arrangement. As we noted earlier, mankind's *vertical* fall from God was caused by the envious archangel Lucifer seducing Eve. At that point Satan replaced God as the spiritual parent of all humanity. There was subsequently a *horizontal* fall as well, occurring when Eve seduced Adam and subsequently Cain slew Abel. The vertical fall denoted mankind's estrangement from God, the True Parent, while the horizontal fall initiated a parallel estrangement of one human being from another. That first fratricide had the effect of dividing the world spiritually into two camps—the satanic, or Cain-positioned, and the righteous, or Abel-positioned. Millennia later this opposition came to be recapitulated on a physical level as the atheistic communist and God-fearing democratic nations, respectively.

On an international level, then, restoration concerned the resolution of this opposition of countries. To accomplish this, it was necessary from the UM perspective for nations to perform specific roles comparable to those of Adam, Eve, and the archangel Lucifer as God presumably had intended these roles to be performed before the Fall: South Korea, Moon's new Israel, assumed the Adam position; Japan (restored to the democratic world after its defeat in World War II) was to be the new "Eve"; and the United States would be the new archangel, or servant that would, by supporting both Adam and Eve, undo the evil of Lucifer.[1] This restoration process, according to Moon, followed an invariable pattern: God "prepared" a "central religion" and a "chosen nation" as the "foundation to receive the messiah" (Moon, 1976). As *The Divine Principle* chronicled, such conditions had existed in the past when restoration was unsuccessfully attempted a number of times, the most famous attempt being Jesus' brief ministry. At that time the chosen nation had been Israel and the central religion has been Judaism. Later, as Christianity became the central religion, Rome became the chosen "nation" and a succession of popes the potential messiahs.

Now, in the latter half of the twentieth century, Moon proclaimed to Americans that the time was again propitious for restoration and that

America had the opportunity to play a central role. In fact, as Moon reiterated to followers in America, because they possessed knowledge of *The Divine Principle,* this attempt would be unique: "This period of providence comes only once in history, no more. There will be no other time you can receive directions directly from our Master, and work with his heart" (MS, 1971b: 10).

The Unificationist theology, representing the "pinnacle" of all previous religious strivings, replaced Christianity as God's new central religion while South Korea became the new chosen nation and America her chief protector. Why was Korea the chosen nation? Obviously one factor was that Jesus Christ purportedly appeared to Moon, a Korean, and had selected him for his sincerity and personal qualifications. Furthermore, on the Korean peninsula at Punmunjom were uniquely massed in armageddon fashion the spiritual forces of both evil and good, North and South Korea. As Moon proclaimed, "That is the only such place on this earth. . . . We have to defeat North Korea, and by defeating North Korea we can defeat all other Communists" (MS, 1971a: 6).

But why was the United States chosen to serve as the servant/protector archangel in this cosmic confrontation? Moon offered several reasons.

First, as *the* major free-world power the United States had the unparalleled military strength to stand up to world communism and was obliged to use that strength *sacrificially* for all people. Moon (1973: 61) observed that the United States had acted previously in a self-centered way and exhorted the country to rise to what he claimed was its God-centered purpose:

> The United States is the leading country in the democratic world, but she has not been able to fulfill that role when she thought of her own interests more than those of other nations. America and Russia seem ready today to throw away the whole world to save themselves. There must be one nation who can sacrifice herself for the establishment of the ideal world.

Second, Moon perceived that its archangelic obligations flowed out of the United States' status as *the* preeminent Christian nation. He maintained that "God can be seen everywhere in America" (1974: 58) and that Americans ought to fulfill a stewardship role for God. Noting the inscription "In God We Trust" on American money, Moon claimed that "it is God's money. Every bill or coin says so. You are the stewards and God has deposited His wealth in your hands. Yes . . . it is God's nation."

Third, America's perceived obligation to the world also flowed from the belief that God Himself had raised the American nation from being a wilderness to the world's most affluent country as part of divine providence.

> America's existence was according to God's providence. God needed to build one powerful Christian nation on earth for His future work. . . . This continent of America was hidden away for a special purpose and was not discovered until the appropriate hour [Moon, 1974: 55].

Reminiscent of the major cultural themes in American civil religion, Moon traced in detail America's growth, including the arrival of the Pilgrims and other immigrants seeking relief from religious persecution, in order to illustrate how America had been divinely guided. (This parallel to American civil religion has previously received an excellent analysis—see Robbins et al., 1976.)

> Their purpose in coming to America was to build a nation centered on God, to establish the land where God could dwell, where they could really share fellowship with each other and rejoice in fellowship with God. This was all in God's Providence, because He needed a nation to serve as His champion for the ultimate and permanent salvation of the world [Moon, 1974: 53-54].

Carrying this parallel further, Moon (1974: 57) compared the trials of George Washington at Valley Forge and his ultimate triumph over the British to David vanquishing Goliath.

Therefore, it is not surprising that Moon interpreted America's political institutions and democratic heritage as being of divine, rather than human, origin and hence obliged to become part of God's providence:

> What is democracy? I want you to know clearly that this is a gift from God. Through democracy He can restore the heavenly sovereignty from Santanic sovereignty without shedding blood. . . . God has been working so hard to give you this environment; that is what democracy is all about. . . . You have assured freedom of speech, freedom of assembly, freedom of publication, and freedom of religion. . . . God created democracy so that in these final days of this dispensation His people, His soldiers, can freely move. This is the environment God provided for 2,000 years so that we could work [MS-416, 1974: 3].

Given the previous understandings, the United States was the logical choice to act as archangel to the new Israel. Concretely, this meant military support of the Park regime in South Korea. For the United States to do otherwise would be to reject the purpose for which God raised it up above other nations and ultimately to imperil its own existence. In a 1971 training session before his first national tour, Moon (MS, 1971a: 6) warned members: "Whenever America withdraws or cancels or stops her foreign aid to the land of Korea, the United States will decline and perish. . . . The future destiny of Korea depends upon the destiny of the United States."

Thus, when Moon analyzed American political and foreign policy, it was natural for him to view Nixon's two-year extension of the period before withdrawal of U.S. land troops from South Korea as "God's will." In one speech to UM members, he put the matter of support for Korea even more bluntly when he said: "there is no way to serve the whole world; therefore, you have to concentrate your efforts toward the restoration of one nation—and this is Korea" (MS, 1971c: 5).

INTERNAL REORIENTATION OF PURPOSE

Thus, the thrust of Moon's tours and rallies, reiterated in all of his major addresses and particularly hammered home during America's bicentennial celebration, concerned three broad objectives: *sensitization* to America's providential significance and obligations; *moral instruction* of Americans in the principles of God-centered conduct; and *unification* against satanic communism, forming a solid front buttressed by one will and sense of mission.

As we have described, protecting South Korea was a vital element in this awakening/learning/uniting campaign. Two other issues were also important. One concerned the stemming of what Moon perceived to be tendencies toward vice and moral decay within American society, particularly in forms such as drug abuse, sexual promiscuity, and pornography. These were favorite themes that Moon drew upon repeatedly in speeches obviously intended as moral instruction for his audiences. In particular, pornography was the subject of a series of demonstrations across the country by hundreds of UM members in 1974. Although drug abuse and promiscuity were targets of much rhetorical energy, Moon and the UM directed most of their efforts internally at members. In fact, such traditional Protestant virtues of sobriety and sexual restraint outside of marriage became earmarks of the conspicuously "straight, Moonie" image and can be traced back throughout the history of the American UM. For example, during his 1965 visit to this country, Moon warned members that alcohol was "an intoxicator" and "one of Satan's best tools" (MS-7[2], 1965: 2).

Almost a decade later, workshop leader Ken Sudo (1975: 69) put sexual contacts and the possibility of improprieties into a distinctly UM context:

> Don't defile your body because it is a temple of God, a residence of God. God wants to live in you. He's made His reservation already, so don't cancel it. . . . Don't make a reservation with Satan.

Similarly, the doctrine of the family—to be detailed later—composed an important part of this ideology. In Chapter 1 we described how UM members were instructed to regard themselves as models of "God-centered love" for all the world. The family was the crucial "building-block" unit for unification and restoration of the world. Because the love within families recapitulated the love relationship between God and man, the True family (as Moon's ideal conjugal unit was termed) became an extremely important referent for members. In 1978 Americans hardly needed to be alerted to the changing conceptions and strains on the nuclear family institution. Thus, UM members spent a good deal of effort trying to spread awareness of, and muster support for, their norm of the God-centered family. They were also severely warned of the consequences for their own deviations from the Unificationist norm:

> If you commit fornication after joining the Unification Church, it is terrible. It is a betrayal against the Lord of the Second Advent and against True Parents. . . . After the blessing [marriage], if someone commits sin, it's completely hopeless. Even Father has nothing to do with salvation then [Sudo, 1975: 136].

Needless to say, proscriptions against homosexuality were equally severe.

The Revisionist Ideology of the West Coast "Oakland Family"

The West Coast's Oakland Family of the 1970s clearly pursued a less doctrinaire course with regard to *The Divine Principle,* theological issues such as the Fall of Man and indemnity, and Moon's strident anticommunism as compared to the East Coast mainstream. This was in keeping with the outreach style initiated in the late sixties by UM missionary Sang Ik Choi following Young Oon Kim's move to Washington, D.C. Choi felt that his mission in the San Francisco Bay area would be more successful in attracting bright young college-age Americans if it deemphasized the UM's heavy Biblical/anticommunist rhetoric that by the late sixties had become passé among the new generation of young adult activists. (That he was likely correct we will see later.)

Choi's successors, Yeon Soo Im and her husband Martin Irwin "Mose" Durst, continued that liberal style into the next decade when the Bay Area missions sought to publically distinguish themselves from the Unification Church of America by organizing themselves into various branches of the Creative Community Projects, Inc. Briefly, the Oakland Family's revision of UM orthodox beliefs ran as follows:

Many elements of the complex maze of numerology, Old Testament history, Satanic threat in the form of international communism, and the need to work off indemnity were either dropped or radically altered. They were replaced by elements of humanistic psychology, reflecting the professional backgrounds of Mose Durst, who studied at the National Training Laboratories in Bethel, Maine, and of Kristina Morrison, his chief assistant, who had completed all but the thesis for her doctorate in psychology. For example, rather than speak of Satan, Durst in his lectures dwelled on human alienation and failure to lovingly communicate sentiments as the true sources of mankind's present dilemmas. Due to faulty socialization, inability to adequately comprehend and cope with the pressures of modern urban life, and a limited vision of what the brotherhood of man could mean, human beings (he claimed) now found their social and personal relationships fragmented and less than satisfying. Without a new principle of reciprocal loving around which people could center their actions and a new model of community based on such loving into which people could organize themselves, there was very little hope for humanity to end its most pressing social problems.

In this treatment the Fall of Man became less an historical event than an existential dilemma all persons encounter.[2] Satan was transformed into raw egotism, and the confrontation with communism simply was dropped ("We don't teach VOC [Victory Over Communism] here," one CCP leader told us in an interview). Rather than working to pay off mankind's accumulated indemnity in order to establish spiritual and physical foundations for the Lord of the Second Advent to bring about God's Kingdom on earth, people strove to self-actualize themselves within a communal setting that allowed them to give emotionally to others and to receive such love from others.

This is not to say that Oakland Family members were unfamiliar with either Rev. Moon or *The Divine Principle.* Indeed, heavy doses of it were provided in weekend and week-long workshops, and most persons recruited for the UM by the Oakland Family were sent on to work for the movement elsewhere with persons with more theological exposure. But the overarching emphasis on Moon's messianic purpose, his legitimation as a charismatic authority, the pervasive threat of communism, and America's unique archangelic role in helping to usher in the millennium were seriously underplayed to the point that the Oakland Family's departure in ideology, despite its many links to Moon's theology, could if need be, stand independent of the latter.

Conclusions

SUMMARY

In this chapter we examined the exportation of Moon's theology to the United States and its ideological extensions in two related but distinct directions. The first, or mainstream East Coast, extension entailed a revision of the UM's original prediction of 1967 as the completion date for restoration as well as a conceptualization of current international events concerning communist and noncommunist nations in the Manichaeistic terms of *The Divine Principle.* In particular it cast the United States in the role of archangel or servant/protector to South Korea. Moon's ministry to this country focused on educating its leaders and citizens in the requirements of this role, calling for a recognition of its duty to reestablish relations between secular/political actions and moral purposes. Dwelling on such issues as the dangers of international "godless" communism, sexual promiscuity, and the weakening family institution, the themes of this first ideological extension directly linked it to America's traditional civil religion which, as we argued in Chapters 2 and 3, had been in decline since the shattering events of the late 1960s.

The second extension, or revisionist ideology of the West Coast's Oakland Family, carried the original Korean-produced ideology forth in a less theological and more humanistic direction. Reflecting the orientations and temperaments of its leaders, this factional variation abandoned much of the religious rhetoric of good and evil and translated the fundamental predicament of modern humanity from original sin into the terms of humanistic psychology. Drawing upon certain popular themes associated with the counter culture of the 1960s, particularly that of self-actualization, the struggle for spiritual purity thus became a quest for individual maturity and interpersonal responsibility.

These two variations existed more or less in a state of mutual tolerance and utility. Each could find analogues for its core concepts in the other, and, as we shall document in the next chapter, transition of members recruited and socialized in the Oakland Family from that humanistic environment to the more theologically oriented UM was relatively smooth.

IMPLICATIONS

The ideology of a world-transforming movement sets forth the rationale for the kinds of relationships its members wish to maintain. We would argue that it is important to the mobilization process that changes in the ideology take place under certain conditions internal or external to the movement:

(1) To explain disconfirmations in specific predictions of future events. If a crisis atmosphere is created by the prediction of imminent cataclysmic change (as a means of fostering internal solidarity), some means must be found for explaining away any "errors" in time timetable of restoration. Techniques for handling this problem include (a) setting a new date for anticipated events along with offering a rationale for their diversion from the original timetable (e.g., Moon's replacement of the 1967 restoration date with three seven-year periods ending in 1981) and (b) defining predicted events as having occurred despite their invisibility to outsiders (e.g., the accomplishment of spiritual as opposed to physical restoration).

(2) To adjust the movement to a new set of conditions. First, the transplantation of a world-transforming movement to a new sociocultural environment may require modifications of the ideology to render it more pertinent to the values and concerns of its new host population (e.g., Moon's designation of a key role for America in the restoration process). If the movement is effective in gaining new members in the new environment, they may then make further alterations in the ideology (see the humanistic revisions of the Oakland Family). Second, changes in the demographic/socioeconomic composition of the movement also may stimulate ideology revisions. Although our observations of the UM did not encompass a sufficiently long time period for such changes to occur, there were indications, for example, that the ideology would be extended to define marital and family relationships more clearly as youthful converts began to form families within the movement.

(3) To cope with the inevitable strains of a long-term movement. For any movement surviving and developing, certain strains and "crisis points" seem inevitable. Primary among these are the problems of schism and loss of the movement's charismatic leader. While schism may have been precipitated by the modification of the original ideology, the event itself frequently leads to further ideological innovations. (There was some potential for such schism in the UM as a result of its innovations on Moon's theology and its separate charismatic tradition, as we shall show in the

next chapter.) Loss of the charismatic founder and leader of the movement also may lead to extensions of the ideology, particularly if these
events occur in an unexpected fashion and the problem of succession has
not been resolved. (Interviews with UM members and leaders led us to
conclude that this question had not been resolved, i.e., whether after
Moon the new ultimate authority in the UM would be one of Moon's sons,
his wife, Mose Durst, current President Salonen, or a coalition of UM
patriarchs.)

On the surface it would seem that altering the ideology would undermine members' faith in its ultimate truth and have disasterous consequences for the movement. Indeed, outsiders frequently are mystified and
even alarmed when changes in ideology, logical inconsistencies, and dis-
confirmed predictions do not have such results. The fact that insiders cling
to their beliefs in spite of these is often used by outsiders to "prove" the
formers' credulity. However, outsiders usually do not identify with the
nature and source of human problems as portrayed by the ideology and
have not experienced the sense of power and confirmatory experiences
that emanate from the movement's strong, communally based social relationships. *It is these social relationships that provide members with
dramatic personal evidence that the ideal life the ideology outlines is in
fact possible and that the ideology itself is true. We would argue that as
long as the basic metaphor remains intact and a strong network of
reinforcing social relationships is maintained, such changes in ideology do
not necessarily pose a threat to the movement.* The ease with which UM
members socialized into either the mainstream or the distinctive Oakland
Family ideological variants (and, as we shall see in the next chapter, moved
from one to the other organizationally) provides evidence of this. The
basic metaphors of love, family, and fall/restoration remained even though
interpretations of and derivations from those metaphors differed.

When changes in the ideology do occur a number of adaptations are
possible which reduce potential strain. First, earlier ideological formulations may simply be forgotten and/or treated as irrelevant (e.g., most UM
members are unaware of the original 1967 date for restoration). Second,
earlier statements may be reinterpreted so as to create consistency with
current ideology or realities (as the UM did, replacing physical with
spiritual victories when events went awry). Finally, earlier formulations
may be treated as allegorical/apocryphal tales (e.g., to an extent Moon's
parallels in history and even the stories of Moon's extraordinary qualities
were treated in this way by at least some members).

NOTES

1. According to one of Moon's 1971 speeches (MS, 1971b), there should have been only one archangel nation but instead three unexplainably resulted. Taiwan was the Asian archangel, the United States was the democratic world's archangel, and West Germany (apparently not included among the latter democracies) was the world-scale archangel. This point is somewhat arcane and probably little understood, if known at all, by many members. It is, however, typical of the complex divisions and elaborations of symbolic/empirical parallels in Unificationist ideology.

2. This does not mean that members were ignorant of, or disbelieved in, *The Divine Principle*'s theology. Durst, for example, in a private interview with the authors (1978), affirmed his belief in the literal truth of Moon's account of such events and the Fall of Man and Cain's murder of Abel. He perceived, however, that the Unification Church's theology and the humanistic revision of it which he helped evolve dovetailed on all significant points, hence there was less need to present both systems to recruits.

Chapter 5

BUILDING THE MOVEMENT:

LEADERSHIP AND ORGANIZATION

A number of factors interacted and radically transformed the Unificationist Movement in the 1970s. Moon's active personal ministry to the American public was perhaps the most dramatic one. His presence served as a catalyst to organizational change by providing both inspirational and administrative leadership and by reducing factionalism within the movement. A second critical factor was the development of innovative patterns in recruitment and fund-raising. The mobilization of these two resources permitted the third major development: the emergence of institutional structures that constituted the means to achieve the movement's goals. These goals included training of leaders, dissemination of the UM worldview, developing careers within the movement, infusing science and other secular institutions with ethical principles, combatting godless communism, and establishing spiritually enlightened marriages. While there was marked increase in the complexity and centralization of the UM, there concurrently existed continued, deliberate resistence to bureaucratization in the form of communal-style organization of activities.

Transformation of American UM Leadership

MOON AS CHARISMATIC LEADER

It would be virtually impossible to understand the course of the UM in the United States during the 1970s without taking into account Moon's charismatic presence and his active involvement in the movement's affairs. For members Moon embodied Max Weber's classic portrait of a charismatic leader, i.e., "as endowed with supernatural, superhuman, or at least specifically exceptional powers or qualities" (Weber, 1964: 398). In this sense, Moon's movement represented what sociologists of religion recognize as the archetypical "cultic" group, centered around a living, awe-inspiring leader who is the medium of ongoing supernatural revelations. By continuously demonstrating and reaffirming his charismatic authority, Moon was able to chart the direction of the movement's growth and development.

By the time Moon arrived in the United States there was already in existence an apocryphal tradition which had grown up around his life and early accomplishments. Some of it was recorded for American members in issues of *The Master Speaks* and *The Day of Hope* volumes. A good deal of the American tradition remained oral. In addition to his communication with Jesus at age 16, a number of other charismatic qualities were attributed to Moon throughout his childhood and adult life. For example, his sense of justice and unyielding morality were recounted as having emerged at a very young age and were soon noticed by others. "If he saw adults taking advantage of innocent children, he would fling himself on the ground and cry, and beat his arms and legs on the floor. Even though his body was bruised and bleeding, he would not cease until the adults relented" (Kim, 1977, Vol. 2: 5).

Later, during his young manhood, after meditating on the tragic life of Jesus, he wept for several days. Indeed, "Once he wept all night long in his room, and in the morning the people in the house discovered that his flood of tears had soaked through the mat ceiling and formed a puddle on the floor below" (Kim, 1977, Vol. 2: 6).

His American followers not only venerated these tales but also constructed new episodes which corresponded to their own experiences. For example, Moon was reputed to subsist on only three or four hours' sleep each night. This personal sacrifice emanated from his "colossal responsibility." When an American member queried Moon on how he was able to maintain such a rigorous schedule, Moon reportedly replied, "If you knew you were going to die in three hours, would you sleep?" (MS-1, 1965: 9). Further, the extraordinary presence radiating from Moon was "felt" by all who encountered him. One apocryphal tale related by an ex-member described Moon's special rapport even with animals. He was reputed to have "such dominion over creation" that members were told "whenever he went to the zoo, all the animals would run over to that part of the zoo" (Enroth, 1977: 108). Similarly, members told of occasions when Moon, reputed to be a master fisherman, would throw a baitless hook into the sea and immediately land an enormous bluefin tuna (Fort Worth Star-Telegram, July 2, 1978).

Moon's charismatic authority was translated into a variety of specific decisions which influenced the shape and direction of the American UM. Many members of the movement, and particularly people in leadership positions, were acutely aware of the linkage between specific movement policies/enterprises and Moon's "inspiration." Moon was credited with inspiring such well-publicized undertakings as the many tours and rallies, the purchases of the Belvedere national training center and the Barrytown Seminary, the UM involvement in several geographically scattered fishing enterprises, and the establishment of the movement's New York-based newspaper, *The News World*. In some instances, such as the tours, Moon himself played a central role in the planning and implementation of events; in other cases, he only issued a broad mandate, such as his instructions to Unification Church leaders in 1972 to purchase facilities suitable for leadership training sessions and to accommodate Moon and entourage when necessary, and left the specific details to UM staff members. Of course, his personal charisma also served as a powerful stimulant to individual members' zeal and dedication. The day-to-day sense of mission with which members carried out their duties flowed directly out of Moon's perceived charismatic example.

One specific instance of the institutional importance of Moon's charisma could be found in the way family units were formed. After the prescribed three-year period of celibacy, members became eligible for marriage, or as the Unification Church referred to the ceremony, the "blessing." Moon himself prescribed the specific occasions on which couples could be blessed, was responsible for conducting the ceremony, and, to varying degrees, for selecting each member's marriage partner. Apocryphal tales grew up about Moon's uncanny ability to select highly compatible pairs of members based on his knowledge of "God's heart and will for each of them." As one member recalled, "Everyone could see after the people were put together that it was just right; they were just the right people for each other" (New Hope News, March 10, 1975). A member's father also allegedly remarked on Moon's "amazing" ability to sense compatibility: "Hal could have searched for a million years and never have found someone with so many complementary points as Lynda."

These sorts of anecdotes served to demonstrate Moon's charisma and, through their retelling, continually renewed his spiritual authority in the minds of members. Moon had met with God, he had survived inhuman imprisonment and torture at the hands of North Korean communists, he had wrestled successfully with Satan, and he manifested dominion over all living things and nature. Thus, it is not surprising that believers found Moon's presence and personal direction of the UM to be awe-inspiring and that his more permanent arrival in the United States dramatically shifted the course of events.

Based on his charismatic authority Moon was able to play a major part in maintaining the UM's ongoing pursuit of its lofty goals. The ideology predicted radical and imminent transformation of the world, but these predictions were not confirmed by events in any obvious way. Through his continuing spiritual revelations Moon was able to redefine the movement's progress in such a way as to create "spiritual victories" when "physical victories" were conspicuously lacking. Similarly the timetable for restoration was adjusted to be more consistent with the movement's real accomplishments and prospects. For example, the original date of 1967 was quickly abandoned and the three seven-year periods culminating in 1981 were, by 1978, being viewed as symbolic.

Simply scaling down goals and creating victories, however, were not sufficient to maintain the high level of personal sacrifice and commitment required by the UM. At least in part for these reasons Moon attempted to maintain UM members' espirit de corps high by making speeches designed strictly for internal consumption in which members were exhorted to continue their sacrifices, the inevitability (if not the imminence) of victory was reiterated, the importance of current projects in attaining the movement's overall goals were stressed, and the dismal fate of those so evil or myopic as to oppose the UM were graphically described. Once the UM became embroiled in controversy, of course, these speeches were leaked and became material for atrocity stories about the movement. The following brief quotations from Moon's speeches are illustrative (U.S. Government, 1978: 314-315):

> so far the world can be against us and nothing has happened. Now when they are against us then they are going to get punishment. So from this time ... every people or every organization that goes against the Unification Church will gradually come down or drastically come down and die.

> ... In the Medieval Ages, they had to separate from the cities—statesmanship from the religious field—because people were cor-

rupted at that time. But when it comes to our age, we must have an automatic theocracy to rule the world. So, we cannot separate the political field from the religious. . . . Separation between religion and politics is what Satan likes most.

MOON'S IMPACT ON UM ORGANIZATION

Immediately after his arrival Moon became convinced of the movement's need for reorganization. Welles (1976: 34) maintained that Moon "had become distressed over the poor progress of the American Church." Reportedly (Welles does not name his sources) Moon "castigated Young Oon Kim and Farley Jones for their lax, overly permissive approach. . . ." Finances were low, authority was decentralized, and there had been relatively little progress in recruitment. For a millenarian group moving inexorably along a theological timetable toward a vague but imminent time of crisis, the 1971 American UM was clearly stagnating.

Moon's serious commitment to building a powerful American UM, and the nascency of its rapid mobilization, began when he entered this country via Canada on a "visitor for business" visa in December, 1971. On arrival, however, rather than a single small but well-disciplined nucleus prepared to carry forth his messianic message, what Moon really encountered were several marginally surviving, loosely connected factions, separated as much by ideological differences as by geographic distance. As mentioned earlier, quite different versions of *The Divine Principle* were in circulation. Sometimes, at least in the Oakland Family, the theological message was deliberately downplayed in favor of a more humanistic, philosophical concern. Control of separate Unification Church centers was decentralized—their living arrangements, as well as their means of contributing funds to the UM, were matters of local decision. Most importantly, work for the UM was part-time. Members held conventional full-time jobs and donated funds and services as they felt appropriate (Personal Interview, 1978; see also Lofland, 1977: 282). Membership was small: reliable estimates of the UM's membership at this time, after twelve years of missionary work, vary between 250 (Stoner and Parke, 1977: 181) and 500 members (Lofland, 1977: 781; Welles, 1976: 34; Sudo, 1975: 316). In sum, as part of a movement with millenarian expectations and global aspirations, the American UM lagged behind.

Soon this would no longer be the case. Moon's arrival reoriented the American UM in ways that irrevocably transformed the lifestyles of its members and unified (without totally destroying) its factions into a more coherent, efficient operation. His first objectives were to consolidate the different factions and publicize the UM message. He also attempted to supplement the American UM resources with the first few of what became a fairly large contingent of Japanese UM members. The latter, despite their language difficulties, provided American members with role models for group-centered behavior. As several informants remarked to us, "Japanese brothers and sisters had better learned how to live the 'sacrificial' life." There are also indications (see U.S. Government, 1978: 318-319) that because of their perceived "trustworthiness" Moon felt they would help "ensure that the proper remittances were made to the national Church."

Clearly, some external funding was requisite because the American UM was ill-equipped to finance any national-scale campaign. The total amount of such funding is currently unknown, but from available evidence substantial sums were likely involved, as Moon himself is reported to have claimed in the early 1970s (U.S. Government, 1978: 337). Testimonies and bank records presented to the "Fraser Committee" investigations (U.S. Government, 1978: 325ff.) indicated that starting in 1971 and continuing at least into the late 1970s large quantities of cash or transferred funds began flowing into UM bank accounts from overseas, principally from South Korea and Japan. For example, one South Korean individual transferred $40,000 to the American UM in 1971; and in the period 1972-1974 Moon's interpreter and former Assistant Military Attache at the Korean Embassy in Washington, D.C., Bo Hi Pak, reported receiving $223,000 in "loans" from an identified Japanese source. Later, in 1975, when the UM bought stock in Washington's Diplomat National Bank, Pak reported being "loaned" $90,000 from the same Japanese source. During a sixteen-month period from late 1975 to early 1977 at least six million dollars were received from Japan by the UM's accounts in the Diplomat National Bank.

Most of this money undoubtedly originated, first from Japanese fundraising teams and the lucrative relationships between the Japanese UM and right-wing Japanese industrialists/politicians (Roberts, 1978), and second from Moon's South Korean businesses (in 1975 Moon's five largest industrial companies, including arms/pharmaceutical/stoneware/titanium interests, had combined assets of $14,970,000—see U.S. Government, 1978: 327) and the Korean Unification Church. How much of this money made its way to the American UM is less clear. Some of it arrived via the Korean Cultural and Freedom Foundation, which had been incorporated in the District of Columbia in 1964 and which originally was directed by a number of persons unconnected to the UM, in the form of "scholarships" and loans between KCFF branches in South Korea and Washington, D.C. Other circuitous routes, such as individual UM members carrying small amounts of cash on their persons across international borders, while suggested (U.S. Government, 1978: 337ff), have not been substantiated.

Initially, Moon and his staff seemed to have misassessed American receptivity to their message in much the same way as Young Oon Kim had in her initial San Francisco missionary efforts, optimistically assuming that the power and logic of both *The Divine Principle* and Moon's personal inspiration would naturally appeal to reasonable people. Coupled with that confidence was the fact that this first tour lacked the "polish" of later tours. Shortly after arriving in the USA, Moon called for eighty-odd volunteers from the various church centers across the nation and hastily trained them in Washington, D.C. as "advance men," albeit with no previous experience. These volunteers also had the task of helping to defray the costs of this first tour by offering candles (typically set in brandy snifters) to the public in exchange for donations of two dollars. Various centers, in particular one in Maryland producing such candles, had been successfully engaged in "cottage" craft industries for some time. In the early 1970s center leaders from other parts of the country, such as Berkeley, visited the Maryland center and helped diffuse the concept of selling such home-produced items. For many, such fund-raising was a novel experience. The tour aided in exposing members to the "solicitation situation" and likely influenced (however much is unclear) the later decision to place members into full-time fund-raising situations with such wares as candles to serve as donor inducements.

Full of enthusiasm but clearly inexperienced in the full-time promotion of their message and prophet, seventy to eighty "advance team" members set out in early February, 1972 on their first crusade, covering seven cities (New York, Baltimore, Philadelphia, Washington, D.C., San Francisco, Berkeley, and Los Angeles—see Kim, 1977, Vol. 1: 3ff). A sample of the revirescent "style" of the tour's publicity can be seen in a full-page advertisement in the New York *Times* of Friday, January 28, for the opening Lincoln Center rally. The ad presented a picture of Rev. and Mrs. Moon with their two children and proclamations: "This is the day of hope, The day of the true family. Sun Myung Moon testifies to the new age revealing God's plan to establish a new world." Obviously confident that Moon's message had popular appeal, the church charged eighteen dollars for tickets to the three successive evening lectures and offered a unique incentive: an "international novel-writing contest" with the theme "Jesus Christ and the Agony of the Cross: God's Will or Man's Failure." A first prize of $100,000 was offered, "for published authors only," with the novel to be based on materials provided by the church. Further, the advertisement promised that the novel would be made into a motion picture.

The UM's *Day of Hope* (Kim, 1977, Vol. 1: 5) viewed ads such as the above as "the first stage of an aggressive, concentrated, and costly public relations campaign." Undeniably, considerable effort on the part of the church members went into the tour. However, as Lofland (1977: 291) maintained in his analysis, other than curious newspaper ads such as the above, "few other media devices were used, and almost no attention was attracted." Matters of effort aside, there is no question that the results from the first tour fell far short of expectations. In each city the press gave the tour generally neutral coverage and treated the Church with polite bemusement, but otherwise little excitement had been generated. Crowds were sparse and unenthusiastic, no doubt in part due to the inexperience of the American staff and to such obstacles as the rather steep admission fee. The popular response was, to say the least, underwhelming.

Establishing an Organizational Base:
National Unity, Recruitment, Financing

Moon's preexisting discontent with the progress of the American UM, coupled with the somewhat disappointing results of his first tour, provided the impetus for fundamental changes both in the American movement's structure and in its style of outreach. Towards the end of this first tour, Moon met in Los Angeles with five key leaders from his Asian and American churches to discuss this situation (Kim, 1977, Vol. 1: 2). Recent events had demonstrated that the movement had extremely low visibility, no single coherent organization that could be called a church existed, and the organizational structure through which the ambitious goals of the international UM could be achieved was sorely lacking. True, the infusion of outside resources had propelled the American UM from a tiny, disjointed, and invisible movement to one which showed some semblence of unity and national exposure. But if the UM was not to be dependent on outside financing (and thereby constitute a drain on the international movement), finding some means of generating a substantial and steady source of capital was imperative. Donations from the incomes of the few American UM members clearly were insufficient. Furthermore, if the UM message was to be disseminated on a national basis and membership to be increased as a means of both spreading the message and raising funds, then more effective recruitment procedures had to be instituted. Finally, if the movement was to manifest the unity internally which it sought to foster worldwide, more commitment of leaders to the *national* movement and not to regional factions as well as more rigorous training of them was essential.

In confronting these problems Moon and the American UM leaders faced a major dilemma: the sweeping changes in the movement which they contemplated required more members, more visibility and money, and yet any one of these elements implied the existence of the others. In order to break through this vicious circle and get on with achieving the movement's larger goals, Moon decided to attack these problems simultaneously. According to the agenda of the Los Angeles meeting, three far-reaching organizational directives were issued by him. First, after consultation Moon ordered the foundation of a new missionary organization that would operate in mobile units or teams as a wing of the UM under the name One World Crusade (OWC). The OWC's principal function was "to evangelize the United States, and further the whole world." As we shall see, the OWC teams radically altered the meaning of full-time UM membership. Second, Moon "assigned State Representatives to establish Unification Church Centers in each of the forty-eight continental states . . ." to work closely with OWC teams in building grass-roots membership. The combination of mobile OWC teams and local centers were designed to increase the UM's visibility on a national scale and facilitate nationwide recruiting. Third, at about the same time Moon instructed Farley Jones (then president of the Unification Church of America) and Philip Burley (Director of the New York church) to purchase suitable facilities at which Moon could reside during visits and which could be used for national training sessions of UM leaders. This national training program would produce greater integration within the movement, more effective leadership, and, presumably, more effective recruiting.

These directives implied financial resources well beyond the American UM's means. Although OWC teams and state centers were to be self-supporting, movement unity required that the national UM have an autonomous financial base and not be completely dependent on local UM groups. It was in the context of researching for a means of fulfilling Moon's directives that American UM leaders "discovered" Mobile Fund-raising Teams (MFTs) which became the principal sources of UM funding by the mid-1970s. As related below, the concept also fit quite well with the new definition of full-time UM membership as well as contributed to the movement's unity and national visibility.

REORIENTATION OF RECRUITMENT AND MEMBERSHIP

Two OWC mobile units were initially formed, commanded respectively by Young Oon Kim and Davis S. C. Kim, Moon's pair of original missionaries to this country. By establishing OWC teams composed of members drawn from centers across the nation, factionalism was reduced and Moon's role as the unifying charismatic leader was given new preeminence. Out of a formerly feudal alliance of de facto separate movements was shaped one truly cohesive movement. Moreover, the mobile unattached OWC teams, with their frequent geographical reassignments and changes in member composition, further mitigated against conflicting local interests and loyalties, as did the national training program (with its later upgradings and revisions) for leaders that socialized them into a more standardized "party line." Additionally, the establishment of state directors and OWC teams opened up a growing array of new organizational positions into which Moon could place talented persons with little regard to theological or factional orientations.

Most significant from an organizational standpoint, the creation of the OWC teams redefined in a fundamental way the meaning of full-time membership for both members and the movement. Full-time commitment to the UM's mission and mobile evangelistic lifestyle now meant the members had to sort priorities in their own lives, a process which in many cases involved "bridge-burning," (i.e., dropping out of school, quitting other employment, leaving home and friends) and that created intense dedication to the movement's goals. From the UM's perspective it meant developing the capacity to plan and execute projects at an extremely rapid pace, drawing on this flexible pool of full-time talent, time, and energy by deploying members wherever needed. For example, OWC teams, although principally evangelistic, were called in temporarily to participate in the fund-raising campaign for the national training center at Belvedere, New York.

Thus, this full-time commitment to evangelistic activities signalled a major change in the UM's self-conception of its mission and the pace at which it would restore the Kingdom of God on earth. After arriving in the United States in 1971, Moon repeatedly told members that time was running out, that these were crucial times. At the end of 1972, nine months after the creation of the OWC, Moon proclaimed to members (MS-300, 1972: 3):

> We must be resolved to work hard while other Christians, other people in the democratic world are at ease without working for the cause of God. . . . We must struggle hard without sleeping, without eating, forgetting about every worldly worry and going ahead with our goal and our vision.

One month later, in a God's Day Midnight (January 1) address at the national training session, he put the timetable even more specifically, comparing the crucial period 1972-1974 to Jesus' brief but significant three-year ministry: "[you] will see that all these three years will be the most important ones in the history of restoration" (MS-314, 1973: 1).

In the eyes of the UM leaders the OWC teams proved effective in their broad mission as evangelistic units. Moreover, their flexibility and mobility were considered to be definite assets. Because the concept of evangelism held a variety of proselytization and financial implications in the context of the church's quest to establish both spiritual and physical (i.e., socio-economic) foundations for God's Kingdom on earth, they could be employed in many different ways. When the original two teams, northern and southern, met in Washington, D.C., in August, 1972, a third team was formed. By December of that year Moon was so enthused with their success that he expanded their number to ten and assigned each a specific region of the country. Young Woi Kim, president of the Korean Unification Church, while in this country for Moon's first tour, predicted fifty vans and 2,000 OWC members in operation by 1974. While the OWC's size never approached that figure, the church continued to expand the number of teams and created International One World Crusade (IOWC) teams made up of Americans as well as foreign UM members. In July, 1973, Moon commissioned the creation of two IOWC teams and forty additional OWC mobile teams. Later he would expand the number of IOWC teams as well.

Another major implication of creating the OWC and state churches followed from the intent that they be financially self-supportive (Kim, 1977, Vol. 1: 2). State centers were to be subsidized initially (i.e., obtaining down payments for property, and the like) through the assistance of the OWC teams. Nine months after their formation when they rendezvoused in Washington, D.C., Moon told the first OWC members:

> By 1974, we must at all costs be able to open big centers in all the states. We have only two years ahead of us. That means, according to my estimation, I have to spend some $40,000 for each state in buying or in paying the down-payment for the centers. So, a total of two million dollars is needed.

This state system was a departure from the earlier policy of establishing centers on an ad hoc basis wherever membership size and finances could support them. Once afloat, the centers were to pay their own way, contributing funds *to* the national headquarters but not draining funds *from* headquarters. This pattern of each unit and project financing its own operations as well as contributing to the national movement's coffers was to be elaborated throughout the 1970s in all areas of the movement. It was this autonomous financing that permitted the rapid proliferation of UM projects in the early-to-mid years of the decade and that underlay the impression among many observers that the UM was growing at an incredible rate.

ESTABLISHING A FINANCIAL BASE

The most striking example of self-supporting/contributing units were the mobile fund-raising teams (MFTs). Their development represented two important features of the UM. First, as far as we were able to determine, Moon never directly created or even suggested them; rather, he did serve characteristically as their inspiration through issuing a general directive, to be discussed shortly, which could have been implemented in other possible ways. Second, once the amazing success of these teams in raising funds had been serendipitously discovered, their activities were brilliantly linked to and integrated with the movement's millenarian theology. As we shall describe in detail, fund-raising became inexorably transformed from a mundane, stop-gap effort into an integral element in each member's spiritual growth.

The first project in which MFTs were employed was in implementing Moon's directive to purchase property for a national training center. After surveying the real estate market and locating a suitable estate (the former Seagrams' family mansion, now referred to as the Belvedere Estate, in Tarrytown, New York), staff leaders realized that they had to raise what by previous standards was an enormous amount of money. The total price of the estate was $850,000, with a down payment of $300,000. Yet, before 1972 total gross receipts for the UM had never exceeded $100,000.[1] Moon's directive to purchase such a center clearly called for some dramatically different source of funds.

In casting about for such a source, then-President Farley Jones and his staff seized upon an organizational innovation—the MFTs—that was experimental at its inception and that went beyond merely providing the cash for the down payment on the Belvedere Estate. Ultimately it altered the most basic resources of the movement and the activities of its members (Personal Interviews, 1978). Prior to 1971 Jones had visited Japan where he witnessed the tremendous success of the full-time, "hard sell" street solicitation techniques that would eventually, for many Americans as well as for Japanese, come to typify encounters with "Moonies." In Japan door-to-door solicitation in neighborhoods was less culturally acceptable than approaching strangers in public places for brief intervals. By canvassing areas of heavy human traffic, such as train stations, city street corners, and parks, the Japanese UM members had successfully raised large sums of money in conformity with that country's customs. In the United States, Jones reasoned, the important factor in fund-raising in public places concerned not so much any folkways about private residence-versus-public solicitation as much as the greater opportunities to encounter potential donors in areas of high population turnover.

Thus, on what appears to have been a trial basis and strictly with the limited purpose of raising the down payment for the Belvedere Estate, president Jones decided to initiate two MFTs, one to work on the West coast and one on the East. Each MFT team was composed of two vans, with five or six persons to a van per the Japanese model. When the West Coast team did not achieve the instant high returns of the East Coast team, Jones ordered the former to make its way cross-country to Chicago. Along route its receipts also grew enormously. Precisely how enormously was reported to the press by UM officials in various interviews along the way. William Torrey, a UM financial official, claimed that all of the UM's 1,500 members (his own membership estimate, apparently, though not inaccurate) had been mobilized in 1972 to collect a total of $500,000 (Marks, 1974). In forty days, reported an Oakland *Tribune* (October 26, 1972) article, three OWC teams that were temporarily enlisted in the Belvedere fund-raising project raised $210,000 by asking donations for the brandy-snifter candles.

The Belvedere project had required $300,000 for the mansion's down-payment. In short order, mobilizing only two MFTs (twenty people) and a pair of OWCs (same size) later aided by a third using the same basic strategies, the UM had raised that amount *and* an additional $200,000. Clearly, Jones' transplanted experiment had succeeded.

How did these teams manage to collect so much money? From our discussions with the current Unification Church National Fund-raising coordinator, himself a member of an original 1972 MFT, it appears that trial and error played an important part in systematizing the lucrative patterns of fund-raising. Originally, members did not possess any ideology of fund-raising that linked it to spiritual development, hence standing on street corners (as the Japanese model had suggested) produced limited returns and proved discouraging to members unprepared for rebuff after rebuff and overall indifference. For a short while, door-to-door solicitations at businesses and apartment houses predominated. Selling candles or simply asking for a donation for "missionary work" in this way could produce an average of seventy to a hundred dollars per fund-raiser per day. Lofland (1977: 287-289) offered the admittedly conservative estimate that members, because they were self-supportive, cleared at least 60% of their gross receipts and thus produced a large return in relation to costs. It is likely that overhead was much lower than 40%, however. Local church centers became, in Lofland's words, "crash pads" for OWC and MFT fund-raisers, as did the very vans driven by the teams. Highly "psyched" by the fervor of the recent tour and the presence of a charismatic leader who thrived on delivering heady lectures loaded with "last days/armageddon" imagery, members put in long hours without the usual distractions of domestic/sexual/recreational/occupational responsibilities and options. Members were continually on the move, living literally out of their suitcases and eating on the run. Most informants who had been "charter" members of these original teams recollected those days with nostalgia for the sense of meaningful hardship, achievement, and fellowship. Their deprivations were regarded as "purifying" experiences "underfire on the front lines." (Also, as we shall see, these early experiences, when related by disgruntled ex-members, became the basis for many of the early atrocity stories that were still repeated half a decade later by the UM's opponents: poor nutrition, minimal sleep, and frenetic hyperactive eighteen-hour days, and even occasionally poor hygiene.)

Realizing that in mobile fund-raising strategies they now possessed the answer of how to amass large quantities of cash to fund the enormous projects required by Moon's mission and that they were now able to do it at a pace consonant with *The Divine Principle*-derived timetable, the UM's staff did not disband the MFTs after the Belvedere campaign. Rather, in a most important development for the UM's financial base, a theological or spiritual significance gradually became attached to fund-raising activities after its initial successes. It became seen as its own form of missionary work, providing a crucible for testing and improving one's understanding of the Divine Principle. The grueling hours and continual rebuffs became spiritual trials of members' capacities to love in the face of hostility, to reach out to and inspire others with their "hearts," and to give nonmembers (however unwittingly) an opportunity to participate in the restoration of God's providence. Such encounters between members and nonbelievers not only provided both with opportunities for spiritual self-improvement but also their aggregate, cumulative effect was to pay spiritual indemnity to Satan for mankind's sins of the past 2,000 years. Thus, counter to the UM's claims that members' misrepresentations or deceptiveness in fund-raising merely constituted "overzealousness," the crucial linking of dollars to spiritual goals so closely almost inevitably led to dishonesty (as UM leaders and members themselves so confided to us). In somewhat the same way that the Calvinist Protestant ethic interpreted wealth as a sign of spiritual merit and the grace of salvation as the source of wealth, the UM interpreted success in fund-raising as the result of a correct spiritual relationship with God and not as the outcome of cleverness or personal talent. Public indifference or unwillingness to donate likewise became an index of a member's incomplete spiritual progress. At this point it became relatively easy for members to substitute means for goals and interpret their fund-raising success as spiritual growth. With that ideological development came the institutionalization of a rationale that apologized for an immensely lucrative form of resource production, locating on a theological level its tensions and problematic aspects in the cosmic battle between the forces of Satan and of God. Such beliefs touched each individual in the UM, in whatever role, and came to be a sociocultural ingredient of the movement indispensible for understanding members' behaviors. They also legitimated a style of resource mobilization that preserved and even reinforced communal living arrangements, not only for the teams of fund-raisers but also for center-members who engaged in such activities to meet expenses, freeing them from other forms of economic enterprise that might have not been so compatible with communalism.

Neil Salonen, who became Unification Church president in 1972, created a third MFT soon after and added a new incentive: a fund-raising contest for members, in conjunction with a similar international movement contest, to be held on Mother's Day, 1973. For added stimulation, a dozen top Japanese fund-raisers who had been brought to this country to help Moon with his first tour were mixed in with the American MFT members.[2] The 1973 Mother's Day competition produced the effect originally intended. It was, in retrospect, a "turning point" for UM fund-raising (as one informant termed it). The untapped potential of MFT members was demonstrated and and many seem to have had their sense of realistic goals pushed higher. For example, the 1973 USA winner (a young college-age woman) grossed $485 in a single day, outdistanced only by a Japanese sister who won the world fund-raising competition by bringing in $525 (accomplishing this feat by setting herself that "condition," or goal, and staying out thirty-six straight hours). The next year, in the World Day Context, the same 1973 USA winner triumphed again at the national level with a total of $612; later she established a church record which stood for several years, collecting an incredible $1,000 in a single day at a New York City traffic signal which possessed extremely long red, and very brief green, lights. The church even organized a "superstars" contest of sorts in June 1974, pitting an MFT team made up of the cream of MFT fund-raisers against an OWC team composed of the "stars" from seven OWC teams. Members who participated in this competition reportedly experienced even greater inspiration and awareness of the new goals within their grasps.

The year 1973 was indeed a turning point for fund-raising. After 1973, with an increase in sophistication about how to approach potential donors and armed with an ideology to offset rejections, plus with a return to parking lots and street corners, the daily per capita gross of MFT members averaged eighty to $120 and higher (up from the seventy to one hundred dollars average prior to 1973). In 1973, three two-van MFTs had been in operation. In 1974, ten new single-van MFTs were introduced, soon to be joined by many more. As of our interviews with church leaders in mid-1978, there were over a hundred MFTs, spread over nineteen regions and under the direct supervision of regional "commanders." Each team consisted of nine members working six to seven days a week.[3] By numerous accounts, between 1973 and 1978 UM fund-raisers were regularly able to produce returns of $100-$150 apiece per day. From 1974 on it apparently became more difficult for the UM to fund-raise as a result of negative publicity and local government harassment of MFTs. However, UM leaders reported to us that overall per capita returns did not diminish significantly; UM members simply worked harder.

Institutionalization

Within a surprisingly short space of time the UM showed signs of transition from its nascent phase of establishing organizational components which were to achieve its major goals (i.e., combatting communism, recruiting young adults, merging theology/philosophy/religion, and disseminating its world view) and the means of generating sufficient financial support to the institutionalization and bureaucratization of its more important undertakings. To a certain extent the formation of distinct, semibureaucratic organizations were merely a result of the rapid expansion of the movement's size, wealth, and range of activities after 1971. The myriad activities, decentralized style of operation and geographic dispersal of members, and property ownership necessitated some central organization.

Beginning in early 1972 there was a surge in UM membership and financial resources as well as in the number and range of the movement's undertakings. Membership grew from a few hundred in 1971 to several thousand by 1978, although there were differing estimates of the movement's largest achieved size. In June 1978 the official UM membership figures given us by the Unification Church's public relations office claimed 7,000 full-time members. Lofland (1977: 315) and UM leader Sudo (1975: 316) both put the core UM size at a maximum of 2,000 persons. The annual budget expanded from approximately $100,000 to several tens of millions during the same time period. In addition to annual gross receipts and elaboration of organizational structures, the UM purchased a variety of property holdings, including land, houses, cars, boats, buildings and businesses, which yielded a much larger total networth.[4] The movement also spawned a remarkably large number of affiliate organizations devoted to the wide range of specific projects which were undertaken in rapid succession, such as the National Prayer and Fast for the Watergate Crisis Committee (formed to mobilize public sentiment against President Nixon's impeachment and the Watergate investigations), the nationwide series of antipornography demonstrations, and the Bicentennial God Bless America campaign. A separate organization often was formed for each project and later dissolved upon the latter's completion, and essentially duplicate organizations in different sections of the country operated under different titles. In this way the organizational structure quickly assumed a maze-like quality which bewildered members and outsiders alike. While these temporary, project-linked organizations were effective in fostering the rapid initiation of a diverse array of activities, they lent little stability, continuity, or direction to the movement's overall goal attainment.

Therefore, it was imperative that the movement create some measure of stability. If the movement was to have the impact its members hoped for and sought, the UM world view would have to be widely shared and accepted. Not far into the 1970s it became clear that even if Moon's public appearances and apocalyptic message captured Americans' attention, a more concerted, long-term effort would be necessary to "change the heart" of America. Correspondingly, if the movement was not simply to be a teen and young adult crusade which attracted the young for a brief stint in a "magical mystery tour" only to lose them to conventional middle-class careers and lifestyles, then opportunities for family formation and occupational careers within (or affiliated to) the movement had to be generated. It was in these directions that the UM moved in the mid-1970s.

LEADERSHIP SELECTION AND TRAINING

As Etzioni (1961: 201ff) has noted, religious movements typically attempt to sustain a relatively high level of charismatic leadership in "line" leadership positions. The charismatic qualities of movement leaders are instrumental in generating and maintaining the intense positive orientation of members, and the ultimate source of charismatic authority legitimates the mundane, daily activities and decisions of the movement. In order to produce this charisma continuously, the UM both selected individuals already possessing these qualities and socialized to instill them. Prior to Moon's arrival, the UM seemed to lack many individuals possessing charismatic leadership potential as well as any regularized means of eliciting or developing it. With the formation of OWC teams the UM moved in the direction of consciously selecting out and rewarding individuals with charismatic qualities. Those who were particularly effective in fund-raising, lecturing, or recruiting found themselves quickly promoted to team leaders' positions in the OWC or on MFTs, as state directors, or as heads of the many special projects sponsored by the movement.

Moon also clearly recognized the importance of establishing an institutionalized means of selecting and training an elite within the movement. The initial efforts in this direction began in March 1973. During the preceding year American UM members had worked furiously to raise funds to purchase a site for a national training center. Prior to that time there had been no long-term training for members and no special training for potential leaders. Throughout 1973 and 1974 Belvedere was used to train the more promising UM members. Shorter workshops (in periods of two, three, seven, and twenty-one days) were conducted at a variety of locations around the country. The longer, more rigorous training in the form of 120-day workshops consisted of lectures on *The Divine Principle* (and related anticommunist material), training in pedagogical skills, and witnessing and fund-raising in New York City. There were no academic qualifications for admission to the training sessions, but there was a written examination which participants had three opportunities to pass.

In 1975 the Unification Theological Seminary was formally established in Barrytown, New York at the site of what had formerly been the Christian Brothers Monastery. Its opening constituted a significant step toward institutionalization of leadership recruitment and training. A largely non-UM faculty comprised academicians with solid credentials, representing a variety of conventional religious backgrounds, was appointed. Students were required to have the normal accredited baccalaureate degrees for admission. The curriculum provided rather standard seminary training with course offerings comparable to other such institutions. The seminary developed most of the standard academic trappings, including the ubiquitous college catalog picturing faculty and students posed in various situations around the campus, and ultimately sought state accreditation. A state charter was initially denied, in part because of the violation that the seminary catalogue claimed to offer a degree recognized by New York State Regents *before* they in fact had received it. A controversy ensued, with UM officials suing for recognition and a number of grievances against the movement, many unrelated to the state charter issue, surfacing among its opponents.

At the same time, there was not full-scale implementation of bureaucratic standards. Academically eligible members were selected for admission partly on the basis of their previous success in fund-raising and/or witnessing activities. Communal elements were also retained. Member-students performed almost all of the seminary's maintenance and service activities, including cooking, cleaning, security patrols of the campus grounds, ground upkeep, and even growing some of the food. Finally, since the movement offered few of the standard occupational outlets for its seminary graduates, newly graduated members might be assigned to any one of numerous unrelated (from an outsider's perspective) tasks.

In addition to the establishment of the seminary, various members of the UM hierarchy were considering plans to erect a church-related college or university. Presumably it would function as other denominationally administered universities where adherents have the opportunity to enroll in programs of higher education conducted within the context of an environment reflective of religious values. Finally, the UM's acquisition of property for fishing operations in Bayou La Batre, Louisiana, included plans for the construction of a maritime academy to train member-workers in the skills necessary to operate these newly acquired enterprises.

DISSEMINATING THE UM WORLD VIEW: *THE NEWS WORLD*

In 1975 the UM (at Moon's inspiration) established its newspaper, *The News World,* in New York City, just as it had done previously in England and Japan. A variety of other publications were established to convey insider sympathetic news to members, such as *The New Hope News* (a newspaper covering movement news), *The Cornerstone* (the seminary house organ), *The Way of the World* (a sort of UM *Reader's Digest*), and *The Rising Tide* (a Freedom Leadership Foundation-sponsored periodical). By contrast, *The News World* was designed to reflect the movement's values in the context of standard news coverage. This theme was clearly sounded in *The News World*'s stated objectives: "While some media can multiply the destructive tensions and inadequacies of city life, a newspaper like *The News World* can help people to understand one another's situation compassionately and thus be a force for unity" (Warder, 1978: 17-18). The editor decried the inadequacy of minority news coverage, control of newspapers by powerful economic interests, and the emphasis on sensationalism, scandal, sex, and violence. He openly acknowledged that the UM perspective influenced the selection and editing process, stating: "I'd be less than candid if I, as the publisher, did not admit that any perception of the paper's purpose and our handling of news and editorial themes are not significantly affected by my religious conviction as a member of Reverend Moon's Unification Church" (Warder, 1978: 37).

The themes stressed in articles included family stability, human rights, and racial harmony. Observing that the paper was committed to an idealistic vision of New York, editor Warder (1978: 26-27) remarked, "Yes, we cover crime and the less noble aspects of the City, but we are searching for the news that is helpful to the reader in his attempt to live in New York City." This idealistic approach to news coverage did not prove immediately attractive to advertisers. Indeed, the paper achieved some (undesired) publicity soon after its inception when it ran advertisements for stores and products without the knowledge or permission of the storeowners or distributors, sometimes reprinting the copy of an advertisement from another newspaper. This practice of *The News World,* apparently an attempt to improve the paper's image by giving the appearance of sustaining prestigious or conventional advertisers, was soon discontinued after outraged merchants and distributors made it publically known that they had never contracted for such advertising, thus proving more of an embarrassment to the paper than a source of legitimacy.

Because the newspaper was subsidized by the UM ($2,550,000 were provided in a five-month period alone at Moon's personal direction—see U.S. Government, 1978: 373-374) and staffed principally by UM members, it was able to maintain its orientation with less concern about advertiser response, operating deficits, and circulation figures than most other dailies. It was also able to afford such relative luxuries as color copy which enhanced its visual appeal. Most importantly, the financial subsidy and use of UM members to produce and distribute the paper allowed members to give away copies of the paper and to combine distributional activities with witnessing. Thus, despite the fact that the newspaper was in one sense an economic enterprise it also was a family business with member-employees living communally and with the formal staff hierarchy sharply limited.

DISSEMINATING THE UM WORLD VIEW: CARP

The Collegiate Association for the Research of Principles (CARP) was an organization whose goals fell somewhere between the UM's overt proselytization and its attempts simply to disseminate its world view. At least in theory, formal conversion to the Unification Church was not central to CARP's objectives; however, it was mandatory that members subscribe to the values and ideas underlying *The Divine Principle.* In actuality there were very few CARP members who were not also members of the Unification Church. In order to associate with the UM youth who shared its ideals but were, for whatever reasons, unwilling or uninterested in formal participation in the UM, CARP chapters were to be established on college campuses. A local CARP constitution stated these broad goals as follows:

> CARP is an educational group whose purpose is to investigate and analyze the ideals, ethics and values that guide social and cultural systems; to provide a vehicle for students to contribute beneficially to community, national, and international needs; and to provide an educational forum for exploring common, universal principles that can solve existing conflict and unify all aspects of human life, including politics, economics, philosophy, science, religion, and culture.

In this sense, CARP resembled the International Cultural Foundation (to be discussed shortly) which attempted to build bridges between the UM and the intellectual community and future leaders of American society.

CARP, like several other UM organizations, was transplanted from the Japanese movement. Although CARP was conceived in the United States as early as 1969, it was first incorporated in the state of New York in December 1973. The first chapter was formed at Columbia University in that year. There was little national, centralized effort devoted to the establishment of CARP chapters in the years to follow. For example, even in 1978 only one UM member was responsible for national coordination of CARP activities. Without a staff and church-subsidized budget or annual dues for members, this official admitted in an interview that CARP lacked the resources to conduct a campaign to establish additional local chapters. Individual UM members attending universities, residents of local UM state or city centers, and members of IOWC teams variously attempted to spark interest in CARP. However, these activities lacked both direction and continuity. As a result, by 1976 there were only half a dozen chapters nationwide. Between 1976 and 1978 the number of chapters rose sharply to twenty-five with a combined membership of between 300 and 400. CARP's formally stated goal was to achieve a predominantly non-UM membership. That the vast majority of members (all but fifteen to twenty) were Unification Church members in 1978 indicated the relative absence of success in those terms. Nevertheless, CARP achieved a visible presence on a number of prestigious campuses, including Stanford, Columbia, Dartmouth, Berkeley, Temple, American, and Howard universities.

DISSEMINATING THE UM WORLD VIEW:
THE UNITY OF KNOWLEDGE

One of the major concerns of the UM was the integration of spiritual and empirical modes of knowledge. From the UM perspective, there was some truth in all of the world's major religions; each had glimpsed some—but only a part—of the essence of God and His creation. Similarly, science through its description and analysis of the natural world had captured some of the fundamental structure and continuities of God's creation. The themes in Moon's lectures contained frequent references to the basic, underlying order of creation reflected in each of these bodies of knowledge. The trend in the West since the Enlightenment had been for religion's purview to shrink and for religion to lose its legitimating functions vis-à-vis other institutions. The UM, however, sought to reverse this trend by more broadly defining what could be considered the "religious" so as to incorporate what were ordinarily defined to be scientific or even political arenas. As one aspect of its central goal of unification, therefore, the UM sought to encourage unity among the sciences (broadly defined to include all disciplines engaged in the systematic compilation of knowledge) and to overcome disciplinary boundaries which were viewed as arbitrary and sterile.

In order to accomplish such a formidable task as forging unity within the multivarious scientific community, the UM clearly needed participation from the scientific establishment itself. Beginning in 1972 the UM sponsored, and Moon specifically returned to the United States from South Korea for, the first Unity of Science Conference. In December 1973, the International Cultural Foundation (ICF) was founded for the purpose of promoting the "search for absolute values" and the unity of science. Working through the International Conference on the Unity of the Sciences (ICUS), ICF sponsored larger and more elaborate conferences each year. The ICF made use of the interlocking communal relationships among various components of the UM by calling on members from all sectors of the movement, including the entire student body of the Barry-town Seminary, to set up and run these conferences. From a mere twenty participants in 1972, the ICUS sponsored annual events which grew to approximately four hundred participants in 1977 at a cost of $500,000 (New York Times, November 28, 1977). As with previous conferences, the 1977 gathering's list of attending dignitaries included a number of prominent scientists and scholars. Some appear to have been attracted by the conference's theme of the search for absolute values; for others the incentive may have been an all-expense paid trip to a "professional" meeting in a major city. Several were Nobel Prize winners who, while they had passed the zenith of their careers, nevertheless functioned as luminaries who lent prestige to the conferences.

Between 1973 and 1975 ICF was responsible for disseminating Unifica-tionist thought to potential future leaders. In March 1973, the first

"100-Day International Leadership Training Session" was held at the recently opened Belvedere Training Center. A similar training session was conducted at Barrytown shortly after the property had been purchased. According to New York Director Joseph Tully, the Unification Church sponsored the session because it felt that youth lacked "direction, purpose and values" and yet they would be "leading various areas in 10 to 15 years." He added, "Unless something is done to give them strength of purpose it will cause problems" (Kim, 1977, Vol. 1: 47). The purpose of the program specifically was to expose students from elite universities (the 1974 seminar included twenty students from Columbia University) to Unificationist thought rather than outright conversion attempts:

> to expose students from top level universities—future national lead-
> ers—to the Divine Principle, Unification Thought and Critique on
> Communism to provide them with tools they will need in the future
> as a foundation for wise leadership. Unlike standard workshops,
> there was no pressure on participants to sign membership but instead
> the emphasis was on laying a good foundation, "planting a seed"
> [Kim, 1977, Vol. 1: 122].

These seminars became an insignificant feature of ICF as participants complained of their confining formats, i.e., noncritical presentations of *The Divine Principle* and thinly veiled proselytization; and the UM achieved few productive returns. ICF thereafter focused the bulk of its resources on the ICUS-sponsored conferences after 1974.

OCCUPATIONAL AND CAREER OPPORTUNITIES

Occupational opportunities associated with the UM were critical to its eventual stability. The movement conceived of itself as more than simply another denomination or religion; it was to be a "way of life." Movement-affiliated industries and businesses increasingly constituted a means by which members could remain involved with the movement on a full-time basis, integrate their work roles with their lifestyle principles, and still pursue something resembling a conventional career. Organizationally, such economic enterprises offered a more stable, long-term source of income than street fund-raising. The latter would arouse increasing controversy if the anticipated movement growth occurred and would not permit "rou-tinized" lifestyles for members.

To an extent the seminary provided career opportunities as graduates would conceivably move into leadership roles, but the latter were limited in number and provided the movement with no external sources of funding. It was the acquisition of the newspaper and fishing enterprises which moved the UM toward its goal of movement-affiliated employment. Particularly the latter seemed typical of the movement's "new thrust" and attracted a good deal of media attention. For example, in articles such as "Moon Sings New Tuna" (quipped by a reader of the national wire services at the Fort Worth Star-Telegram, October 31, 1976) it was reported that the Tong-Il Fishing Company of New York, an UM-owned enterprise, purchased 5% of the entire east coast tuna catch for processing and exportation to Japan in 1976. Soon thereafter, International Oceanic Enterprises (likewise, UM-owned), through a subsidiary company, began fishing operations off the mid-Atlantic coast. A shipyard and seven hundred acres of land slated to become the site for a fish-processing plant were purchased in Gloucester, Massachusetts for two million dollars. In July, 1978 the company was actively negotiating for ocean front property in the same area to support its fishing fleet operations. Perhaps the most controversial "fishing" purchase was one of seven hundred acres of land valued at two million dollars and an adjacent ship-building marina for three million dollars in Bayou La Baltre, Louisiana, a small fishing village of 5,000 just south of Mobile, Alabama. This site was earmarked for a seafood processing plant, a boat-building enterprise, and a maritime academy.

At the same time the expansion of career opportunities and new organizational positions was not accompanied by an erosion of the movement's communal lifestyle. Most members who entered into responsibilities closely resembling those of jobs in larger society continued to reside within the communal group. For example, the majority of the national staff of the headquarters of the Unification Church in downtown Manhatten by day engaged in conventional paralegal, public relations, or accounting jobs but maintained residences in the UM's communally organized hotel (the former New Yorker) for token room and board costs.

COMBATTING COMMUNISM

The fight against communism was an obvious feature of the UM since its inception in war-torn South Korea and flowed directly out of Unificationist theology. The UM's Manichaeistic perspective of the world as divided into two opposed camps, the satanic/communist and the divine/democratic, led to America being depicted as the archangel or guardian of the forces of restoration and God. Of particular importance was the latter's defense of South Korea, the new Israel, against North Korea and its communist anti-Christ, Kim Il Sung. Thus, what was to most observers a political/ideological conflict became for UM members ultimately a religious one.

UM members' concerns with combatting communism were reflected organizationally in their early support of the Korean Cultural Freedom Foundation (KCFF), formally created by non-UM persons in 1965 as a private foundation to strengthen ties between the United States and South Korea. Although nominally unaffiliated with the Unification Church, KCFF was supported by many UM leaders, notably Bo Hi Pak, and also provided financial support to the UM in a variety of ways already indicted. (In fact, Moon's status as a permanent resident alien in the United States, issued by the Department of Labor, came shortly after February, 1973 when his wife, sponsored by the Korean Cultural and Freedom Foundation, was granted such residency because of her "expertise" in preparing Korean cuisine.) KCFF sponsored the Korean "Little Angels" children's dance troupe which toured the USA and appeared with Moon during his tours, attracting enthusiastic audience response. KCFF also initiated "Radio Free Asia," a radio broadcasting format the goal of which was to "broadcast the truth behind the Bamboo Curtain" (Kim, 1977, Vol. 1: 246). During the Vietnam war Radio Free Asia sought information on American servicemen missing in action through its broadcast facilities. Initially, at least, KCFF was able to attract a number of prestigious Americans to endorse its cause. Its letterhead, for example, included names such as Dwight D. Eisenhower, Harry S. Truman, and Admiral Arleigh Burke.

UM-affiliated anticommunist organizations grew out of The International Federation for Victory Over Communism (IFFVOC). The Japanese branch of IFFVOC was the immediate precursor to a similar American organization, the Freedom Leadership Foundation (FLF). FLF was conceived by Moon and established in the United States in 1969 by the current Unification Church President Neil Salonen as a tax-exempt, nonprofit organization. Salonen continued to serve as its chairman into the end of the 1970s. Formerly a membership organization which at one time nominally numbered all Unification Church members among its constituents (Marks, 1974), FLF moved toward operating principally as an "educational" organization. Foremost among its activities became the publication of *Rising Tide,* a biweekly anticommunist newspaper with (before 1978) an average printing run of approximately 7,000. For several years FLF also ran a college campus "education" campaign under the auspices of the Committee for Responsible Dialogue. Conservative lecturers such as Fulton Lewis III, Phillip Abbot Luce, and William Rusher were also sponsored as part of such educational campaigns.

The primary goal of FLF was to "advance the cause of freedom against the forces of Marxism-Leninism" which were seen as a powerful and growing threat. Consistent with this goal, the FLF's *Rising Tide* gave extensive coverage to terrorist campaigns, human rights violations in the Soviet Union, and genocide in Cambodia. The organization publically took positions against *détente* with communist nations, for U.S. opposition to communist expansion, and against U.S. military withdrawal from South Korea. In their effort to combat the "tyranny of communism" FLF members individually stressed "promoting a critique of Marxism-Leninism, living their lives according to the Divine Principle, and working toward a God-centered democracy."

The vigor with which the UM supported FLF goals fluctuated over time. The organization was rather modestly staffed and funded initially; 1974 estimates of its operating budget were between $50,000 and $60,000, and its full-time staff numbered approximately eight. Press runs of the *Rising Tide* remained in the 7,000-8,000 range. But in mid-1978 a new cohort of thirty full-time and thirty-seven part-time UM members were trained at the UM New York headquarters for FLF work. As the 1977 FLF Secretary-general, Michael Smith, noted, the UM "had always intended to expand FLF." Smith attributed the recent expansion in part to the "speed up of communist victories in the world" (Personal Interview, 1978). The newly trained FLF staff members were dispersed to various states to strengthen FLF's "educational" objectives. Press runs of *The Rising Tide* were expanded to 60,000-80,000 copies in order to effectively promulgate FLF's perspective, and staff members worked to organize lectures and debates by political and academic figures to emphasize the worldwide communist threat.

MARRIAGE AND FAMILY FORMATION

Family formation was a matter of the greatest importance to the UM, for the new God-centered families created by the unions of spiritually "pure" members were to be the basic building blocks of the restoration process. On joining the Unification Church members vowed to maintain a three-year period of celibacy so that prior to entering any human marital relationship they would first learn the "true meaning of God-centered love." It was to the task of learning unselfish, "heartistic," loving relationships with others and with God that members dedicated much of their time and energy during this period.

Because the movement began to achieve its spectacular growth only in 1972, the issue of marriage, referred to as a blessing by members, and family formation did not immediately arise in the United States. By 1975 marriage and family formation was becoming a more imminent concern for members as well as UM leaders. Many members had now lived in a "crisis" and "crusade" atmosphere for several years while involved in fund-raising and witnessing activities and naturally began to consider marriage, child-bearing, and moving closer to living more routinized life-styles. From an organizational standpoint, providing predictable marriage/child-bearing arrangements increased the probability of members forging permanent relations with the movement and intergenerational continuity in church membership. Particularly in light of the church's encouragement of large families (Moon himself had a goal of a dozen offspring) and discouragement of birth-control/abortion, families would serve as a con-tinuing source of UM growth.

Up to 1978, Moon himself has blessed virtually all American couples whose unions have been sanctioned by the church. Because "blessings" occurred only at Moon's inspiration and marriages typically were arranged (i.e., Moon or other UM leaders, recommended appropriate mates) large weddings took place only at periodic intervals. There were several such ceremonies in the last two decades. Thirty-six couples were blessed in Korea in 1961, seventy-two more in 1962, 430 in 1969, 790 in 1970, and, most recently, 1,800 in 1975. A few Americans were included in the 1969 and 1970 ceremonies, but the first major American blessing took place in 1975 with the union of 120 American couples among the 1,800. The increased emphasis on a more settled lifestyle was reflected in plans for an imminent blessing of several thousand couples on three continents in late 1978 or early 1979, and UM leaders' insistence that the transient living styles characteristic of the early and mid-1970s were only temporary and would soon become less prominent.

Resistance to Bureaucratization

But while the UM experienced a distinct trend toward institutionaliza-tion and bureaucratization by the mid-1970s, at the same time it con-sciously and deliberately resisted this trend in several identifiable ways. The result was the establishment of a "limited bureaucracy" in keeping with the UM's dual characteristics of both a movement and a large organization.

Rigidity was discouraged by Moon's ongoing revelations about the means to be used in creating the ideal world—new roles, projects, and needs meant that bureaucratic structures could never firmly develop around the same set of priorities. An office or staff set up to accomplish some goal (e.g., Young Americans for a Just Peace) could realistically expect to find that goal eventually dropped or superceded as Moon's revelations led the movement to new evolving purposes. For this reason Moon explicitly told high-ranking UM staff personnel that no individual was to serve in any organizational position longer than three years. Indeed, during the authors' visit to the Unification Church's national headquarters we were informed that the entire staff was about to be replaced in one of these triannual turnovers.

The natural tendency in bureaucratic structures is for structural growth and differentiation to accompany functional specification (i.e., the creation of new posts and positions to handle one or more specific tasks). The UM resisted this trend by maintaining a minimum permanent staff (there were no more than two dozen permanent staff persons in the entire national church headquarters as of summer, 1978) and by creating temporary, ad hoc committees which provided the manpower for tackling specific tasks and which were loosely supervised by the permanent staff. Members of such committees might be drawn from any of the UM's divisions such as the OWC teams, specific ministries such as the Washington, D.C. "capitol" ministry, or staff members themselves. Working with the staff, the committees would then be dissolved when the project was completed (or terminated) and the committee members reassigned to other tasks. For example, the Bicentennial God Bless America Committee, the National Prayer and Fast for the Watergate Crisis Committee, American Youth for a Just Peace, and Project Unity all operated for a fairly short time and then were disbanded. In this way, projects could be undertaken and resources mobilized with only a small permanent core of staff persons coordinating them. (Chapter 9 discusses in detail a prime example of this strategy—the "Frontier '78" publicity campaign.) In addition, the number, composition, leadership, and area of operation of MFT and IOWC teams, state and local Unification Church centers, and specific project-oriented committees constantly shifted. Thus, individuals never were in one place or position long enough to develop the sort of entrenched personal career interests that are endemic to more crystallized bureaucratic structures.[5] Members even reported a sense of "adventure" and novelty in this continual juggling of responsibilities and titles.

At the same time, despite this tremendous amount of organizational fluidity, continuity was maintained at the top of the organization by three related factors. First was the board of directors and officers of the Unification Church of America, which provided the movement with formal stable leadership. A second source of continuity was an informal "council of elders" made up of original Unification Church members and patriarchs who, with Moon, acted to monitor the direction of the UM and weigh the virtues of important decisions. Third was what the Fraser

Committee (U.S. Government, 1978: 372) referred to as "a pattern [in the UM] of interlocking directors, officers, and stockholders." For example, that source and our own interviews revealed that many of the Unification Church's 1977 directors (Mose Durst, Joseph Sheftick, Neil Salonen, William Bergman, Edwin Ang, and Michael Warder) were also members of the more informal council of elders, *and* that the names of the majority of these persons appeared repeatedly on UM transactions and directorships. Thus, Neil Salonen concurrently appeared (among other posts) as both president and a director of the Unification Church of America, president of the Freedom Leadership Foundation, a director of the Korean Cultural and Freedom Foundation and of the International Ocean Enterprises, and a major stockholder in both Tong Il Enterprises and the Diplomat National Bank. Likewise, Mose Durst was president of National Educational Development Services, Inc. and Creative Community Projects, Inc. as well as a director of the Unification Church of America and a member of the council of elders *and* a major stockholder in International Oceanic Enterprises. Michael Young Warder, editor and publisher of *The News World,* was also a director of the Unification Church, secretary of the International Cultural Foundation, director of International Oceanic Enterprises, and a major stockholder in Tong Il Enterprises. Similar lists of titles could be assembled for Edward Ang and David S. C. Kim as well as for Bo Hi Pak and other UM leaders.

In addition to Moon's direct emphasis on avoiding bureaucratic rigidity while preserving stability in the movement's leadership was an UM norm on returning to "grass-roots" tasks such as witnessing and fund-raising periodically to keep a perspective on the ideas of the UM and what, in other religious institutions, might be termed "humility." For example, we learned that President Neil Salonen had decided to pioneer his own witnessing mission on the West Coast in addition to his presidential church duties. Even more surprising, we encountered a former Unification Church president inconspicuously enrolled at the UM seminary as a student. And Michael Young Warder, editor of *The News World,* periodically went out on the street hawking newspapers. Such grass-roots activities were a source of considerable pride to those engaged in them and served as an example of proper humble attitudes to UM members.

Finally, as we have mentioned repeatedly, whenever possible the UM continued to maintain members in self-sufficient, communally organized lifestyles. Similarly, it drew upon its own membership and their energies and skills insofar as feasible to staff and manage its various projects and enterprises. When special needs occurred, as with the annual ICUS conferences and getting *The News World* started, labor from other parts of the movement, such as seminary students, was borrowed temporarily to make up the shortage.

The Persistance of Factionalism

In Chapters 2 and 4 we described the existence of a less theologically concerned faction of the UM on the West Coast of the United States. During the mid-to-late sixties it had been oriented in this liberal direction by Korean missionary Sang Ik Choi who perceived the limitations of attempting to attract many persons with the ponderous theological tactics of Young Oon Kim. When Kim moved the American UC's headquarters to Washington, D.C. in 1966, Choi and his colleagues were left relatively free to develop their own humanistic brand of Unificationist ideology which eventually culminated in the International Reeducation Foundation. The beginning of Moon's American crusade, as we have seen, greatly retarded this sectarian trend when Moon mobilized virtually every available member to provide the manpower either for work on his specific projects or to raise funds to finance the latter. Thus, by the heyday of Moon's Day of Hope tours in 1972-1973, Choi's IRF had been, functionally at least, absorbed into the larger UM and many of its leaders deployed elsewhere.

However, in 1973 New Education Development Systems, Inc., was founded in San Francisco by Martin Irwin ("Mose") Durst, a Ph.D. in the humanities with social psychological/sensitivity group training, who had married Yeon Soo Im, one of Choi's original band when it arrived in the Bay area in 1965. NEDS was intended as an umbrella organization from which specific groups and projects would emerge; each was dedicated to general, noncontroversial educational and charitable purposes such as "to provide expanded educational opportunities . . . and to promote, interest, and unite groups working to expand educational opportunities" so as to "promote the general welfare" (California, 1974).

There was nothing in this self-description of NEDS that directly or indirectly alluded to religion or UM ideology, and in fact, the tact chosen by the corporate enterprises of Durst and the West Coast Oakland Family—as those persons associated with NEDS and its best known spinoff organization, Creative Community Projects, Inc., became known—carried on the deemphasized theological bent of Choi minus the IRF's straightforward disclosure of its ties to the Unification Church. The CCP's public image of an ethically concerned, nonreligious educational community of persons seeking to restore the integrity of human relationships and thereby improve the world at large was promoted in its literature which members distributed and fostered through the claims of its street missionaries.

Yet there is evidence to demonstrate that the NEDS/CCP organization was, simultaneously, both an integral part of the UM, working closely with the Unification Church of America *and* a branch of the UM with strong sectarian tendencies. The CCP was an important recruiting arm of the UM, by its own account sending thirty to fifty new members each month into a variety of movement organizations and activities (Personal Interviews, 1978).[6] The CCP's workshop locale, to which college-age persons would be invited for weekend and week-long training seminars, was a picturesque 600-acre ranch in Booneville, California, the deed for which was transferred (for tax purposes) to the Holy Spirit Association for the Unification of World Christianity in May 1975 (Allan, 1975). Throughout the mid-to-late 1970s Durst served as one of the Unification Church's directors and, as a member of the council of elders that oversaw the affairs of the UM, was in fairly frequent contact with President Neil Salonen and other movement officers. The national office of the Unification Church apparently considered the CCP's centers in San Francisco, Oakland, and Berkeley as its own offices as well, according to the 1974 Unification Church Directory of Centers which included the former centers on its list. Moreover, checks paid to the order of NEDS were at one time deposited in a Unification Church account (Ross, 1976; also Personal Interview, 1978).

Yet CCP, as the major organizational component of the Oakland Family, manifested a number of characteristics that indicated a growing sense of identity separate from the mainstream UM and that could, in time, provide the basis for a schism between the East and West Coast organizations. Briefly, the most important characteristics were:

IDEOLOGICAL DIVERGENCE

The Oakland Family was more apt to stress self-actualization and mastery of ego at the expense of mentioning Satan, *The Divine Principle*'s historical-Biblical development, and the national/international timetable of events, as proclaimed by Moon, for the restoration of God's Kingdom on earth. Restoration, as we heard it used by Oakland Family members, referred more to a general principle of positive, constructive loving action than to any specific historical process.

DIVERGENCE IN EXPECTATIONS OF LIFESTYLE

Members of both the mainstream UM and the Oakland Family displayed a great deal of rhetoric about the ideal family. However, the term was not always used consistently between them. Whereas the mainstream Unification Church used the term with a double meaning—to refer to those persons caught up as peers (i.e., brothers and sisters) in Moon's millenarian

movement as well as to the nuclear unit of parents and children which
would be modeled after the True Parents and their "sinless" children (i.e.,
the Moons)—the Oakland Family's members used the term generally only
in the former sense. Mainstream members openly acknowledged that they
"endured" celibacy for a temporary period only, to be followed by more
conventional, desirable, and theologically imperative conjugal relations. It
was our impression from our visit to the Bay area centers that the Oakland
Family was dedicated to a permanent communal model of living, with no
immediate expectations among many members that their communal
celibacy would be replaced by conventional heterosexual relations. The
family had great theological importance to mainstream UM members: only
through heterosexual marriage (and not through some communal, symbolic kinship relation) could individuals recapitulate the androgynous
nature of God. The Oakland Family appeared to have discouraged this
aspect of sexual relations along with its deemphasis of theology.[7]

BUREAUCRATIC SUPERVISION

The Oakland Family's leadership structure did not operate under the
same regulations as other branches of the UM. For example, the former's
members were not required to shift positions of responsibility periodically,
nor did permanent CCP members expect to be eventually transferred to
some other branch of the UM or to another locale outside the Bay area.
From interviews and discussions with other observers it appeared more
than likely that the CCP's outstanding success in recruitment for the UM
earned it a "hands-off" privilege with regard to Moon's prescriptions on
"limited bureaucracy" and mandatory turnover.

ELITISM

A final, more subjective but nonetheless real characteristic of emerging
sectarianism was the attitude of many in the Oakland Family that they
were set apart from the rest of the UM by their superior dutiful adherence
to what they perceived to be the heart of Moon's inspiration. This can be
best illustrated by two separate comments: first, from a rank-and-file
member who had been in the Family for two months' time; and second,
from an executive officer in CCP. The first comment was offered spontaneously in a conversation on the differences between the Oakland
Family's and mainstream approaches to conversion and reasons for the
latter's success. The member noted matter-of-factly, "Of course, it's considered that we in the Oakland Family are living the Principle most fully."
Most fully, that is, in comparison to the rest of the UM. He went on to
mention the general consensus among other members as to this belief.

The second comment was made in a tape-recorded interview with one of several high-level executives of CCP in response to a question about the reasons for their relative success in recruiting members for the UM:

Oakland Family Official:
The heart of Oakland is the heart of God. We take very seriously the Principle. . . . We try to live the Principle. . . . The question [concerns] putting it into practice. The point is how do you make it real . . . living a God-centered life.
Interviewer:
I hate to put words in your mouth, but it sounds to me as if you're saying that you do this more successfully. . . . The logic seems to be that if in fact you're able to draw more people in, and love is the basis of all this, then what you *are* actually is more successful in living the principle than some other areas [of the movement].
Oakland Family Official:
Of course.

Again, confirmation of this elitist view was made matter-of-factly rather than with any trace of smugness or arrogance. Moreover, it was the interviewee's view that Rev. Moon had often openly acknowledged as much and that others in the UM also regarded the Oakland Family as the prototype for realization of *The Divine Principle.* This perspective was *not* shared by many persons in the UM both at rank-and-file and executive levels, however. In fact, national UM officials used such words to describe the Oakland Family as "immature," "irresponsible," and "principalistic" (i.e., living an extension of the philosophy contained in *The Divine Principle* but not strictly adhering to the theology itself). These leaders also stated that the Oakland Family had ignored instructions not only from national headquarters but even from Moon himself.

SEPARATE CHARISMATIC TRADITION

Finally, there were indications in 1978 that Durst, as president of the CCP/NEDS network and active executive of the Oakland Family, was emerging as a charismatic figure in his own right within the UM. Specifically, apocryphal stories began to surface and be repeated, notably in the CCP's initial weekend workshop at the Booneville farm, concerning Durst's romance and marriage to Yeon Soo Im (known to Family members as "Ooni") as well as about his unique leadership status. Sociologists engaged both in covert and overt participant observation in the late 1970s observed this trend of building a legend about Durst (Personal Interviews, 1978). With an emphasis on Durst's role and the concomitant watering down of orthodox UM theology, it could be realistically argued that a subcultural base of heroic tradition was being constructed around the figures of Durst and his wife that would legitimate the already present sectarian tendencies of the Oakland Family.

Do these sectarian characteristics of relative organizational/ideological autonomy and an emerging self-identity of superior purity in the Oakland Family imply a future schism in the UM? The possibility, admittedly, does exist. The Oakland group evolved a distinct humanistic philosophy that could stand on its own without reference to *The Divine Principle,* an encapsulating lifestyle, and an effective technique of recruitment. And, like ` other branches of the UM, it had a strong degree of economic self-sufficiency. Yet there was one major factor mitigating schism: the overriding, intense personal loyalty of Durst and his wife to Moon. Durst and his assistants accorded to Moon all the awe and devotion due the classic charismatic leader in Weber's ideal type. With a conception of their own work firmly rooted in the ultimate millennarian goals of Moon, it would be unlikely that factionalism would result in splinter movements while the unifying charismatic figure's influence was still prominent.

Conclusions

SUMMARY

The UM fairly early began to construct both written and oral traditions of apocryphal stories testifying to the charismatic authority of Sun Myung Moon on such points as his legendary wartime suffering and adventures, his rapport with the spirit world, and even his ability to gauge which UM members would make the best marital partners for each other. Moon's arrival in the United States in 1971 brought this authority directly into the operation of the American UM and had a significant impact on its organization. Though Moon, like other UM leaders, initially misassessed the level of potential public interest in his message, through his direct mandates for reorganization of recruitment and training as well as through his inspiration for various other projects the movement began to pick up momentum and expand its resource bases. In particular, Moon's establishing of One World Crusade evangelistic teams composed of full-time members and the serendipitous discovery of full-time fund-raising tactics (the latter an experimental response to Moon's direction to leaders to purchase new leadership training facilities) overcame simultaneously several fundamental obstacles to mobilization of financial and membership bases.

Within a short time signs of processes of institutionalization appeared along with the UM's rapid accumulation of money and members. These could be discerned in the more systematic recruitment and leadership training procedures, the creation of various UM-sponsored media for disseminating its world view and combatting communism, the creation of new occupational and career opportunities, and the gradual expansion of its married membership. This is not to suggest that by the late 1970s the UM had either resolved all its major challenges or completely institutionalized. Indeed, throughout the decade the movement was confronted with the continuing problems of factionalism and pressures to bureaucratize its coordinating structures. However, the UM was able to strike a workable, if precarious, balance between communal movement characteristics and the minimally necessary bureacracy as well as to tolerate pragmatically some factionalism so long as the latter contributed to the overall world-transforming effort.

IMPLICATIONS

Leadership. World-transforming movements typically are founded and/ or led by charismatic figures. From the standpoint of a given movement's members those charismatic qualities which the leader is thought to possess are perceived as inherent qualities. While it undoubtedly is true that a leader develops a number of specific skills associated with his or her charisma (such as oratorical ability and the capacity to inspire members' awe and confidence in the leader's judgment) that come to be regarded as part of the "charismatic personality," *charisma is in fact largely a socially constructed attribute. Ultimately, its source is to be located not in the independent claims of the leader to extraordinary or supernatural sensitivities but rather in the mobilization requisites of the social movement organization.* Evidence of this assertion lies in the fundamental fact that even if outsiders perceive the existence of such specific personal qualities in a leader, they do not feel compelled by them as do members of the movement. (Movement followers, in turn, develop ad hoc ideologies that typify potential members with such labels as "open-minded" or "closed-hearted" to account for this differential response.) Further evidence is that such leaders frequently do not publicly announce their own supraordinary status but allow others to "discover" it. This, of course, maximizes the opportunity for followers themselves to create a charismatic tradition. Moreover, group-generated charisma builds the sense of drama which followers experience by their membership in the movement.

This perspective on charisma is important because it highlights the organizational salience of charismatic leadership. World-transforming movements envision a world based on principles, such as pure love or conditionless trust, that literally fly in the face of the reality of everyday life as it is experienced in conventional society. The construction of a charismatic individual who embodies qualities that will characterize the new order has important consequences for the organization and its membership:

(1) The leader becomes a role model whom members can emulate. By attributing through collective effort ideal features to an individual who becomes the locus of loyalty, members reaffirm their personal commitment to each other and to achieving the values for which the movement stands. An ever-visible, if rarely attainable, standard thus is present to orient members' behaviors within the group.

(2) The struggles and sacrifices which members of such movements must inevitably endure are rendered less onerous by comparison to the extraordinary personal trials of the leader as constructed in the form of apocryphal tales. Similarly the leader's accomplishments, literal and symbolic, past and present, provide members with a vicarious sense of victory.

(3) The extraordinary qualities embodied by the movement leader give members a sense that the movement is linked to powerful forces that will assure them ultimate victory. Thus, their enterprise is perceived as unique, and, however slim the probabilities of total success may seem from the perspective of outsiders or the history of such movements, *this time* success is considered attainable.

Organization. World-transforming movements are characterized by tension among ideological, communal, and bureaucratic imperatives. Ideologically, such movements are pushed toward creating organizations that promote transformation of each major social institution and maintaining egalitarian relations among members while communal imperatives foster diffuse role expectations as a result of the groups' insulation and interdependence. Bureaucratic organization, by contrast, involves specific role expectations and a clear-cut hierarchy of coordination.

Among the first organizational problems which such movements confront are those of mobilizing the basic resources of membership and money. Our data suggest that such organizational problems tend to be resolved, initially at least, in a manner consistent with communal organization principles and are resolved most effectively when congruence between ideological, communal, and formal organizational needs can be established. For example, this occurred when the OWC and MFT teams were organized communally and the UM ideology was expanded to legitimate spiritually such functional activity. However, as mobilization continues, pressures toward bureaucratization mount for several reasons. First, the larger the membership of the movement and the number of its constituent organization units, the greater the need for a central coordinating bureaucracy and specialized administrative roles in each organization. Likewise, an increase in a movement's financial resources requires not only greater supervision and accounting of income and expenditures but also mechanisms to ensure a flow of income at the new, higher level. Third, the conventional bureaucracies with which movement organizations must deal in the larger society expect exchanges to be conducted in a rationalized, routinized manner. Failure to do so results in conflict, suspicion, and breakdowns of communication (e.g., conflicts between the seminary and New York State Regents, *The News World* and advertisers, and the UM's public relations with the media). Fourth, the recruitment of members creates pressures to provide careers and the opportunity for mobility within the movement as cohorts of members proceed through the life cycle. Finally, the persistence of factionalism, rival charismatic figures within the movement, and varying interpretations of the theology all produce pressures toward orthodoxy. This manifests itself institutionally in such ways as an emerging definition of "authentic" scripture, formal theological training, specification of credentials for interpreting scripture, and ultimately, with the advent of new generations of members, the development of "Sunday schools."

The pressures toward bureaucratization clash with the imperatives of the theology and communal lifestyle. In such cases of conflict it appears that organizational exigencies supercede or at least compromise ideological purity (as when UM ideology was extended to legitimate the importance of lucrative fund-raising). A variety of mechanisms can be created to reduce this conflict. Some of the tactics for resolving these conflicts that emerged from our data were:

(1) Creation of a series of ad hoc organizational units to accomplish specific, short-range projects that disband upon completion of a task. In the UM this tactic created a large number of prestigious but temporary leadership roles without creating permanent offices or hierarchies.

(2) Limiting the size of the elite stratum by assigning each elite member leadership status in several different wings of the movement.

(3) In the middle ranks the emergence of vested interests in offices was deterred by periodically reassigning members to different tasks, teams, and geographic areas.

(4) In the lower ranks high turnover among novitiates functioned to reduce the competition for upward mobility. Given organizational expansion, the number of upwardly mobile members was roughly commensurate with the number of new leadership positions.

(5) In the more formally organized components of the movement there was an expressive emphasis given to even ostensibly instrumental activities. Many specific projects (e.g., the antipornography campaigns, support for the Helsinki Human Rights Agreement of President Carter, discussed in the following two chapters) were conducted largely for their symbolic value to members as they had little visible impact and were short-lived.

NOTES

1. Neil Salonen (UC president following Jones) gave this figure in an interview with *Washington Post* reporters that was widely reprinted. See, for example, the Charleston, West Virginia *Gazette-Mail*, March 3, 1974.

2. Before his first seven-city tour, Moon told the advance members assembled in Washington, D.C. for the pretour training session that he had brought over twelve Japanese both for their skills in raising money and as models for Americans on the tour to emulate. He promised to bring more if they were successful (MS-300, 1972: 11). However, there does not seem to have been any direct connection between their initial presence at Moon's behest and the slightly later formation of the MFTs.

3. MFTs had not always maintained such a taxing schedule. Originally (i.e., in 1972), team members rested two out of every seven days and worked only eight-to-five shifts, a relatively "soft" life by later standards. The coming of the Japanese en masse in 1973 (Lofland [1977: 285] noted *600* "imported" foreigners, primarily from Japan) changed all that. It is more than likely that Moon brought them into the American movement as role models to set a new, rigorous standard for the "laid-back" American members (MS-300, 1972). The zeal of the Japanese fund-raisers, working twelve hours a day, seven days a week, challenged (and, no doubt, embarrassed) the Americans. The easy hours and middle-class weekends disappeared. When President Neil Salonen eventually permitted MFTs one day off every other week, few felt justified in taking advantage of it (Personal Interviews, 1978).

4. It should be noted that some of the more spectacular financial estimates printed in the press were based on the fallacious assumption that all property was owned outright. In fact, many holdings were financed through minimal down payments and long-term mortgages.

5. By 1978 Unification Church President Neil Salonen had already served a six-year term of office. Our impression from an interview with him on this point was that Moon and other UM elders preferred the continuity of his leadership in what was a crucial stage of the movement's development.

6. Despite its obvious connection to the UM, the CCP publically downplayed and even denied any connection with the Unification Church, a source of frequent criticism by outsiders. The authors as well encountered this often belabored denial in contacts with street missionaries in San Francisco. That the group may have deliberately concealed this relationship on tax returns has been alleged by investigative reporter Andrew Ross. In a published series of articles covering the activities of Moon and the UM, Ross (1976) noted that "On July 28, 1973, NEDS filed IRS Form 1023,

an application for tax-exemption. Question 5 on the form asks: 'Does the organization control or is it controlled by any other organization? Is the organization the outgrowth of another organization, or does it have a special relationship to another organization by reason of interlocking directorates or other factors?' Martin Durst, the president of NEDS, who signed the form, checked the two 'No' boxes."

7. When one colleague requested that the San Francisco center members fill out a questionnaire on marriage expectations, employing such standard UM terminology as the blessing (UM marriage ceremony), center leaders denied him permission on the grounds that most members would be unable to answer because *they were unfamiliar with such terms as blessing.*

pg 163

MOBILIZING VISIBILITY AND LEGITIMACY

In order to awaken the world to the dangers of its present state as well as to the imminent opportunity for the millennium, the UM needed to reach as many people, and as quickly and persuasively, as possible. For some time UM leaders had assumed that merely making the ideology available would ensure its acceptance. When Moon arrived in the United States leaders felt that his prophetic, charismatic presence would ignite public interest. However, in the face of almost complete public indifference to Moon's first American tour the movement's leaders were forced to formulate a more systematic strategy for generating large audiences to receive its message. The specific tactics involved an artful combination of advance publicity and gala public occasions which served as "media events." This mixture of better funding, improved coordination of advance public relations, deliberate solicitation of endorsements, and sheer ballyhoo indeed made the UM, as some of our informants put it, a "household word." However, achieving legitimacy required much more than simply large sums of money and skillful public relations. The UM quickly attracted fundamentalist Christian opposition (among other sources) and eventually became entangled in the Watergate scandals, much to its detriment.

The Strategy: Tours and Media Events

From 1972 to 1974 Moon and the UM conducted five major Day of Hope tours across the United States. The first was the modest seven-city tour of February-March 1972, discussed in the previous chapter. The second, and probably the most successful overall, was the four-month 21-city tour beginning in October 1973. Immediately after, a third and more ambitious 32-city tour was undertaken beginning in March 1974 and continuing into May. The fourth tour, unlike the others, did not feature Moon as the keynote speaker; rather, Bo Hi Pak, Moon's interpreter, conducted this ten-city tour himself over a two-month period following the end of Moon's third tour. Finally, from September to December 1974, Moon launched an eight-city tour that was, in many respects, a culmination of the past two years' experience in producing grandstand media events as well as a high-water mark for the UM's efforts to garner publicity. (Interspersed among the tours or following them were also a number of other campaigns and one-time rallies. During the 32-city tour, for example, the UM conducted an antipornography drive in a number of large cities. Two of Moon's largest rallies—the June 1976 one in Yankee Stadium and another the following September at the Washington Monument—were not part of any tour.)

Each tour served essentially two functions: first, the obvious—to reach the American public and disseminate Moon's ideology; and second, to provide experience and training for UM members that would wield them into a more cohesive movement. President Neil Salonen said as much in an October 1973 interview (Basham, 1973) when he announced the 21-city tour's three goals:

The first is to fulfill the role of John the Baptist by proclaiming the Second Advent, telling people that God is speaking again today.

The second is to intensify the work of members in a lot of cities. The tour is a shot in the arm for the local groups.

The third purpose is the training of members, both in local groups and those on the tour.

FUNDING

Unlike the first tour with its minimal investment in advertising and promotion, future tours were lavishly financed. The church poured over a quarter of a million dollars into the 1973 21-city campaign.[1] One year later Salonen stated publically that the 32-city tour was costing the church over $400,000.[2] By late 1974, when Moon conducted his final eight-city tour, the church was reportedly spending between $300,000 and $500,000 *for each city* (Lofland, 1977: 296). The money came largely from the same lucrative fund-raising tactics that had paid for the first tour and the church's expanding property holdings. Some cash did result from ticket sales (at three dollars per lecture on the second tour), but this was likely a minor source. As mentioned below, the church was in the habit of giving away more tickets than it sold to ensure maximum attendance at its functions. An unknown but probably limited amount also came through the movement's international organizations. For example, it appears that one advertising agency whose home offices were in Japan was instructed, at unspecified cost to aid in publicizing the tours (Personal Interviews, 1978).

ADVANCE PUBLIC RELATIONS WORK

Moon's first Day of Hope tour in 1972 was characterized by inexperienced advance teams and a general lack of sophistication. From the top down, UM members had believed that the sweeping power of their message alone would take popular hold in grass-fire fashion. It did not, and the 21-city tour, beginning in October 1973, significantly improved on these points. Moreover, what can be generalized to each tour and rally following the 1972 "trial balloon" also holds for subsequent rallies (e.g., at Yankee Stadium and the Washington Monument) as well as, in part, for other later church-sponsored endeavors, particularly its antipornography drive and annual Unity of Science Conferences. Never again did the church leave anything to chance in public relations.

The Chicago stop on the 1973 21-city tour was exemplary of this new, smoothly coordinated strategy. According to a Chicago *Sun-Times* (December 15, 1973) description, the team of [seventy to one hundred] young "well-barbered, conservatively dressed" church members began preparations for Moon's reception and three-night speaking engagement several weeks in advance of his coming. (In July 1973 Moon originally created two *International* One World Crusade Teams (IOWC) composed largely of Germans imported expressly to help with the advance work. In September, shortly before the tour began, he created two more such IOWC teams for the same purpose.) A sound truck was hired to drive through the downtown and suburban shopping centers. Full-page advertisements were placed in Chicago newspapers. Members canvassed the city streets, buttonholing pedestrians to buy tickets. Posters proclaiming the events were placed in store windows, on commuter transit platforms, on trees and lampposts in city parks, and on the sides of buildings. Various influentials whose professional backgrounds that bespoke respectability (military personnel, clergy, businessmen, and politicians) were cajoled into attending a pre-speech banquet with complementary tickets and expensive prime rib of beef dinners. Prestigious halls were rented: the Ambassador West Hotel for the banquet, McCormick Place for three successive nights of speaking. The press was of course invited. A similar strategy had been followed in New York and Washington, D.C. on that tour as it was to be in other cities on other tours.[3]

The nonillustrious who came to hear Moon were drawn in largely because of UM advance teams' energies on the streets. For example, in a 1975 training lecture to UM members, church patriarch Ken Sudo (1975: 315-317) explained how the UM had been able one year earlier to attract an audience of 20,000 to the eight-city tour's inaugural Madison Square Garden rally through sheer footwork. The New York Unification Church had put 300 local members to work over a period of two months, and 700 IOWC members were added for one month's time. Sudo calculated that together these thousand members logged 30,000 "man-days" in advance work, stopping passers-by on the street, following up contacts with phone calls, carrying publicity literature such as posters and leaflets throughout the city, and so forth. Similarly, Lofland (1977: 295) reported that UM members gave away tickets to persons on the street in exchange for their names and addresses. Soon after UM members in teams called on those same persons, often repeatedly, to encourage attendance at the rally, on the average of 120 homes per member.

For the planned Yankee Stadium rally in 1976, Sudo expressed the official optimism that the UM could attract a crowd of 200,000. To do so, however, utilizing the same advance work strategies, he estimated that 10,000 workers would be needed. Admitting that the church only possessed 2,000 full-time members, many of whom were in IOWC teams overseas or who could not be spared from MFTs, Sudo spoke of a "drastic" change forthcoming in style of witnessing that was to rapidly build membership and provide the manpower to publicize the Yankee Stadium rally. This was the now defunct program of "Pioneer Witnessing." "Pioneers" were to go alone into areas as missionaries and attempt to make two to three committed, full-time converts per month. The latter would be trained over the next ten months and then, as Sudo put it, "from morning until night give away tickets, tickets, tickets. . . ." But, as Lofland (1977: 326) noted, the Pioneer Witnessing program was unsuccessful in America, as "many of the pioneers became disoriented, dejected, and rejected, and they defected." Still possessing only several thousand full-time members one year later, the church only managed to half-fill Yankee Stadium with about 25,000 persons (many of whom, as we shall see, were not terribly interested in Moon's message). Nonetheless, the fact remains that having mobilized the capital to underwrite such extravaganzas and the cheap manpower to help promote them, Moon could create audiences to hear his message where otherwise no audiences previously existed.

However, two other related factors complemented this effort. One was the tours' prestige-by-association tact of inviting luminaries to expensive banquets and soliciting their rubber-stamp endorsements. The other was to embellish the above media events with as much fanfare as possible.

COOPTING LUMINARIES

By "luminaries" we refer to those prestigious individuals who stand in the public eye as gate-keepers of traditional or important values. They are elites whose opinions of a person, place, or event "stamp" it with legitimacy or illegitimacy. They were the sort of persons sought by Moon's advance teams with a fair amount of success, at least during the earlier tours. Moon's deliberate strategy for incorporating them in his publicity campaigns was simple: his teams would create in the minds of the general public and among community luminaries *the impression* of a widespread acceptance of movement and message, *at least long enough to expose both groups to what he had to say*. To do so his advance teams capitalized upon one simple fact about the movement: few persons knew much about Moon or his ideology, and first impressions, at least, made him out to be simply a Korean evangelist in the mold of a Billy Graham. His clean-cut followers and their often ambiguous statements of purpose reinforced that image.

Luminaries were coopted in one of two ways. First, advance teams contacted the offices of governors, mayors, representatives and senators and asked for statements of good wishes, honorary citizenships, declarations of specific dates as Days of Hope and Unification, and so forth. Thus, Moon became an honorary Kentucky Colonel, an honorary Colonel and Aide-de-Camp of Mississippi, and "a very outstanding Phoenician" (i.e., a citizen of Phoenix, Arizona) to name just a few such designations.[4] Across America the tours were greeted, as a result of this advance work, in official letters and certificates by such disparate officials as Georgia Governor Jimmy Carter, Alabama Governor George Wallace, and Los Angeles Mayor Tom Bradley. By our count of such entries in the UM's two-volume *Day of Hope* chronology, the governors of no less than 26 states and the top executives of at least 178 cities provided Moon with honorary titles and good wishes over a four-year period, all in connection with his Day of Hope tours.[5]

Later observers would sometimes wonder how the UM managed to obtain responses from so many public officials who knew so little about

Moon the man and his religious movement. Would not they have been more cautious? Did they simply hand out honorary citizenships, greetings, and proclamations of special days indiscriminately without some screening? The answer was: frankly yes. When the Dallas *Times Herald* (October 23, 1973) questioned Dallas Mayor Wes Wise on his issuing a proclamation of a Day of Hope and Unification for Moon's 21-city tour visit (despite protests by local clergy), Wise's defense of his actions was typical. Wise admitted that he knew little about Moon or the UM and further stated, "unless he's preaching something really radical, I would extend the same courtesy to any visiting religious leader." No screening, nor any established review procedures, existed, and the proclamation was not viewed by the mayor's office as an endorsement of either Moon or the UM. Commenting on the fact that the mayor of Dallas regularly received numerous similar petitions for such proclamations, his assistant reported that Mayor Wise had signed 126 proclamations for special days, weeks, or months in the previous three to four-months period. As one member of his secretarial staff noted, "There are just jillions of them."

Along with such proclamations, the advance teams used the traditional political strategy of seeking appointments for Moon to meet luminaries in order to have photographs taken of them shaking hands or apparently engaged in meaningful conversations discussing their "mutual" interests. This technique harkened back to 1965 when Moon was able to have a fully photographed visit with former President Dwight D. Eisenhower. The UM's *Day of Hope* volumes proudly displayed such photographs showing Moon with Richard Nixon, Senators Hubert Humphrey, Strom Thurmond, Edward Kennedy, and James Buckley (who would eventually become a vocal UM opponent when both of his godchildren joined the UM), and other national figures.

Ancillary to these two versions of the first coopting technique was the practice of soliciting good wishes for special events, such as the 1973 21-city tour's "kick off" rally at Carnegie Hall, by inviting dignitaries who had a low probability of attending. They in return usually telegrammed their polite regrets which were read at the event, and in this way courtesy replies were transformed into letters of endorsements, such as the following:

I WISH TO EXTEND MY CONGRATULATIONS TO YOU ON THE
OCCASION OF THE INAUGURATION OF YOUR 1973 DAY OF
HOPE TOUR. NEW YORK APPRECIATES THE CONTRIBUTION
OF THE UNIFICATION CHURCH TO THE LIFE OF OUR GREAT
CITY. I AM SURE THAT YOUR NEW PROGRAM WILL HERALD

WORTHY OF YOUR FINE EFFORTS. I HOPE THAT YOU WILL
ENJOY CONTINUED SUCCESS IN YOUR WORTHY ENDEAV-
OR.

MAYOR JOHN V. LINDSAY

In similar telegrams, William F. Buckley, Jr., sent his "heartiest best
wishes," Senator Strom Thurmond wished the group success in its "campaign for Christ," and Senator Jesse Helmes expressed admiration for
Moon "as a Christian in our increasingly secular society. . . ."

Thus, the UM relied on a "snow-ball" tactic whereby the movement
created the image of Moon being endorsed by various prominent persons
in order to facilitate gathering further endorsements and derive prestige by
association. No one was more aware of its effect than Moon himself who
encouraged his followers:

> When you go get the proclamations in your various cities and you
> meet the Mayors, it is easy, because your foundation has been laid.
> All you have to do is show other proclamations, other letters, and
> say what other people have done to honor Father [cited in U.S.
> Government, 1978: 348].

The second and more visible method of coopting luminaries was to
provide them with free invitations to expensive banquets usually held the
night before Moon was to begin speaking. At these Moon customarily gave
only brief remarks of welcome and short excerpts from his speeches.
Because these events were intended more to court local opinion makers
and provide media events of "big-name" persons attending Moon's tour
than actually to convert such people, his role in them was truncated and
his polished American church president, Neil Salonen, did most of the
speaking.

The Chicago stop of Moon's 1973 21-city tour was typical of this tact.
Over 200 guests, including political, military, religious, and business leaders, were introduced to Moon and the reception party and read congratulatory telegrams from a variety of other prestigious figures, including former
President Richard Nixon.

This pattern of staging well-publicized media events studded with
famous and influential people in sumptuous surroundings was repeated in
every city and at every major rally from 1973 to 1976 and the scale of the
banquets expanded. To inaugurate the Madison Square Garden rally (the
first of the 1974 eight-city tour), *1,600* dignitaries were invited to the
Waldorf Astoria Hotel for a roast beef dinner at the estimated cost of

$40,000. And, as Lofland (1977: 295-296) noted, the pattern of relative ignorance about Moon, *The Divine Principle,* and America's role in the last days of God's providence on the part of those attending continued. Indeed, "Most guests were reported not to know why they had been invited or who Moon might be: it was a nice free dinner." In other locations, guests received their tickets sometimes third or even fourthhand.

FANFARE

The style of the UM's tours and rallies clearly incorporated a large degree of fanfare. Included here would be the large number of luminaries wooed into attending Moon's functions and lending their importance. And, as mentioned earlier, Salonen made a practice of further exploiting this form of prestige-by-association through ceremoniously reading various telegrams of good wishes and communiques of regret from other famous persons unable to attend. Included also in this style would be the work of the advance teams with their sound trucks, media ads, and so forth.

However, advance publicity and famous guests aside, the media events themselves were conducted so as to maximize their potential for spectacle. Drawing on a range of resource talent within the movement, the UM was able to put together a fairly impressive context for the delivering of Moon's message (though, as we shall show, that did not prevent many persons from exiting in midperformance once the thrust of his message became apparent). For example, the large, prestigious halls rented by the tours were typically draped with thematic banners and both American and UM flags (carrying any of several logos). The male UM members who acted as ushers as well as security guards were frequently dressed in tuxedos. Often the UM arranged with local police to provide special security (in the early tours they ejected protesting members of the audience; later they functioned simply to separate outside picketers from the audience inside) that lent the impression of a serious and important event. Moreover, with a membership drawn from the young, well-educated middle class, the UM could draw on a substantial number of talented musicians. These included singers and instrumentalists in groups such as a gospel folk-rock band called Sunburst, various smaller brass and string ensembles, and a thirty-person choral group called the New Hope Singers, "whose smiles were so broad they one-upped the Up with People Chorus" (Chicago Sun-*Times,* December 15, 1973). Moreover, tours and rallies also featured a colorful Korean folk dancing troupe and an endearing group of singing/dancing Korean children known as "The Little Angels."

Fanfare was not restricted to such formal events. A prominent example of it outside the lecture halls was the antipornography campaign which began in 1973 and surfaced periodically from then on as an issue that garnered publicity. Seeing an issue for which there already existed a substantial public base of support, the UM conducted a series of local demonstrations in cities against smut stores, often with the cooperation of clergy. Typically, a city campaign featured antiporno statements in newspapers and even on radio and television as well as a travelling 350-member troupe of UM members with posters and placards decrying pornography's debilitating effects. A prepared "open letter to the city" was often presented to prono shop owners as well as to the media. News releases from the Unification Church were issued. That these were principally media events was demonstrated by the facts that they occurred sporadically, never went beyond street demonstrations, and lacked the organizational commitment directed in other efforts to gain visibility and legitimacy.

LIMITATIONS OF STRATEGY

We do not mean to leave the impression that these media events were unqualified successes. Far from it. Two not insignificant factors concerning the public performances of Moon himself ought to be emphasized. First, one does not rewrite the basic meaning of both the Old and New Testaments and then, in lecture format, easily persuade an entire culture (including powerfully entrenched religious institutions and millions of adherents) that this new interpretation is superior. The psychology of religious commitment is too complex. As the UM learned, creating an audience was only half, not the whole game. Second, the incongruity of a prophet who claimed to understand the Bible better than all the Western theologians and scholars taken together but yet who could not express that truth without the aid of an English-speaking interpreter remained a persistent stumbling block. In the end, better publicity for the tours and rallies only accented it. The format of first Moon speaking several sentences in excited Korean, then Bo Hi Pak calmly translating, back and forth for well over an hour, was a poor draw. A typical example was Moon's stop in Burlington, Vermont during his 1974 thirty-two-city tour. There 5,000-6,000 free tickets to Moon's lectures were distributed, including to the usual elite banquet-night crowd. While the press account of Moon's speech (e.g., "Moon at the podium, then stomping across the stage, tight fist often upraised, quickly shifting from smiles to tones often snarled out in angry vehemence . . .") was less than flattering, its description was nevertheless accurate. After the *three-hour* speech, many in the audience left the Ramada Inn "shaking their heads, murmuring disbelief, and stopping in the lobby or outside the inn doors to express their skepticism of the phenomenon they had just witnessed" (The Burlington

Free Press, February 18, 1974). As Jonathan Kwitny, in *The Wall Street Journal* (September 20, 1974) summed it up: "In the long run . . . the most damaging factor to Mr. Moon may be the tedium of his own appearance."

The Impact of Opposition on Visibility and Legitimacy

Ironically, the movement's initial lack of visibility proved to be a mixed blessing. Had the UM been successful earlier in conveying Moon's theological message to large numbers of Americans, these tours might have encountered much greater initial resistance. Yet it was precisely because the UM was able to "pass" as just another evangelistic Christian group, without much serious investigation by outsiders into its core beliefs or their implications, that the first tours proved as successful as they did. For example, in reviewing early newspaper coverage for the period 1972-1973 we found that journalists clearly perceived Moon's entourage as simply part of an evangelistic revival, an impression that many members held of themselves as well and thus saw no reason to challenge. However, when both the media and the public became more familiar with Moon's ideology and its wide-ranging implications for traditional American institutions, militant opposition rather quickly emerged.

PLANNING AND STRATEGY PROBLEMS

The declining effectiveness of the later tours can in part be explained by internal matters of planning and implementation. At least two major factors can be identified. First, because the UM's tactics for drawing large crowds to Moon's speeches could not be indefinitely repeated in any one locale, the tours' itineraries progressively shifted away from large metropolitan areas to middle-sized (and smaller) cities in less densely populated states. For example, the first tour stopped in cities such as New York and Los Angeles. The second tour incorporated a number of large cities, such as Detroit, Boston, and Atlanta, but also smaller ones such as Omaha and Tulsa. Moon's third tour trekked to such regional "outposts" as Laramie, Fargo, Missoula, and Burlington.[6] Given the limited stature of local luminaries who were attracted to these functions, the tours concomitantly lost their national media appeal. A speech at Carnegie Hall drew more press attention than the same one delivered in a Rodeway Inn.

Second, following the success of 1973's 21-city tour, the movement's expectations for the impact of future campaigns rose sharply. Indeed, immediately after that tour's completion, Moon and his staff threw themselves into hastily planning and launching an even bigger 32-city tour within a month's time. And, as the tours progressed, events were staged on an increasingly grander scale to attract larger and larger audiences. For example, the inaugural lecture of Moon's final eight-city tour was held at Madison Square Garden in September 1974, to accommodate 40,000 persons. Later, the keynote speaking event for the UM's Bicentennial God Bless America campaign took place in Yankee Stadium.

However, in order to generate the size crowds necessary to stage a respectable media event, the church members found themselves in a dilemma. They could draw large crowds by the usual frentic level of preevent publicity (i.e., papering billboards, walls, and public places with posters, using sound trucks and leaflets in the streets, and the like) and, most importantly, by the distribution of enormous quantities of free tickets. (To insure a respectably sized crowd of 40,000 at the Madison Square Garden rally for Moon's eight-city tour, church members reportedly gave away almost 400,000 tickets—Daily News, New York, September 19, 1974.) Yet such ticket-holders, unlike those of the first and second tours who paid anywhere from three to eighteen dollars to hear Moon speak (or unlike the luminaries at each who were wined and dined free of charge), felt little obligation to sit through one of Moon's tedious sixty to ninety minute discourses. Hence, it was not unusual in the later tours for as many as 50% or more of the audiences to exit by the middle of Moon's speeches. This they did in droves at the September 1974 Madison Square Garden rally: Moon spoke from 8:00 to 10:20 p.m., but ten minutes into his speech the crowd began walking out; by 9:30, two-thirds had left. At the Yankee Stadium rally in June 1974 the practice of distributing free tickets created pandemonium. Not only did the majority leave well ahead of Moon's conclusion, but, in Lofland's (1977: 323) words, "groups of young, male toughs, amounting to several hundred people, roamed the stadium, fighting, robbing, setting off smoke bombs, attacking [Moon's] security forces and generally making a sour scene." The adverse consequences of indiscriminately inviting New York City in toto to such functions began to hit home.

FUNDAMENTALIST CHRISTIAN OPPOSITION

Aside from a few unorganized, isolated instances of opposition, the first two tours were largely unmarred by formal demonstrations against Moon and his movement. However, by early 1974 and the 32-city tour, opposition had grown both more vocal and better organized. Throughout the country evangelical Christian clergymen and associated groups began to appear at each of the campaign's publicized stops to "greet" Moon with fundamentalist leaflets, full-page anti-UM newspaper advertisements, and public demonstrations. Often state-level denominational organizations and local/regional interfaith councils would forewarn their colleagues of the coming tour in areas where it was scheduled to stop. For example, upon Moon's arrival in Berkeley in January, 1974, a coalition of seven evangelical campus and community organizations (such as the Intervarsity Christian Fellowship and the Christian World Liberation Front) presented a standard set of fundamentalist criticisms of Moon and the Unification Church, i.e., that he was un-Christian in proclaiming his own messianic role and in offering a new set of scriptures to complete and interpret the Bible. In Salt Lake City on the same tour one group distributed tracts during Moon's lecture alleging that the UM was "deeply involved in the occult, practices marriage by witchcraft, and is deceptive and dishonest" (Deseret News, April 27, 1974). These protests sometimes disrupted Moon's speeches, as at a rally at Burlington, Vermont where "members of the audience stood up unexpectedly to voice their faith in Jesus and to disdain Reverend Moon's predicted coming of a new messiah" (Vermont Cynic, February 21, 1974). Local pastors delivered anti-UM sermons in which they lambasted Moon and his theology with such statements as that of one Baptist minister who said: "Any man who claims he is Christ is an infidel" (Clarion-Ledger, Jackson, Mississippi, March 25, 1974). There is evidence that such attacks gradually began to have an adverse effect on the tour's ability to mobilize whatever limited legitimacy could be had from the endorsements of regional luminaries. For example, both the governor of South Dakota and the mayor of Sioux Falls had signed the usual proclamations of good will making Moon an honorary citizen in their respective jurisdictions, but after some counterpublicity about Moon's movement and letters of complaint they withdrew these before his arrival (The Des Moines Register, April 9, 1974).

Perhaps the most vitriolic account of Moon and his 21-city tour was penned by syndicated religious columnist Rev. Lester Kinsolving who summed up Moon's lecture performance as an "interminable harangue [resembling] a tobacco auction conducted by an ex-drill master of the Kamikaze corps during an earthquake" (Dundee Sun, Omaha, Nebraska, November 15, 1973).

ENTANGLEMENT IN THE WATERGATE CRISIS

A more costly opposition, at least in the short run, was generated by Moon's defense of President Richard Nixon during the Watergate scandal.

Moon claimed in November 1973, while visiting in Korea, that God appeared in a vision and told him to forgive Nixon (Washington Post, November 10, 1977). On the basis of that vision, Moon maintained that "At this moment in history God has chosen Richard Nixon to be President of the United States" (Kim, 1977 v. 2: 246). Hence, the archangel Nixon, despite his errors and misjudgments, required forgiveness from the American people in order to perform effectively those tasks necessary to fulfill God's last days providence, i.e., maintaining a staunch barrier against communism, particularly in South Korea. In effect, because of God's will for Nixon to remain, Moon claimed the American people lacked the authority to remove Nixon.

This support, church spokesmen tirelessly reiterated, was in the long-run interest of the institution of the presidency and was not meant to preserve the power of Nixon the man.[7] In the course of offering a defense for what he alleged were Nixon's excesses and abuses, Moon issued a number of statements which not only ran headlong against prevailing public/media opinion but which also reflected extreme insensitivity to the basic precepts of American democracy. For example, two quotes, the first by Moon, the second by UC President Neil Salonen, exemplify this point:

> even before he published the Watergate statement, he knew that Nixon was wrong, that the President was lying about not being involved in the Watergate cover-up. But he knew that in a world where evil already prevails, the President must have that kind of right, even the right to dissolve the Senate and House, if necessary [New Hope News, New York, August 20, 1974].

> if necessary, President Nixon should have taken all the tapes at the very beginning and destroyed them and said that many things may have been done which were right or wrong, and he would repent for the things which were wrong, but called the people to support him for the sake of the continued strength of the nation [Daily News, New York, July 25, 1974].

Despite the fact that Nixon's support from even his own party continually eroded, Moon persisted in releasing such endorsements justifying Nixon's continuation in office and calling for an end to the Watergate investigation. The UM released full-page advertisements with that message in dozens of newspapers across the country at a cost conservatively estimated at $72,000 (Marks, 1974). Moon also appeared publically with Nixon and arranged noisy demonstrations on the latter's behalf, as in December 1973, at the official lighting of the national Christmas tree. Soon after, when UM members sang carols in Lafayette Park, the belea-

guered president left the White House to thank them personally, reinforcing such support.

Moon's support-the-president campaign, under the banner of "Forgive,
Love, Unite," came at a time when national political leaders were attempting to forge a delicate bipartisan consensus to pressure for Nixon's resigna-
tion, and it proved embarrassing to them. As an illustration, the planning
committee of the January 1974 Annual Presidential Prayer Breakfast had,
by mutual agreement, explicitly declined sending an invitation to Moon.
Yet, through White House aide Bruce Herschenson (U.S. Government,
1978: 341) Moon obtained one and arrived at the Washington Hilton
Hotel along with some 2,000 enthusiastic UM members who demonstrated
outside in the name of the Unification Church's National Prayer and Fast
for the Watergate Crisis Committee. Later that same day Nixon enter-
tained Moon briefly in the White House. Publicity for the UM's activities
in support of Nixon, as Lofland (1977: 293) noted, "somewhat overshadowed" the 32-city tour occurring at the same time.

MEDIA NEGATIVITY

Until mid-1974 the UM was able to project a relatively favorable, if
unconventional, image of itself to the public through the media without
serious contradiction. The fundamentalist Christian opposition had
succeeded in bringing to light some of the more controversial elements of
the UM doctrine, but the press simply treated this controversy as intra-
mural squabbling among sectarian Christians. Moon's public and outspoken endorsements of Richard Nixon during the Watergate investigations of 1973-1974 largely reversed that public image, however. In the
period of a few months the UM shifted in the public eye from being
simply a curious sect to something possibly conspiratorial and threatening.
It was at this point, during winter, 1974, that the media became aware of
and investigated the complex, multifaceted structure of the UM. Questions
began to be raised about the UM's domestic and foreign political involvements, sources of funding, methods of recruitment, and the implications
of its ideology. At this juncture the organized groups of disgruntled UM
members' parents and ex-members which had been gradually coalescing
throughout the decade (more fully discussed in Chapter 8) began to seek
out and gain credibility from various media. Increasingly the UM's
opponents, rather than the UM itself, influenced the content and tone of
media reporting; indeed, by 1975 it was hard to find anything resembling a
positive newspaper article on Rev. Moon or the Unification Church.

Within this negative trend, however, media coverage vacillated between
portraying the UM as an aggregation of quixotic "oddballs" and presenting

it as a dark foreign conspiracy. For example, of the former, in early 1975 the Korean Unification Church sponsored in Seoul, and with Moon presiding, the largest (1,800 couples) in a series of mass marriages of UM members, a small percentage (6%) of whom were Americans. The press in covering the marriage was true to its pattern of having a laugh at the UM's expense whenever possible in its reporting. A not unrepresentative sample of headlines and what journalists refer to as "kickers" from press reports of the wedding ceremony included: "Take a Number," "All Together Now," "But Who Gets to Kiss the Bride?," "Say, That's a Lot of Rice," and "The I Do's Will Be Deafening."

Much more damaging to the UM were the atrocity stories disseminated in the press by the UM's increasingly vocal critics. Newspaper articles recounting conspiratorial allegations and antidemocratic motives of the UM proliferated, with titles such as "Cult Called US Greatest Threat," "The Korean Satyr Who Seized Nixon" (dwelling on the allegations from the early 1950s that Moon had engaged in sexually initiating females into the Korean Church), "Cult Compared to Nazi Youth Organization," and "The Moon-KCIA Connection."

The largely negative media coverage of the UM was suggested by our own review of 150 New York *Times* articles dealing with the UM between January 1973 and June 1978. Most (37%) were neutral because many articles merely contained details of UM legal controversies, land purchases, and the like. The remainder of the articles had some valence; only 4% were predominantly positive, 25% were balanced, and 37% were predominantly negative. Most of the articles and most of the negativity occurred after 1974 when UM critics became more vocal, visible, and organized. The sample did not include articles published during the fall of 1978 in the wake of the Frontier '78 public relations campaign which probably were more balanced in character.

Conclusions

SUMMARY

From 1972 to 1974 the UM made a concerted effort to remain conspicuous in the public eye by, among other strategies, conducting a series of five speaking tours across the United States for Moon and his interpreter Bo Hi Pak. The tours performed two primary functions which were recognized by UM leaders themselves: first, to disseminate the prophetic message of Moon in order to reform and morally unite Americans, and second, to build members' morale and train them for future UM work. Lavishly funded, each tour was staged on an increasingly grander scale and marked by improved public relations sophistication on the part of advance team members. The latter systematically created publicity through a variety of tactics, such as cajoling well-known figures to attend or indirectly endorse the rallies by associating their prestigious names with the latter and "loading" each stop on each tour with enough fanfare and entertainment to qualify it as a media event that would reach publics beyond merely the audiences who attended Moon's speeches.

There were, however, limitations on the UM's strategy to make Moon a household word. Two were implicit in the format of the tours themselves. First, the oratorical performances of the non-English speaking Moon himself were characterized by a tedium that quickly bored audiences. When the essentials of his message did strike home, fundamentalist Christian opposition rapidly emerged. Second, after the earlier tours had stopped at major cities and presumably "used up" both luminaries and available audiences (without whom media events were impossible to stage), UM leaders were forced to plan later tours in progressively smaller cities and less densely populated areas, which in turn mitigated against the tours' publicity value. In addition, the tours gradually became overshadowed by the UM's embroilment in the Watergate investigation due to Moon's outspoken defense of President Richard Nixon. This involvement in late 1973 and early 1974 was perhaps the single factor contributing most to the increasing skepticism and critical reporting of the media's coverage of the UM.

IMPLICATIONS

Leaders and members of world-transforming movements frequently overestimate the impact of their ideologies on those to whom it is introduced. Because for many in the movement the ideology is perceived as absolute truth, members come to equate understanding with believing. That is, if only one will listen to the message, he or she will also believe (e.g., this perspective accounts for the UM's heavy emphasis on the content of its ideology in recruitment and socialization activities during the early 1960s and the high hopes for Moon's first national tour in the U.S. in the early 1970s). Initially, then, there is in such movements a concerted effort simply to make the truth known. Movements gradually become more realistic about their prospects for immediately winning the hearts and minds of the entire society and begin thinking in terms of a nucleus of the faithful who will begin the transformative process and gradually gain broader acceptance of the movement's goals by becoming living examples of its truths.

Once a movement has discovered the difficulty of even getting others to listen and that, far from being perceived as self-evident truths, the ideology is often regarded as bizarre or even heretical, the movement begins to incorporate a more systematic organizational strategy for gaining social visibility and legitimacy. These twin objectives become a major focus of movement activity and have important organizational implications. First, creating visibility and legitimacy for the movement provides a major outlet for full-time participation in the movement, one which meshes nicely with proselytization and fund-raising activities. Of course, to the extent that the former efforts are successful the latter become easier and more effective. Second, the movement is unlikely to witness immediately the radical institutional restructuring it forecasts; gains in visibility and legitimacy therefore constitute visible signs of success which increase internal solidarity.

The problem that a small, largely anonymous world-transforming movement faces in generating social visibility and legitimacy is that they must be created simultaneously within the context of restraints imposed by a strategy of persuasion. Because both social visibility and legitimacy are qualities conveyed by those who respond to, not initiate, action, the problem is a relational one. The social visibility of a group refers to a collective response to acts by that group; in this sense sheer "noise" does not in itself create social visibility. The legitimacy of a group refers to the number and power of individuals who support it (or at least its right to exist). Legitimacy obviously cannot be achieved without a certain degree of visibility. Visibility may be generated independent of legitimacy, but high visibility paired with low legitimacy yields "notoriety" which of course undermines persuasion as a strategy for producing social change.

Perhaps the simplest means for a movement to spread its message and control both the presentation and content is the purchase of air time on radio or television or space in printed periodicals (a tactic which the UM did occasionally employ). However, "advertisement" is perceived as "propaganda" (as contrasted with "news" which is defined as "information") by the media and the public because the presenter is in virtually complete control. Because the presumably independent analytic-evaluative role of the media has been removed the resulting presentation has less legitimacy. Social visibility also is uncertain because advertising usually does not call for a collective response.

Some visibility accompanied by greater legitimacy can be generated by such means as creating charitable or culturally supportive organizations (e.g., the UM's Korean Folk Ballet troupe and numerous touring musical groups) or participating in culturally legitimate events or celebrations (e.g.,

UM's participation in America's bicentennial celebrations). Frequently, however, these sorts of activities allow a movement little opportunity to express its uniqueness as nonpartisan and/or reaffirmation of commonly shared values are stressed. Indeed, a movement which, for example, uses a presumably charitable or service organization for proselytization, fund-raising, or publicity is accused of operating "front groups" and such groups are denied legitimacy. Thus, while legitimacy is accorded by virtue of the activity itself the opportunity for achieving visibility for the movement is limited (although the event or activities may produce con-siderable visibility).

It is possible to achieve greater visibility if the movement itself sponsors events at which it exerts a greater degree of control and which focus more directly upon its interests and message. An event of sufficient size, novelty, color, and the like will produce visibility in the form of an audience and through media coverage will generate public interest. The creation of an audience is particularly important because it can create visibility and legitimacy simultaneously. In addition to a substantial gathering being news in itself, the individuals in attendance constitute a group which grants legitimacy by consenting to enter into that social relationship vis-à-vis those directing the event and other members of the audience.

If the movement lacks visibility or legitimacy it may well be forced to create motivations for attendance which are peripheral to its real interests (e.g., the UM's provision of free tickets, dinners, and entertainment). Even with such inducements some measure of legitimacy is required. This is often achieved by creating themes for the event which are easily linked to central cultural values (e.g., Moon's themes of "Day of Hope" and "God Bless America" during the tours) and associating prestigious individuals' names with the movement or event (e.g., the UM's emphasis on attracting local or national luminaries to its tour events or reading congratulatory telegrams from such individuals).

The greater the amount of social visibility and legitimacy a world-transforming movement seeks to create, the more vulnerable it becomes to the forces it thereby sets in motion. Very large audiences, for example, require either lavish inducements for participation or a compelling mes-sage. In either case questions arise concerning the source of funding, movement leadership, and the full content of the ideology. Similarly, the more specifically movement-oriented statements or activities with which social notables are asked to link their names the more information about the movement's purpose, organization, and activities is required. *Because world-transforming movements inevitably violate some social norms (see*

Chapter 8), in general the greater the visibility such a movement achieves the lower its legitimacy. As a result, these movements frequently ally themselves with conventional groups and causes (e.g., as the UM did in defining itself as a Christian group) despite the constraints this imposes. The alternative is to risk a situation of high visibility and low legitimacy in which case the movement effectively loses control over the publicity it receives (e.g., the atrocity stories regularly appearing in the media about the UM). The media may feel obligated to "expose" the movement for what it "really is" and prominent figures dissociate themselves from it. However, the charges of front groups and deception levied against such movements emanate from the organizational dilemma of attempting to create visibility and legitimacy and not necessarily from any inherent strategy of deceptiveness on the part of the movement.

NOTES

1. Interview with Linda Merchant, Unification Church public relations spokesperson, in the Dundee *Sun,* Omaha, Nebraska, November 15, 1973.

2. Interview with Neil A. Salonen, the Burlington *Free Press,* Burlington, Vermont, February 18, 1974.

3. At the Washington, D.C. prespeech banquet which hosted a number of prominent national politicians there was an added touch: each of the 500 distinguished guests at the fifty reserved tables received a "personal gift" from Rev. and Mrs. Moon—a three-and-one-half ounce jar of Il Hwa Korean Ginseng Tea (Moon's company's brand), wrapped in gold paper and a red ribbon.

4. One unsolicited honor occurred when Moon was sarcastically named April's "Guru of the Month" in the Honolulu *Star-Bulletin* (March 16, 1974).

5. Lofland (1977: 296) reports similar figures, mentioning honorary citizenships in 73 cities and special days declared for him or the UM by 153 governors and mayors.

6. The seven-city (first) tour visited New York, Philadelphia, Baltimore, Washington, D.C., Los Angeles, San Francisco, and Berkeley. The 21-city (second) tour included New York, Baltimore, New Orleans, Omaha, Chicago, Seattle, Philadelphia, Dallas, Minneapolis, Kansas City, San Francisco, Boston, Tampa, Cincinnati, Tulsa, Berkeley, Washington, D.C., Atlanta, Detroit, Denver, and Los Angeles. The 32-city (third) tour included Portland (MN), Burlington, Manchester, Providence, Hartford, Princeton, Wilmington, Richmond, Charleston, Raleigh, Columbia (SC), Birmingham, Nashville, Louisville, Indianapolis, Milwaukee, Des Moines, Little Rock, Jackson, Wichita, Albuquerque, Phoenix, Las Vegas, Laramie, Sious Falls, Fargo, Missoula, Boise, Salt Lake City, Portland (OR), Anchorage, and Honolulu.

7. Among many of the UM members whom we interviewed, this was the most difficult of Moon's pronouncements to accept. Many revealed to us that they had spent long hours thinking and praying about this issue before reconciling themselves to supporting the president.

Chapter 7

RECRUITMENT AND TRAINING:

DEVELOPING COMMITMENT

Previous chapters have examined the way in which the UM as a world-transforming movement mobilized several key resources: ideology, visibility and legitimacy, leadership and organization, membership and finances. This perspective treated resources, human and nonhuman, in the context of their utility to the movement and to the achievement of its goals. In that sense we have examined the movement from the top down. However, an understanding of the organization and operation of the UM (or other social movements) also requires viewing the movement from the bottom up. The latter perspective is critical because at the individual and communal group levels the ideology was more *legitimating* and *justifying* than *determining* of individual behavior and group structure. The ideology offered a critical analysis of the past and present and a vision of the future; in so doing it justified and legitimated the formation of a radical community, one which broke with the goals and means of conventional society. Once formed, however, these communally organized groups developed requisites of their own quite apart from the movement's overarching ideology and organization. It was the requisites of these groups *as communal groups,* then, that largely determined individual behavior and group structure.

Some evidence of this is provided by the literature on communal groups which demonstrates remarkable continuities among groups with very disparate ideologies (see, e.g., Kanter, 1972a; Coser, 1974). A somewhat parallel observation emerged from our own research. As we have noted in several chapters, the Oakland Family diverged significantly from the orthodox, mainstream UM ideology. There were also some important differences in recruitment tactics. Yet, what was most striking was the similarity in the structures of the UM's communal groups. Further evidence can be found in the relative day-to-day unimportance of UM ideology to many of its members. As reported in our previous research (Bromley and Shupe, 1979), individuals who had been UM members for several months or even longer had at best a sketchy knowledge of *The Divine Principle.*[1] In fact, in some of the more candid interviews members acknowledged to us that their primary attachments were to the communal lifestyle itself, or to the high moral standards that members set for themselves, rather than to the movement's goals and ideology. It was apparent that as long as members conformed to the norms of the communal group their statuses were secure.

Other evidence of the importance of the structure of the communal group for behavior (as opposed to the ideology or movement goals) was apparent from a variety of communal activities relatively unrelated to movement goals or which emerged within the communal groups and were later justified theologically. Group singing, for example, which occurred before and/or after virtually every gathering, served an important expressive, solidarity-producing function. Sometimes the songs were explicitly religious, but often they were not (e.g., "If I Had a Hammer," "Blow'in in the Wind"). All emphasized the themes of social betterment, optimism for change, and unity of purpose. Clearly, the collective activity was often more important than the substance of the lyrics. An even more important example was the rationale which developed for fund-raising. As reported in Chapter 5, the MFT concept emerged serendipitously out of the necessity for raising a large amount of money (to purchase a residence for Moon and a training center) in a short period of time. It was only after the MFTs had surpassed anyone's grandest expectations as a fund-raising technique that members were provided with a theological rationalization for it. Similarly, in the 1970s the UM adopted those proselytization techniques that led people to begin acting out appropriate role behavior rather than waiting for intellectual conversions. These new techniques were utilized because they integrated people more readily into communal activities as well as enhanced spiritual understanding or growth. Indeed, it was precisely these techniques which "caused" people to participate in the UM without deep ideological commitments. Finally, even those practices which derived most directly from the ideology (e.g., celibacy) were rigidly adhered to, we would argue, in large measure because of their group-sustaining functions. It may have been theologically necessary for members to remain celibate, but for young adult males and females to live continuously side by side and yet not compete for one another sexually it was organizationally imperative.

Viewed from this perspective the critical resource which the UM required to mobilize at the communal group level was member commitment. In this chapter we shall examine the structural features of UM communal groups that fostered this commitment.[2] Following Kanter (1972a: 68ff; 1972b) commitment can be analytically considered along three dimensions.

First, the *instrumental* involves the individual's orientation of self relative to the rewards and costs that are involved in participating in a group. The individual must find "what is profitable to him is bound up with his position in the organization and is contingent on his participating in the system; he commits himself to a role." This is achieved by inducing sacrifice of something valuable, on the one hand, and investment of personal resources in the group, on the other. Second, the *affective* concerns the individuals' emotional attachment to people in the group. Emotional commitment is engendered by attenuating relationships which obstruct the individual's total emotional involvement in the group and building the individual's primary loyalty and allegiance to the group so that he experiences intense feelings of "we-ness" and "oneness." Third, the *moral* is the degree of "moral compellingness" of the norms and beliefs of the group to the individual. The individual's former identity is rejected and a new identity is assumed such that the group's authority becomes a moral necessity in terms of the individual's own self-identity.

In the discussion that follows we shall examine how the structure of UM communal groups fostered commitment in each of these areas. The process of evolving commitment has been divided into three stages— recruitment and initial socialization, full-time membership, and deepening involvement and commitment.

Recruitment and Initial Socialization

RECRUITMENT

If individuals are going to be persuaded by a movement to make major sacrifices and commitments, then some combination of maximizing the attractiveness/salience of its message and lowering the costs of initially experiencing its truth must be found. Initially the problem for a movement is to bring potential members to a low but crucial level of involvement. One approach is for recruitment to be directed at those for whom the movement's diagnosis of the present state of affairs and vision of the future seems sufficiently compelling to warrant even the limited sacrifices of time and energy called for. Another is for recruitment to be directed at those for whom the group might be less attractive but the cost of initial inquiry very low. In practice the UM integrated both these recruitment tactics and sought to stress them simultaneously.

The UM directed recruitment efforts at Americans in their teens-to-late twenties. These were the persons unencumbered with career/domestic commitments and for whom the cost of experimenting with the UM would be lowest. UM proselytizers typically recruited in places where they would be most likely to find such persons, e.g., public parks, shopping malls, libraries, city streets, bus and train stations, and centers of countercultural activity, such as college campuses and certain key urban areas (e.g., San Francisco-Berkeley). They also systematically looked for any visible "symbols" of transience or independence, such as backpacks or persons alone rather than in obvious heterosexual pairs. The following sample of statements taken from UM members recollecting their circumstances when they were recruited reflect this tactic: "I had just graduated from high school but hadn't found a job yet."[3] ... "I was attending a Unitarian convention as a youth delegate after graduating from high school. I decided to backpack through the country and gradually work my way back home." ... "I was looking for work in Minneapolis after hitchhiking around the country for awhile."

The most immediate problem for missionaries was to establish contact with strangers. This was solved by any one of a large number of creative approaches. For example, one IOWC team "conducted" a door-to-door brief survey of "attitudes toward world problems." A widely used technique (dating back to the early 1960s) was to advertise in the classified sections of newspapers for idealistic persons for Peace Corps-type work and set up "interviews" with them. Sudo (1975: 358) contains one member's account of how she would canvass libraries and strike up conversations on the basis of book titles which she noticed persons reading. We personally spent an afternoon watching Oakland Family members, both surreptitiously and later with their knowledge, operating an "information booth" near Fisherman's Wharf in San Francisco. There members would pick up on slogans printed on T-shirts (e.g., "Hey, are you from Michigan?") or items that people might be carrying, such as guitars, to catch their attention.

After initiating a conversation, UM members were characteristically vague in their descriptions of the group which they represented and portrayed its goals in general, innocuous terms. Taylor (1976: 32) reported how at different times in his participant observation study he was invited by street missionaries to a lecture "on world peace" and once was told in the initial conversation: "We are trying to build a community where we can live together in joy, peace, and brotherhood." Along with a description of the group individuals received invitations to dinners and lectures to learn more details, implying little or no commitment beyond these events. For example, one UM member recalled:

> One day while walking in Golden Gate park on my way to school, this Chinese-American girl, she came up to me and said, "Are you interested in a meaningful way of life?" I said "Yes." She said, "How about an international community where we get together and study Principles of Living? Why don't you come over and see?" So, then I went over to their center [Kim, 1976: 29].

At this point the UM was willing to allow individuals to self-select on any of a number of bases. Statements of initial interest that we encountered when interviewing UM members included curiosity, naiveté, and even romantic attraction: "I went to the [church] center and heard a lecture . . . [that] explained many things I had questions about and explained the relation between science and religion." . . . "[After attending a lecture] I was impressed with their determination." . . . "The people cared more than other places I had been." . . . "I was not terribly tormented with theological doubts or anything like that . . . [but] I was very interested in experimenting with communal living and had been a very socially concerned agnostic." . . . "I felt a great deal of appreciation, admiration and love for my spiritual mother."

There were some differences in approach among different UM groups. For example, groups in the mainstream theological tradition, such as the IOWC team which we observed, immediately and (if anything) proudly displayed signs of this affiliation. Pictures on walls, color slide shows or movies, and lectures clearly linked their efforts to Moon and the Church. Conversely, the Oakland Family, or Creative Community Project, Inc., departed from the mainstream practice, initially downplaying religious themes and in particular any connection with Moon or the UM (as indicated in Chapter 5). This strategy actually cast a wider net for the nonreligiously idealistic and on first encounters appealed to many persons who otherwise would not have responded.

INITIAL SOCIALIZATION

We define *initial socialization* as the period between an individual's first participation in an organized UM function (i.e., dinner/lecture/weekend workshop) and completion of the first one or two workshops, that is, up to three or four weeks in the movement. Our previous research (see Bromley and Shupe, 1979) showed that 30% of the persons who joined the UM did so within one week, 60% within one month. Only 20% waited as long as two months. In both wings of the UM, the format for the introductory evening was essentially the same, with only the content differing. A typical format involved this sequence: each "guest" taken to an UM center by a host (usually the street missionary who had first encountered him) or met there by the latter, the host introducing the guest to other UM members with plenty of what Taylor (1978: 31) termed "getting-to-know-you" questions, exuberant song singing and group introductions before the buffet dinner, dinner itself, and then perhaps more entertainment (more songs, and the like) before a one-hour lecture and/or slide show. At this point all that was expected of the individual was that he or she be polite and attentive. In return, UM members were effusive in their attention to, and interest in, the guests. Toward the end of the evening guests were warmly and persistently urged to return for a different lecture the following evening or a weekend workshop.

Once an individual had agreed to participate in a workshop, the UM was in a much stronger position to begin building commitment. Individuals were available to the UM on a 24-hour basis, and so it was possible to convert even normally private aspects of life into collective activities. Workshops involved a carefully orchestrated continuous schedule of activities, each of which was in some way designed to build instrumental, affective, or moral commitment. The following illustration of this process is taken from Taylor's (1978) detailed account of his participant observation of both a weekend workshop and subsequent week-long workshop at the Booneville farm of the West Coast's Oakland Family. We have relied on this example both because it was the single most comprehensive report available (though we had access to various other papers, such as Ayella, 1975, and numerous journalistic accounts) and because in the mid-to-late 1970s the Oakland Family was the most successful center of recruitment of all the UM branches. Many of the same processes and techniques of building commitment, however, were used elsewhere in the movement in one form or another.

In return for payment of a modest "registration fee" of eighteen dollars and giving up a weekend's time, potential recruits were bussed to a pleasant rural locale about hundred miles from San Francisco. There they found a rigorous, fast-paced schedule of group activities with lectures and discussions on humanistic topics interspersed among recreational activities such as swimming and volleyball. At the instrumental level newcomers quickly learned that in temporarily sacrificing outside activities they attached themselves *totally* to the group. Upon arrival a "buddy system" paired each newcomer with a Family member who literally focused all his or her attention on the novitiate. Taylor found that at one point his host doted on him to the point of even following him into the bathroom.[4] Newcomers were explicitly told that they should "participate one hundred percent" and that "no one can do anything alone;" indeed, total participation of all individuals in every event, with these events strung into a nonstop series of activities, was the norm. On the first morning of the workshop Family members woke newcomers early with cheery songs and exhortations to begin "the greatest weekend" of their lives. Beginning at 7:30 a.m. newcomers were propelled into closely timed activities sometimes lasting as little as ten minutes and others several hours, exercising and singing for forty minutes before breakfast, then a group walk, song practice, lecture, lunch, dodgeball, conversations with buddies, more lectures, dinner, preparation of skits, group "testimonies," more meetings, and finally bed. The steady momentum of this schedule never let up, prompting one informant to later comment to Taylor: "The weekend with its many lectures and group activities seemed to rush forward. . . . the activity was so intense and incessant I had no time to think about it. The only time I had for myself was during sleep."

The Oakland Family applied deliberate affective pressure through a series of techniques strongly reminiscent of those employed in sensitivity group training in order to build a sense of communion and solidarity among newcomers. Nonfamily members were disparaged as significant others and objections or hesitations to total participation on the part of newcomers were characterized as negative. Individuals were encouraged to drop inhibitions and participate fully in expressive activities such as introducing oneself to as many persons as possible in thirty seconds, engaging in pantomime games and exercises that otherwise might have seemed "silly," "group hugs," and frequent, vociferous cheers. They were also subject to a number of "rules" that clearly had the effect of segregating each newcomer not only from skeptical outsiders (e.g., almost total discouragement of phone calls or lack of privacy for what few were put through) but also from fellow novitiates. Taylor's report is replete with anecdotes wherein two newcomers would momentarily be left "unguarded," begin to exchange pleasantries or impressions and then be quickly split up by Family members. Newcomers were to talk only with "advanced" members not likely to express "negativity." Newcomers were also urged repeatedly to stay with their groups, rely on their buddies, and participate fully only as parts of the group. In this way, Taylor noted, "members effectively can sustain the appearance of harmonious unity." Moreover, he commented that "besides pressures to cooperate with group life, no one is allowed to express questions, concerns, or opinions that threatened members' continually reified definition of the situation" (i.e., outside the discussion groups where such doubts could be formally expunged). At the same time, in exchange for surrending freedoms of inquiry and reflection, newcomers were "love-bombed," i.e., showered with constant attention and "overwhelming kindness" that often had the desired effect. One young woman observed by Taylor reported:

> I was raised back East. We were always moving from one place to another—always uprooting and having to go to another school . . . living in poverty and corruption. I was always afraid of people with hate in their hearts. . . . It's so wonderful to be in a place where you don't have to feel that fear. It's so hard to explain! [She blushes and is on the verge of tears.] When I first came here, I didn't know what Karen meant when she ran up and hugged me, and said, "At least you're home, welcome!" But now I know what she means. I am home!

A prime strategy used by the Oakland Family to build the moral dimensions of commitment and transform self-identities was to carefully arrange for members to testify (with all the appearances of spontaneity) as to the unhappiness in their earlier lives and the immense difference since joining the Family. Taylor observes that "As assistant group leaders, members' primary concern is to express through informal testimonies how their lives have been transformed since they met the family." Thus, while it may have been early to initiate identity changes in potential recruits, it was possible for UM members to model appropriate identities in front of novitiates. Acting as role models, their stories were intended to inspire others to provide similar anecdotes and further erode the social personae of newcomers. Taylor later interviewed one person who left the workshop and commented:

> People would tell their stories of before they'd joined, mostly of having been a long-haired hippie, atheistic or spiritually trippy, who was living a self-indulgent life with drugs and sex, and was really deep-down unhappy. Then he'd found the Family and been transformed into a joyous, virtuous child of Heavenly Father. Everyone

works very hard, and this is seen as an inevitable product of such a transformation giving all you've got in loving service.

Such testimonies usually occurred in small, circular "seminar" groups of approximately seven to ten persons, one-half of whom were Family members. Newcomers who could provide not only positive sentiments about the group but also denigrate their preworkshop lives were of course rewarded with praise and love. Those who did not were chided good naturedly but persistently until they too could say something positive. Lectures emphasized the "natural person" who realized "his highest potential by contributing himself to a collective effort to help build the 'ideal world.' " To immerse one's identity in the group and its goals, to not react on the cognitive but rather on the affective level, was to self-actualize one's potential and emerge as this natural person. Thus, one group leader told newcomers:

> Think of three things you would like to improve in yourself. If you have three things you want to change, and try one hundred percent, just think what you could do in a week! . . . Write down a list of things you want to improve in yourself, then evaluate them at the end of the day. I will talk with each of you individually during the week to help you actualize your goals.

In the "eleventh hour" the final effort to convince potential recruits to accept this new vision of the ideal world founded on unconditional love and to pursue self-actualization through the Family was made. The exuberant, exhausting pace culminated in the extension of an offer to newcomers for them not to leave but spend the next week in further exploration of their potential. The lectures built to this theme and "buddies" did their best to turn the emotional ties constructed during the previous thirty-six hours into another stage of commitment. Those who wanted were returned to San Francisco by bus; the rest remained. According to Taylor's observations, about half the newcomers chose to stay on for the week-long seminar, a figure which coincided with our own rough estimate based on conversations with Oakland Family leaders. (During the week-long workshop, we might mention, the orthodox theological message of the UM was introduced.) This fairly high proportion is not surprising considering the high amount of self-selection that originally occurred at the recruitment stage (and some initial attempts during the week by Family members to screen out "undesirables"). Nor is it surprising then that most persons who go on to take the longer workshops eventually become members. While a slightly better than 50% success rate would be a poor one indeed for a group that supposedly possessed mysterious "brainwashing" powers, the secrets of "spot hypnosis," and other techniques alleged to the Family, it was quite respectable when one remembered that the Family drew virtually all of its recruits as total strangers off the streets of the San Francisco Bay Area with only vague promises of what they could offer. The success of the Oakland Family lay not so much in any "mystical" powers to recruit and beguile on initial contact but rather in the operation of a combination sensitivity training/boot camp socialization experience repeated weekend after weekend on a year-round basis. Thus, the convincing quality of its workshops had an almost theatrical nature: members producing moving testimonies, affection, cheers and tears on cue, all with the appearance of spontaneity rather than systematic planning and practice.

FULL-TIME MEMBERSHIP

Full-time membership is somewhat more difficult to define. Members often did not make a formal declaration of membership immediately (though membership forms did exist) and participation in workshops was not a sufficient criterion because some individuals "joined up" UM groups in transit without having participated in any workshop. Nevertheless, if an individual chose to participate in one of the longer workshops (i.e., several weeks) this was usually a good indication that he or she would go to become a full-time member and, more importantly, it was in these longer workshops that the process of building commitment was intensified.

By the end of several weeks' participation in workshops the UM usually had begun to build strong, deep ties to the movement. Few individuals at this point were likely to detach themselves although there was a high attrition rate among members at least for the first several years of their participation. At this point when individuals clearly had taken up residence and were involved full-time in the movement they were called upon to: (1) begin making major sacrifices of their former activities and invest themselves totally in the movement; (2) to disengage from former relationships outside the movement as well as relationships inconsistent with the requirements of communal group activity and attach themselves emotionally to a new network of relationships within the movement; and (3) to reject their former sources of identity and develop a new set of priorities by which to judge themselves.

INSTRUMENTAL

On joining the UM many individuals began severing their ties to their former lifestyles (as part of the desocialization process—see Dornbusch,

1955; and McHugh, 1966) and by so doing increasing their investment in the decision that they had made. One specific manifestation of these initial personal sacrifices was the abandoning of material possessions such as automobiles, stereo systems, other electric appliances, furniture, and even houseplants. These items were often sold and the money donated, sometimes along with bank savings (ranging from a few dollars to $15,000 among our respondents) to the UM. Not infrequently such sacrifices were considerable:

> When I joined the family I was very blessed with a lot of material possessions: I had a sports car (Pontiac Firebird); $4,000 in a bank, a $3,500 console Hammond organ I bought while I was a musician for seven years; color television; a portable organ and amplifiers. . . .
> My engineering books, deep freeze, etc. were sold by me personally because I attached little value to them except monetary. My money I gave to the church (they didn't ask me to, I decided based on my understanding of what it meant to be a disciple of Rev. Moon).

Careers and career aspirations as well, not at little personal sacrifice, were also jettisoned. Respondents reported giving up careers as musicians, quitting graduate training in such fields as business and psychology, and dropping out of medical school. One young woman recalled: "Giving up my job was emotional, four years of sweat and tears to become the first woman civil engineer in New Zealand caused me a lot of pain to give up." In addition, other obviously meaningful activities were sacrificed. For example: "I gave up volleyball—I had played in a league and represented my country (Iceland) in two international matches."

Throughout the first few years that individuals spent in the UM they engaged in other sacrificial activities designed to promote their own spiritual growth. Two examples of this were fasting and "setting conditions." Fasting, which usually restricted a member to drinking water (or sometimes fruit juice) but prohibited eating, was intended to serve a three-fold purpose: (1) purification of the body; (2) an existential coming to terms with the meaning of life and death; and (3) demonstrating self-control and commitment to the movement by undergoing the same physical rigors that Moon himself once endured. Manifesting this self-control was tangible evidence to oneself and to others that one was totally committed and to be taken seriously. A seven-day fast was required of each member sometime during the minimum three-year term between joining the UM and receiving the blessing of marriage. However, members fasted on a voluntary basis relatively frequently for a variety of spiritual reasons for periods of several weeks or even a month. Even longer fasts, in the face of greater challenges, were also reported. For example, the first two Pioneer Missionaries to Finland undertook a forty-day fast (after the example of Jesus' forty days in the wilderness) to prepare themselves spiritually for the difficult task ahead. When one member was unable to continue the fast after twenty days, the other pioneer "indemnified" her partner's failure by extending her own fast to sixty days (Personal Interviews, 1978).

"Setting a condition" referred to a process in which members attempted to make contact with the spirit world and mobilize its forces in achieving some restoration-related goals. If members were able to set up the proper spiritual conditions, these would act as a magnet to draw spiritual forces and influence human events. The means of making the situation propitious for the presence and intervention of spirits typically involved prayer and/or fasting. For example, Moon's tours and the three major rallies at Madison Square Garden, Yankee Stadium, and the Washington Monument were held to meet conditions providentially set for him in his quest for world restoration. UM members routinely "set conditions" for myriad purposes related to their own roles in this restoration process. One UM missionary stated: "I found that the majority of my people came in response to a prayer condition. I did a 21-day prayer condition—it was just half an hour reading *Master Speaks* and praying. People came directly from these conditions" (Sudo, 1975: 343).

Perhaps one of the classic examples comes from one member's description of the conditions set by the movement's legendary star fund-raiser (previously mentioned in Chapter 5):

> She would pray for people to come with money, and she would get incredible things to happen. Incredible donations. And it was because she was challenging God and challenging Satan and challenging the parking lot. . . . I heard she laid many conditions: prayer conditions, and cold shower conditions, and through this experience she could understand that it's not herself but God who raised the money. Therefore, through establishing conditions God could do it through her [Sudo, 1975: 21].

Thus, the activities necessary to set conditions could be extremely arduous. The fund-raiser just discussed, in meeting her goals, had solicited money for twenty-four hours straight in the rain on a busy street in New York City when she alone raised $1,000 in a day without rest. Other UM members would frequently begin fund-raising early in the morning and continue well into the evening, often on the basis of such conditions, for days or even weeks at a time. Prayer, too, consumed a great deal of personal energy. Rather than being merely a ritualistic observance, prayer involved channelling one's total energy and attention into communication with God. Even a few minutes of such activity could be exhausting (and exhilerating).

At the same time, as members "detached" from their former lifestyles and statuses, they involved their personal resources more deeply in the movement. One clear illustration of how totally a person's time and energies could be consumed on a day-to-day basis by movement activities can be seen in the typical round of life or routine in the "day of a Moonie." The following from our own participant observations represents a summary of such a day for an IOWC team member:

On an average day members of the group arose by 6:00 a.m. At 6:30 there was a short period of physical exercise followed by a prayer meeting consisting of songs, prayers, and a spiritual "message for the day." Members rotated leadership of the prayer meetings in order to provide each with the exposure to the responsibility and opportunity for expressive leadership. Breakfast was served at 7:30. If there was a need for an organizational meeting, it was held after breakfast. Otherwise, the next hour was used by members to take care of personal needs and prepare for the day's work beginning at 9:00 a.m. Members were assigned to either a witnessing or a fund-raising team. Each team, consisting of half a dozen or more members, was provided with transportation to a pre-determined locale. There the members of each team canvassed the area on foot either singly or in pairs from shortly after 9:00 a.m. until early afternoon when the team reassembled for lunch. After a lunch break of approximately one hour, work was resumed until 7:00 p.m. If guests were expected for dinner (i.e., if proselytizers anticipated meeting any of their day's contacts), some or all of the members would return to the center to have dinner and meet with the guests; otherwise, all members would continue to witness or fund-raise late into the evening. For those who returned to meet with guests, there would be two-hour presentations or lectures and discussions with the guests beginning around 7:00. Dinner was served about 9:00 and afterwards there was follow-up discussion with guests. The latter usually left by 10:00 or 10:30, and a prayer meeting for members followed at 11:00. The members who had returned early began to retire shortly after the prayer meeting. This daily schedule was flexible. The group might "take a day off" for rest, cleaning the center, their vans, and so forth, attend a movie, or simply lounge around while reading, writing letters, or talking. If fund-raising and witnessing quotas had not been met, the group might put in a number of eighteen to twenty-hour days. In any event, the schedule was demanding and relegated little free time for extraneous (i.e., individual) purposes.

Admittedly, fund-raising and witnessing teams members led a more hectic lifestyle than members in established centers, but our observations of persons in the latter situations led us to conclude that they too led just as consuming, if slightly less hurried, schedules.

Yet, at the same time it is important to emphasize how challenging and even exhilerating this schedule could be and that these feelings contributed to members' affective attachment to the group. For despite the fact that the daily schedule was usually long and rigorous, the nature of the activity or where it took place changed often. Members working on mobile teams had the opportunity to visit cities across the country and not infrequently travelled abroad as well. Constantly witnessing and fund-raising in locations varying from college campuses to airports to bars lent variety to what otherwise might have been monotonous routine. Further, members were shifted frequently among UM projects. They might work in an agricultural commune, work on several special projects such as the "God Bless America Campaign," tour a number of cities on a fund-raising team, or play or sing for one of the movement's several touring musical groups, all in a relatively short period of time. Short of "joining the navy" there was no other way for many youth to "see the world" so inexpensively.

Not only were members completely encapsulated in group-related endeavors throughout each day, but each individual contributed in some vital way to the sustenance of the whole and in return had many personal needs fulfilled by every other group member. A division of labor existed in which different individual members were responsible for such tasks as buying and preparing food, repairing clothing, providing transportation in and maintenance of group-owned vehicles, or even giving haircuts. Any additional requisites, such as dental or medical care, which could not be provided by other UM members were paid for by the group at the request of the individual. This total dependency of each member on the group, on the one hand, and his or her feelings of importance to and responsibility for the group on the other were in themselves very effective in building individual commitment.

Finally, our observations at several locations also revealed how members invested virtually all of what in conventional society are regarded as personal possessions in the collectivity. For example, when members received "Care Packages" of cookies, sweets, and the like from their families, the contents were shared and made available to all. Even personal clothing was exchanged for use on occasion. More importantly, all proceeds from fund-raising activities were turned in to team leaders or center directors, hence most members had little if any spending money. Money was simply distributed to members when requested for specific needs.

AFFECTIVE

The UM also sought to build commitment to the movement by emotionally detaching individuals from important relationships outside the UM or those which might reduce communal solidarity within the movement and facilitating affective ties which would link the individual more closely to the communal group. Assuming full-time membership in the UM, then, entailed almost immediately attentuating or even renouncing certain relationships external to the group. There were a variety of reasons why relationships with outsiders were attenuated. First, one solution to the problem of maintaining a high level of motivation and expectation in the face of events which were potentially disconfirming of UM ideology was to withdraw from the outside world. Except for highly structured, ritualistic contacts with nonbelievers (i.e., through fund-raising or the pseudo-*Gemeinschaft* of proselytization overtures and weekend workshops), all relationships were insulated within reinforcing environments of the like-minded. The latter contexts prepared members psychologically for their frequent forays into the unresponsive world of indifference and hostility and furnished unconditional support for their perseverance as well as for their defeats. Thus members were at least strongly encouraged to disengage from nonreinforcing contacts that could not be handled in highly ritualized (i.e., impersonal) ways, principally from former intimates, family members, and friends who often were numbered among the nonsupportive or even the hostile. As one UM leader told Sontag (1977: 63):

The church has not . . . encouraged members to go home frequently. Young members get the impression that is wrong, that it is something they should not want to do.

A second reason was that members tended to see all of their activities and relationships in religious terms. It was difficult to share this pervasive world view with nonbelievers (see Kornhauser, 1962, for a discussion of this same phenomenon among political activists). Outsiders, with their "fallen" interests, could not be expected to be sympathetic with the movement's goals. Even if neutral they would only constitute a drain on a member's time which could otherwise be put to use in pursuit of the restoration. Third, given the demands of totalistic involvement, it was difficult to sustain such relationships on any regular basis.

The following quotes illustrate how members interpreted such disengagements in their own pasts:

> I left my fiance of three years although we were very harmoniously learning to love each other.
>
> It was difficult to commit myself to the church, because my mother was all alone and I felt responsible for her. I saw, however, that Jesus had demanded from his disciples to leave their relatives for him. . . . My relationship with my best girl-friend got cut off, because she was a strong Christian and could not accept my new religious commitment.
>
> Because of my very close relationship to parents and brothers and sisters, I spent all my time, love and money on them. Now I transferred all that to a man I had not yet met except I thought of him as my new father.

When members were not "harbored" in such environments, as was the case with the Pioneer Witnesses whom Moon sent in 1975 *on an individual basis* to separate areas of the country, defections were high. In the late 1970s Moon still assigned individual Pioneers to the more than 120 countries where he conducted "missions, and the drop-out rate of these from the UM was more than fifty percent" (Personal Interviews, 1978).

Relationships which posed a threat to the movement's uncompromising demands for solidarity and single-minded loyalty were also closely controlled. Sexual relations, one of the deepest emotional unions between human beings, constituted perhaps the prime example of this (see, e.g., Barker, 1978). Total celibacy to the point of abstaining from even the most "innocent" of romantic attachments, was normatively, and in reality fairly strictly, followed prior to marriage. Moon required each member to remain celibate for a minimum of three years and often longer after joining the UM. Members openly spoke of problems experienced in coping with sexual desires and quenching them through a combination of frequent prayers and cold showers. Yet, despite the enormous theological significance of the sin of fornication, such self-denial appears to have been beyond the abilities for some members in both centers as well as out in the field in MFT teams and elsewhere (Sudo, 1975: 128).

Yet, at the same time individuals' attachments to their families and other loved ones as well as opportunities for immediate sexual/emotional gratification were exchanged for deep involvement in the communal group and its diffuse rewards. This oneness had the effect of creating strong feelings for, and attachments to, the group. Members literally shared all activities. They lived, slept, ate, worked and played together. Their daily schedules, literally from dawn until dark, were coordinated and predicated on the assumption that all members could invariably depend on one another. To disregard this network of functional interdependence was, for any negligent member, at the same time to know that he had "let down" all other members in failing to meet his responsibilities. By the same token, to "hold up one's end," even in the performance of relatively mundane tasks, expressed an indirect but self-recognizable sense of solidarity and lent an unmistakable uplifting feeling of satisfaction to each individual. Characteristic of the affect resulting from such interdependence were these three comments, one from an ex-member of the UM and the other two from our respondents. One member said, "I am going to stay because I have a responsibility to this group. I am doing the most good for myself and the people here." Another member put it this way: "If it could be like this around the world, what a world this could be!" An ex-member stated:

> In a way it [life in the church] was a wonderful experience. Because of the closeness of the people and the cooperation and having a purpose in life. There is so much enthusiasm and consideration. . . . There is so much hope, and you can feel that. . . . There is a tremendous satisfaction in every day (Sontag, 1977: 55-56).

The two primary activities of many UM members, witnessing and fund-raising, were ostensibly instrumental in nature but had important expressive functions as well. For example, fund-raising activities build affective ties whether or not the activity was instrumentally successful. If the group met its goals it was because everyone had contributed their share of effort and the group was able to take pride in this achievement or even some time off for collective recreation. If members were not successful in fund-raising the response of the group typically was to close ranks and support each other all the more. The expressive importance of what might appear to be instrumental activities is exemplified in the following accounts of UM projects.

One of the Unification Church groups we observed spent several days preparing and conducting a cleanup campaign in the city of Houston, Texas to show the UM's civic-mindedness. Large posters were painted announcing the project, and despite the fact that the project had no visible impact on the cleanliness of city streets members proudly displayed and photographed the small mountain of plastic trash bags that they had filled.

On another occasion, when pornography was the source of considerable controversy in Houston, the same UM group laboriously prepared paper clothing which they spent one night clandestinely pasting over sexually suggestive posters and billboards throughout the city.

However, the incident which best illustrated the expressive nature of such group projects occurred when the Houston Unification Church center received instructions from church headquarters in New York to gather signatures on a petition supporting the human rights provision contained in the Helsinki Agreement and endorsed by President Jimmy Carter. The members of the center, along with members of a visiting IOWC team, gathered together on a Mother's Day Sunday morning and divided into teams. Each team was instructed to attend a local church service and then to solicit signatures for the petition. The leader of the center referred repeatedly to the petition as the *Helenski* Agreement. Because most members appeared to be unfamiliar with the agreement, he read it aloud. Someone eventually asked where "Helenski" was. After considerable conjecture and discussion of its location by members, one of the authors contributed the fact that the mispronounced city was in Finland. After futile attempts by members to interpret the broader meaning and significance of the Helsinki Agreement, they concluded that the petition was one in support of human rights. Thereupon they enthusiastically left to solicit signatures. Because the members themselves had little understanding of the petition, they were not very successful in explaining it to those whose signatures they requested. As a result, they obtained only a few dozen signatures. Despite the fact that the group did not achieve its instrumental goals, this occasion was exploited for its expressive value. When the group reassembled for dinner, the leader conducted a debriefing session in which members were encouraged to recount individual and team experiences. Considerable positive reinforcement was offered for accounts which stressed the members' efforts to express love for others even in the face of adversity, the importance of carrying forth the group's message despite apparent failure, and the success achieved in spiritual growth even if the signature-gathering efforts had fallen flat. The members whom we had accompanied had earlier seemed dispirited by their lack of success in soliciting signatures, but the collective reaffirmation of group values revitalized their spirits.

In these three cases UM groups made short-lived efforts to become involved instrumentally in solving social problems. Their efforts, not surprisingly, had little lasting impact and the groups made no efforts to follow up their initial activities. However, members took considerable pride in their "acomplishments" which they perceived as evidence of their social involvement and efforts to promote change. Thus, whatever the external consequences of these and other projects, they obviously played an important expressive role.

MORAL

The development of moral commitment is crucial to preserving the stability of communal groups, for as individuals' identities change to fit closely the values and norms of the group conformity is exerted internally rather than externally. Violation of group norms becomes less likely because individuals are conforming to their own expectations and sense of morality as well as the group's. Immediately upon joining the UM members' identities began to be reshaped. Some of the mechanisms were purely symbolic. For instance, the date on which a member first encountered an UM missionary became his or her "spiritual birthday" and that missionary became the latter's spiritual parent. Rev. Moon and his wife were then designated as one's True Spiritual Parents, in a sense demoting the status of the biological parents.

Physical appearances as well as personal habits were also targets of transformation:

> Things which I did to reinforce my commitment to change included a complete transformation in my wardrobe . . . , my hairdo, and to some extent my language (not so much slang or worse words). I did these things very deliberately because I *knew* they would hasten an internal rebirth.
>
> I used to wear very casual clothes. When I joined the church, I began to dress much more neatly in order to conform to the standard of members. I also shaved my beard. . . . I used to lead a very sexually oriented life, both in thought and practice, but when I joined the church I found . . . that I was no longer interested in sex, and comparatively free from sexual thoughts.

These early external changes were followed by internal changes in self-concept which continued indefinitely. This was indicated by the changing criteria by which individuals came to judge themselves. The primary criteria, consistent with the requisites of communal life, were selflessness and an ability to love others unconditionally. For example, John stated:

> I am a person who has found hope for achieving perfection in my life. Before I joined the church this was measured by external criteria (successful business and living environments). Now I define

perfection in terms of my relation with God and people and creating a happy family.

I studied the Divine Principle again and again, and finally the message changed my life. I now know how to love others fully. I am no longer worried about my physical appearance, because now I spend most of my time loving others, not myself but others. I am happy because I am a new person.

When we asked UM members to contrast their current perceptions of themselves with those prior to joining the movement we received the following type of responses. With respect to their former lives members recollected: "My life was far too self-centered. It kept me from growing and understanding God." . . . "I was living a selfish life. I hadn't thought about giving to others. I spent much of my time painting." . . . "I lacked true genuine love." . . . "I lacked love. I didn't interact with others as siblings should in a family." In sharp contrast were their statements about their new identities: "I am a child of God desiring to change the world for all people." . . . "I am a child of God, a member of the Unification Church and a person interested in making a better world." . . . "I am a person who is trying very hard to help God and the world and to fulfill the inevitable." Statements about members' goals also closely reflected these new priorities: "All I want to do is develop a relationship with God." . . . "The goal is to reach a pure heart—that equals perfection." . . . "The goal is to relate to one another as brother and sister with God as the parent." If these statements appear to be merely "parrotting the party line," that is precisely the point. Members routinely discussed their motivations in such terms not only to us and with each other but also in their personal prayers and other sacrificial activities.

Because such internal changes were very important to the group, there were ongoing attempts to encourage and monitor them. However, because they occurred on an internal level, they had to be either monitored by individual members themselves or by the group through public confessions. Very little in the way of group confessional activity occurred within the UM. Members on occasions gave testimonies which included a description of their former fallen lives and celebrated their new found freedom. In many of these descriptions members provided the not unexpected exaggerations of former sins and indiscretions along with the sudden discontinuity of conversion. These testimonies not only served to distinguish members' former from present careers but in their own minds also functioned to impress novitiates with the power of membership. For example:

I was finding value in the wrong things. I used to get high on marijuana, acid and cocaine every week. . . . Now I am going in a definite direction instead of constantly changing.

I was drifting. I had no sense of purpose. The major difference in my life since joining the Church is that I have a clearer idea of what I want to accomplish for myself and others.

Apparently, the only instance where all members engaged in confessional activity was shortly before the blessing when a personal "autobiography of sex" was required to be submitted to the True Parents. More commonly many members kept personal diaries in which they recorded their own spiritual progress. Naturally prayers also included confessions in the course of asking for divine strength to improve.

Once individuals had abandoned old identities which were inseparable from faults of "egotism," "selfishness," and "pride," they developed new self-concepts which drew strength from their transcendental relationships to the group and its ideology. Concurrently, they also sensed new levels of insight into the world and its problems, or as Amy said, "much deeper feelings of purpose and direction." Similarly, Virginia commented, "The church has brought me to the point where I can see things as a whole, how they need to be."

Members genuinely felt that their accomplishments were not their own, that in times of triumph they were possessed of a God-centered, spiritual energy that worked through them. (Indeed, one of the sternest rebukes which one member could give another was to accuse the latter of "being off-center.") Thus, as one member commented about success in fund-raising:

Fund-raising is probably the most amazing way to know God. It is not salesmanship or personality that brings in contributions—it is God. Hence, fund-raising is successful when God is there and not when He is gone."

An even more graphic statement of the quasi-mystical experience into which the practice of solicitation was sometimes translated can be seen in the vivid, almost sensual imagery of one member:

I felt the spirit world zinging around me. I felt that every cell in my body was alive.

But she too admitted the importance of her connection to this larger power:

Whenever I felt it was my own skill or when I became arrogant, the contributions would stop for a few hours. Then I would pray and get recentered and gain inspiration. Then I would go back out on the street.

Deepening Involvement and Commitment

Based on discussions with UM leaders and observers, for most individuals who joined the UM membership lasted only two or three years. Thus, most members did not remain in the movement long enough to advance to a point where lifetime commitments were formed. Further, since the movement's rapid growth began in the early-to-mid 1970s, sufficient time had not elapsed for those who appeared to be permanent members to have developed stable, long-term lifestyles within the movement. However, a few observations can be made about the emerging pattern of deepening group commitments.

The period following assumption of full-time membership was the time of the most continuous and intense personal sacrifice. Fasting and other ascetic practices designed to further spiritual growth presumably did not need to be as severe as higher levels of spirituality were achieved. Still, members did continue periodically in acts of self-denial to sustain and build their spiritual strength. Unification Church President Neil Salonen's personal pioneer mission to Seattle and *The News World's* editor Michael Young Warder's periodic hawking of newspapers on the streets of New York certainly were acts designed to maintain their humility and "sacrificial heart." The only movement-wide sacrificial act for all UM members of which we were aware was the forty-day period of celibacy required for all previously unmarried members following marriage. As one member put it:

Through this separation we can really build the foundation of family spiritually on which to value our marriage. I am sure at the end of this difficult period of separation, there will be a more solid foundation [Kim, 1976: 22].

Merely by staying in the movement, members' commitment continued to deepen. By the mid-1970s the UM was beginning to develop occupational opportunities within the movement (e.g., a fishing industry, a newspaper). Those who did not become involved in movement affiliated economic enterprises usually worked on church-related projects. One's career became so entwined with the UM that the chances of transferring out of a movement-related job into a similar "outside" position continually declined. Not only were some of the skills nontransferable but also the nature of the organization mitigated against mobility. The movement provided none of the formal, standard *individual* job benefits that could be transferred, such as life and health insurance, retirement pensions and social security contributions. Furthermore, individuals did not accumulate personal assets such as houses, automobiles, and savings accounts. Thus, with advancing age individuals had committed a larger and larger proportion of their potential lifetime assets to the movement. Of course the movement's stigmatized status also worked against easy transition to more conventional organizations.

The pattern for affective relationships was somewhat more complex. While some old friends might be lost, frequently there was an opportunity for reconciliation with parents and other relatives. A number of members reported to us that their parents had initially been distraught over their joining the UM; however, as their lifestyles stabilized parents gradually, if reluctantly, became more accepting of their status. Nevertheless, the individuals' affective ties to the movement continuously deepened and broadened. Perhaps the single most significant event was marriage. By marrying within the church the individual's family life also was tied to the movement. The marriage partner was also without exception a UM member and children would of course be raised in the church. If a member were to leave the church he or she would be giving up not only a religion but also a family because apostasy was primary grounds for divorce. Similarly, marital problems constituted a threat to one's religious status. Thus, an individual became enmeshed in a tightly woven, interlocking set of relationships that strongly reinforced each other.

By the time an individual had been in the movement a number of years, his former identity had been relegated to the past and the new identity was well established. However, the individual continued to experience higher levels of meaning through group membership and feelings of connectedness with spiritual forces and events. For example, individuals who were blessed experienced their marriage as a relationship that transcended mere physical or emotional union:

> Our marriage is for God. First thing is, then, I have to learn to respect my wife and she had to learn to respect me. I have to see her not only as my wife but as a daughter of God. She has some mission for God. She has to see me in terms of that, not just that she is good for me and I am good for her [Kim, 1976: 22].

Thus, members could even consider remaining married to partners with whom they experienced significant personal conflicts or could entertain the idea of sacrificing their own sense of identity for the sake of what was regarded as a spiritual union.

Conclusions

SUMMARY

In this chapter we focused on the UM "from the bottom up," i.e., on the basic communal units within which UM members operated on a day-to-day basis, emphasizing how their commitment was generated and maintained. As we stressed, those radical communal groups so functional to a world-transforming movement such as the UM, in meeting their own requisites qua communal organizations, possessed a calculus of building commitment independent of the goals of the movement and its ideology. While UM ideology initially justified the formation of radical communal groups, it was the latters' organizational requisites, rather than the ideology, that determined individual behaviors and group structures. Thus, we examined those mechanisms through which the UM generated membership commitment along instrumental, affective, and moral dimensions. It recruited those young persons for whom the cost of initial inquiry and experimentation with the UM's communal lifestyle was lowest and who were also the most idealistic. Because the imminence of the anticipated restoration left little time for intellectual/belief conversion, the UM developed techniques to socialize individuals quickly into those roles necessary for the maintenance of communal groups. It encouraged persons to sever their links to former lifestyles, relationships, and material holdings in order to foster the growth of new self-identities firmly grounded in the UM's fortunes, needs, and aspirations. As members remained in the movement, their permanent commitment generally became stabilized over several years, fostered by the gradual, almost inextricable linkages of such members to the movement through occupational careers as well as the formation of families along UM approved lines. Thus, over time, after so many alternative career opportunities and possible life trajectories had been foregone and after so much of members' lives and resources had been invested in the movement, separation from the UM became less and less conceivable.

IMPLICATIONS

As we pointed out in Chapter 1, the ideology of a world-transforming movement legitimates a variety of organizational relationships: sacrifice of conventional lifestyles, insulation of members from the corrupting influence of the contemporary social order, egalitarian relationships among members, and a leader-disciple authority relationship. *The form of organization most consistent with these characteristics of a world-transforming ideology, of course, is the communal group.* In communal groups usually there are clear physical and social boundaries with the outside world and a tendency toward self-sufficiency; roles are diffuse; there is a striving for relationships of pure benevolence; the emphasis on moral involvement, mutual support, interdependence, and harmony leads naturally to egalitarian relations; and the movement itself or a single charismatic leader constitutes the source of authority. Both ideology and communal organization imply intense commitment: the world-transforming ideology if the massive social change it envisions is to take place, the communal group if its viability as an ongoing organization is to be sustained. It is not surprising, therefore, that world-transforming movements typically have communal groups as their basic organizational unit.

Ideology constitutes legitimation for the kind of relationships members wish to sustain. The ideology therefore stands as the formal, ultimate symbolic system in terms of which members' activities and relationships can be understood and explained. *However, because the demands of the ideology and lifestyle are highly congruent, on a day-to-day basis the organizational requisites of communal life can produce the type of behavior called for by the ideology without any necessary invocation of the latter.* For example, once an isolated, autonomous community (by virtue either of physical isolation or continuous physical movement) has been established, the necessity of daily sustenance and survival in themselves provide members with evidence of the salience of contributing to the group somewhat independently of ideological strictures related to segregating oneself from corrupt society. Further, the fact that members are in reality mutually interdependent upon one another for food, shelter, companionship, recreation, and so forth fosters egalitarian relationships even without legitimation from a set of universal principles, all-powerful deity or other sources of supreme authority. *Whatever the source of relational patterns within the basic communal units of world-transforming movements, it is clear that intense commitment is imperative if the movement is to sustain itself. As a result, building and maintaining commitment is perhaps the most fundamental concern of world-transforming movements.*

One of the major problems which world-transforming movements face in attempting to build commitment is that typically they are able to exercise only limited selectivity in their recruitment efforts (e.g., recall particularly Lofland's description of the UM's almost complete lack of selectivity in the early 1960s); hence their reliance on intensive socialization of new members in the context of communal organizations. Such movements encounter difficulty in recruiting new members because it is unclear precisely what type of individuals can most readily be attracted to the movement and because, even if the movement had a clearly defined concept of the "ideal convert," the movement often lacks the social visibility and legitimacy to attract such individuals (see Chapter 8, for example). As a result, world-transforming movements frequently seek to reach that general segment of the population for which it perceives it has the greatest appeal and which at the same time is not committed to alternative lines of action (e.g., in Korea the UM concentrated early recruitment among refugees dislocated by the war. In the United States the UM's OWC teams centered activity on college campuses, counter-culture centers, bus stations and airports where socially unencumbered youth could be found).

Because world-transforming movements lack selectivity in recruiting, individuals who do choose to affiliate with the movement may have a variety of different motivations for doing so (e.g., individuals were attracted to the UM on the basis of the ideology, communal lifestyle, a personal relationship with a member, or the "loving atmosphere" of the group). The immediate problem that the movement faces, then, is to elicit behavioral conformity necessary to the communal group and hopefully to produce commitment such that each member sustains and builds internal solidarity. *The most effective means of integrating members into a communal group is to provide a clearly defined role into which the individual can move and begin acting immediately. Communal groups offer an ideal environment for building intense commitment because the individual can be provided with a diffuse, encompassing role that offers an immediate sense of efficacy, involvement, social and emotional support, and clear sense of purpose.* Then, whether or not the individuals have the ideologically appropriate motivations, they can conform to the requisites of the communal group. The appropriate role-playing behavior may precede commitment in the psychological sense and the development of deeper commitment may occur more gradually *if* the individual remains in the movement. As described in the foregoing chapter, the communal group creates commitment through constructing role requirements which have the effect of disassembling the individuals' former social involvements, affective attachments and basis of identity external to the movement and providing an encompassing set of social relationships and affective support and a new source of identity within the movement.

There are a number of forces at work which threaten commitment maintenance. First, and most important, behavioral conformity creates the appearance of commitment, and while conformity is rather easily produced by the structured roles into which new members are placed commitment is not thereby ensured. Because conformity in itself does not offer a stable basis for continued participation, there is constant concern and pressure in communal groups to demonstrate moral commitment (e.g., keeping diaries, offering confessions and testimonials in which members emphasize their continual struggle for selflessness, harmony, and the like). However, the stronger such pressures are the greater the cost to individuals of remaining in the group. Second, defections may be frequent (the dropout rate in the UM's seminary graduating classes was estimated at 15% per year) particularly to the extent that role-playing behavior precedes commitment. However, defection also occurs at later stages of membership as the personal costs of a true quest for selflessness and purity (as ideologically defined) take an increasing toll on the individual. Defection is, of course, demoralizing and forces the movement to engage in constant recruitment without experiencing real growth. Third, there is the threat of disillusionment with the movement's progress in attaining its goals. While the movement can counteract this to a certain extent by promoting a crisis atmosphere, redefining goals, and so forth, the tremendous energy and involvement required of individuals becomes difficult to sustain if there is little visible progress. Fourth, if the movement does prosper there is a tendency for bureaucratic organization to emerge which conflicts in turn with communal solidarity (see Chapter 10). Finally, social repression, while it may reinforce ingroup-outgroup sentiments, is discouraging to members who have chosen to change the world through persuasion. A bitter, hostile response raises the question of whether the world is capable of receiving the truth. *While intense commitment is the principal source of a communal group's strength, then, it also is a source of vulnerability. Commitment is a resource which must constantly be replenished if the group is to survive, and therefore, it often assumes priority over the movement's goal-oriented activities. Thus, preservation of communal solidarity rather than transformative goals becomes the primary determinant of movement activity.*

NOTES

1. A similar lack of theological knowledge and sophistication among the UM members on the West Coast who had belonged for a number of months was discovered by Ross (Personal Communication, 1978).

2. For a more social psychological analysis of the recruitment/socialization pro-

cess from the perspective of the individual joining the UM, see Bromley and Shupe (1979).

3. Unless otherwise indicated, all quotations in this chapter were taken from our own interviews conducted with UM members during 1977-1978.

4. Another anonymous colleague who underwent the Oakland Family's weekend workshop commented that his host's attentiveness took such extremes that when the former happened to look away from his plate during a meal the host reached over and peeled his banana (Personal Communications, 1978).

PART III

THE MOVEMENT IN TURMOIL AND CONFLICT

PREFACE

Chapters 8 and 9 examine the dialectic of controversy and conflict over the Unificationist movement in the mid-1970s: first, those normative violations and deviant actions of the UM which aroused public ire; second, the emergence of a countermovement, organizationally spearheaded by disgruntled families of UM members but generally reaching into all major institutions of American society to enlist support to obstruct and slow the UM's expansion; and third, the UM's attempts to counterattack their nemesis through a variety of public relations campaigns and outright legal confrontations. Chapter 8 examines the types of conflicts the UM experienced in its relationships with the larger society. Those internal strategies that proved most effective in mobilizing resources for the UM were also ones that provoked public outrage and demands for the movement's repression. Though the anticult countermovement began around the same time that Moon arrived in the United States, its growth and visibility did not begin gaining momentum until the mid-1970s when the UM had already reached its zenith and was encountering increasingly negative publicity. This countermovement's strategies and tactics against the UM, and particularly deprogramming, generated controversy as well. Chapter 9 analyzes the ways in which the UM publically resisted anticult movement opposition and harassment through assertion of its legal rights, seeking favorable media treatment, and instituting organizational changes.

The data in Part III were obtained from UM files and documents, newspaper articles, and our interviews with executives in various bureaus of the UM's national headquarters. Information also came from informants, publications, and observations of the anticult movement, spanning the same two-year period as our research on the UM.

Chapter 8

RELIGIOUS INNOVATION AND REPRESSION

The conflict which the UM increasingly experienced during the 1970s centered primarily around four issues: the nature and content of the UM's theological and ideological expectations, UM organizational style, the UM's recruitment and socialization methods, and its fund-raising tactics. It was a conflict derived from the fact that those mobilization techniques most closely related to successful achievement of the movement's *internal* goals were the same ones that eventually provoked intense hostility from larger American society. Much of the impetus for social repression of the UM came from the anticult movement (ACM) that was principally staffed and funded by the families of youthful UM recruits. The ACM was to a relatively great extent successful in directly obstructing the UM's operations and expansions by fostering negative stereotypes of the UM's purposes and way of life and to a lesser degree through controversial deprogrammings. As we shall show, more than any other single factor it was the vociferous persistence of the ACM that triggered social control reactions by governmental and other institutions.

Innovation and Conflict

THEOLOGICAL INNOVATION AS HERESY

Despite the absence of a formal criterion for heresy, American religious culture does contain a number of sacrosanct symbols and·myths as well as sacred statuses to which ordinary persons may not aspire lest they draw moral indignation and be accused of pretentiousness and blasphemy. As Moon presented the solution to the problem of theodicy, or evil coexisting in the world with an all-powerful righteous God, all previous religions worldwide were incomplete in their particular revelations of truth, and Jesus had failed to accomplish his divinely commissioned task. This essentially reduced all other established religious bodies to a status inferior to Moon's Unification Church, transformed Jesus from a unique personage to merely an unsuccessful aspirant to a cosmic role, and designated the course to restoration as outlined in *The Divine Principle* to be the only viable way to reestablishment of mankind's true relationship to God.

While this theology was extremely effective in fostering among UM members a powerful sense of uniqueness and a certainty of belief in a final answer to eternal human struggles, it also generated intense outrage by the gate-keepers of traditional religion and morality. For example, from the standpoint of orthodox Christians, Moon's doctrine negated the Trinity, Jesus' divinity, and the integrity of all Biblical history. Moon sounded this theme in a number of widely quoted speeches:

> In 1960 I performed the holy wedding—the wedding of the Lamb that the Bible predicted. There the first heavenly family was established upon the earth. That was the equivalent in significance to the very moment of the crucifixion of Jesus. . . . I consummated the heavenly plan. This was the most historical day in the history of God [Kim, 1976: 28].

This constituted heresy, all the more so infuriating to traditionalists when the UM continually attempted to pass as simply a bonafide Christian group in its many public enterprises. Too, it threatened the balance of American Christian pluralism with its rhetoric of establishing *the* catholic church. While such rhetorical ecumenical appeals were acceptable within a pluralistic context, they never were cast in such specific terms of organizational and doctrinal hegemony. Another factor contributing to the sense of outrage was the UM's evasive or thinly veiled allusions to Moon as the Lord of the Second Advent, the new Christ come to complete Jesus of Nazareth's unfinished work. These allusions provoked an even more severe reaction because the UM would never clearly confirm or deny publically Moon's messianic role (one that from the UM's standpoint was achieved rather than ascribed, hence to be established). Thus, UM opponents were never presented with a clear target to attack (for examples of such evasions, see Chapter 1).

ORGANIZATIONAL STYLE

The creation of a theocratic order meant the elimination of what were, from the UM's perspective, arbitrary institutional boundaries, particularly between religion and science, education and religion, church and state, and economics and religion. The UM defined "the religious" in such a broad way that it overlapped into what most outsiders viewed as "the nonreligious." Thus, UM members felt limited constraint to operate within the normative regulations of existing institutions, creating a plethora of quasi-religious and nominally secular organizations that were designed to achieve the UM's multifaceted goals (and which came to be referred to by UM critics as fronts). At the same time each of these institutional domains was closely and zealously guarded by spokesmen and gate-keepers. Many of these arrangements and boundaries (e.g., church and state) had been laboriously negotiated over decades or even centuries in this country and often represented tacit, fragile understandings between institutions. Predictably, the institutions involved responded with alarm and condemnation as they saw the delicate equilibrium upset.[1]

One example of this redefinition of institutional boundaries was Moon's outspoken defense of then President Richard Nixon on the basis that the latter presumably possessed a divine mandate to hold office. This was seen as a blatant instance of religious intrusion into a political controversy heavy with partisan overtones. There were also indications that, archangelic roles for Nixon and America aside, Moon recognized the practical advantage of such a defense, both in terms of his reputation in Korea and in this country, to his movement should Nixon survive impeachment (U.S. Government, 1978: 342) A second example concerns UM members' involvement, at least for a limited period of time, in what for all intents and purposes was political lobbying activity with congressmen.[2] As the Fraser Committee (U.S. Government, 1978: 338-339) noted, the UM saw its activities in a different light: "A Capitol Hill public relations team, organized to develop contacts with Senators and Congressmen, was . . . characterized as part of an effort to remind legislators of spiritual values." Finally, some of Moon's numerous hyperbolic speeches to UM members, some of which were "leaked" to the press, suggested political ambitions and (to put it mildly) autocratic pretensions. Such statements as those in Moon's notorious 1974 Parents' Day Speech at Jackson, Mississippi (MS-416, 1974a) in which Moon proclaimed, "Some day . . . when I walk into the Congressmen's, or the Senator's offices without notice or appointment, the aides will jump out of their seats, and go get the Senator . . . saying he must see Reverend Moon," and "Let's say there are 500 sons and daughters like you in each state. Then we could control the government.

You could determine who became Senators and who the Congressmen would be," were circulated widely as evidence of his political aspirations.

One of the most exasperating features of the UM's organizational style was its continuous formation of affiliated groups which carried many separate functions. These allowed the UM to broach religious institutional boundaries with impunity because they merely had to contend that these groups were "not the Church." While staffing and funding patterns clearly belied these arguments in many cases, it proved difficult to present hard evidence of violations of the UM's religious status. Thus, for example, when Congressman Donald Fraser's House Subcommittee on International Relations attempted to subpoena Moon as a witness for its investigations, UM spokesmen declined to have him appear on the grounds that Moon technically was not an officer, employee, agent, or member of the Unification Church of America, a legalistic but otherwise absurd separation of the movement from its most integral personage.

RECRUITMENT/SOCIALIZATION

Two aspects of the UM's recruitment/socialization procedures aroused public ire and controversy. First, the timetable laid out in Moon's theology did not permit the UM the luxury of slow, incremental growth through ordinary generational reproduction. At least a core of dedicated members had to be recruited almost immediately "to establish the base" for world restoration. This meant that the UM was dependent upon the larger society it was condemning for its growth. Second, the central element of Moon's *Divine Principle* was the creation of spiritually perfect, God-centered individuals and families which would be the building blocks of the new order. In order to achieve this spiritual purity UM members had to segregate themselves from the fallen world except for highly structured, ritualized contacts.

As a general strategy to recruit members rapidly and simultaneously generate intense commitment, the UM emphasized the affective rather than the cognitive aspects of recruitment/socialization. Teaching a complex theological system was impractical due to the movement's self-imposed time constraints, such a lengthy process limited effectiveness in creating and sustaining the crisis perspective embodied in the UM's ideology, and the limited appeal of a millenarian religious message to many potential recruits. As we discussed in Chapter 7, what proved effective was initially to downplay theological orthodoxy and segregate and encapsulate potential recruits in (1) an atmosphere of intense, positive reinforcement (e.g., love-bombing them), and (2) in a continuous round of activity that provided limited opportunity for intellectual reflection and that enmeshed the individual in appropriate role performances even before conscious commitment to the values underpinning the role or redefinition of self occurred. Thus, new members were immediately treated as brothers and sisters, involved in the witnessing and/or fund-raising activities of the group, urged to take up residence in the communal setting, and discouraged from maintaining close links with former associates, possessions, and lifestyles. In a very real sense, then, each member of the movement became dependent on and obligated to every other member on a continuing day-to-day basis, leading to a great sense of responsibility which had (at least in the eyes of anticultists and much of the naive public) an enormously powerful and somewhat mysterious ability to promote identification with and conformity to group expectations.

It was the combination of (1) initial deception (or "packaging"), (2) an emotionally charged socialization process which mitigated against an intellectual, critical perspective while drawing the individual into a network of encompassing role obligations, and (3) the subsequent severing of conventional ties which provoked outrage, particularly on the part of upper- and middle-class parents. To parents and other outside observers the rapid conversions and (apparently) deep commitments of new members were both difficult to understand and disturbing. They found it almost beyond comprehension how such profound behavioral and attitudinal changes in people they had known so intimately could occur in such short periods of time. Not only were the conversions rapid, but families found it extremely difficult to maintain communications with young converts because the latters' views had become highly ideological, with new emotionally based points of orientation and vocabularies of discourse, and members were constantly on the move with their whereabouts frequently unknown even to the leaders of the decentralized UM. Unable to maintain ongoing communications with their children and to explain these phenomena in a common sense model of conversion, they turned to models implying coercion and manipulation (e.g., brainwashing, "spot hypnosis," or even the use of "mind control" drugs). Even those opponents of the UM who did not accept the brainwashing type of explanation decried the movement's hard-sell socialization tactics.

FUND-RAISING AS AN ECONOMIC BASE

The conflicts between the UM and larger American society over the former's fund-raising tactics derived directly from the UM's ideology and organizational goals. As discussed in Chapters 5 and 6, the imminent millenarian thrust of the UM required that young members with few if any skills, services, or products of value to the larger society somehow generate large-scale economic resource accumulation. These were necessary to achieve widespread visibility leading to a rapid impact on societal institutions and to assure financial independence sufficient to support the encapsulating environment that would maintain the spiritual purity of members. At the same time, as Chapter 7 documented, members had to obtain sufficient legitimacy to raise funds, recruit new members, and gain acceptance for its cosmic message.

These three requisites in turn necessitated that economic resources be generated quickly, with a minimum of nonproselytizing contact with fallen outsiders, and without having to train members in saleable skills or diverting them into production of goods or services. Furthermore, such resources needed to be gathered in such a way that economic activity became a reinforcing extension of religious values. Simply requesting donations satisfied all of these requirements. No real skills, services, or products needed to be developed (hence a low overhead). The contact with the donor was superficial, ritualized, and rationalized as of spiritual benefit to both parties in the exchange. Moreover, this technique proved capable of amassing staggering amounts of capital in a relatively short time.

The tactical solution to these organizational problems, as we have seen, was the creation and proliferation of MFTs which moved rapidly about the country "exploiting" local charitable markets. The funds that they gathered in this way were used almost exclusively for the further development of the movement. Thus, they contributed little or nothing to the welfare of the local community in which they were raised and as some unknown but presumably finite percentage of available charitable dollars were skimmed from the local economies. From the UM's point of view, fund-raising was an essential part of the process of world salvation; from the perspective of nonmembers who did not share this vision, it was nothing more than a self-serving "rip-off." Further, the UM's ideological justifications for the spiritual importance of its fund-raising practices and vague representations of itself as a Christian group led rather easily to members' half-hearted efforts to identify themselves in terms meaningful to potential donors or to outright misrepresentation (i.e., "heavenly deception"). To some extent such "half truths" were legitimated by Moon himself:

> Telling a lie becomes a sin if you tell it to take advantage of a
> person, but if you tell a lie to do a good thing for him that is not a
> sin. Even God tells a lie very often [Kim, 1976: 7].

To outsiders it seemed incongruous that persons holding such lofty spiritual ideals of truth and love could at the same time deliberately engage in shabby day-to-day deceptions; hence charges of hypocrisy or that the UM's ubiquitous smiling fund-raisers were "brainwashed" were forthcoming from critics. Finally, in the eyes of the mass of UM opponents, these tactics constituted manipulation, not only of donors but of the youthful members whose labors were exploited in the service of a movement with goals of mere financial aggrandizement. At a time when young adults were customarily building their own futures, ACM critics charged that their precious years of youth and opportunity were being squandered on activities of no personal or social intrinsic merit.

These conflicts over fund-raising tactics were all the more frustrating to UM opponents because social control was so difficult to exert. The UM's status as a religious organization sharply constrained the legal pressures that could be brought to bear. The extreme mobility of fund-raising teams meant that by the time community members could be made aware of the UM's presence the MFTs had already moved on. Further, despite massive efforts by anticultists to expose the UM and its practices, the public by and large remained ignorant and apathetic. Thus, the UM was often able to pass as a Christian group or as just another local charity without serious challenge from most of those whom it approached for donations. Finally, the fact that most Americans had a reservoir of discretionary funds available to them meant that many were willing to give persistent, earnest young fund-raisers small amounts of money rather than take the time to question the solicitors' purposes or affiliation. Therefore, individual UM members were able to raise large amounts of money despite being discredited through sheer dint of effort. For all these reasons, then, UM opponents were not terribly successful in cutting off the root sources of support for the movement which only served to intensify the level of ACM rhetoric and efforts to attack the UM on other fronts.

The Anticult Movement

As has been shown, the UM committed a number of cultural violations, and for many of these violations there existed institutionalized control mechanisms to censure or apply sanctions to the movement. However, for that institution upon which the movement had the most profound and immediate impact, i.e., the families from which UM members were recruited, there was no representative, organized form of redress. Faced, from their own perspective, with a great loss, family members had the greatest incentive to attempt in various ways to thwart the UM's expansion, extricate individuals from the movement, and make others aware of the perceived imminent danger. While other institutions through their bureaucracies took an interest in the "problem," it was only the patchwork of families that directed all of its efforts and resources to dealing with the latter. This was in large part a function of the fundamental motivation of these families from the outset to "recover" family members from the UM and other cults. Although this countermovement was never able to achieve a viable national organization or funding base because of its highly particularistic orientation, it was, for reasons to be discussed, able to play a major role in harassing the UM in the mid-to-late 1970s.

It was no accident that the deprogramming or anticult movement (ACM) emerged in the United States roughly about the time that Moon arrived in 1971 and initiated the first of his nationwide tours. As reviewed previously, the nation was undergoing a major religious revival. The ACM began not as any well-integrated network of formal organizations but rather as a spontaneous campaign or collective behavior carried out by small, local ad hoc groups or single families (and sympathizers) of young persons who had joined the Children of God (COG) and other radical elements of the late 1960s Jesus movement (and *not* in opposition to the Unification Church specifically).[3] At first, individual families of young adults involved in COG believed their fears for the latters' safety, their anxiety over rumors of substandard living conditions and authoritarian asceticism, and their confusion at their family members' rapid conversions to be unique. Gradually, however, contact with families reporting similar experiences and "horror stories" led individual families to identify themselves as an outraged public in the sense which Mills (1959) used the term, i.e., translating "private misfortune" into a public issue through the sharing of grievances.

It was not until a year later (in 1972) that a group of such like-minded parents, relatives, and friends gathered in San Diego and founded "The Parents' Committee to Free Our Sons and Daughters From the Children of God Organization," later shortened to FREECOG (Free Children of God).[4] Genuine feelings of desperation resulted from parents' inability to "bring their children out" and officials' apathy or failure to act against COG; from the unsavory stories of exploitation, sexual irregularities, and malnutrition told by apostates or those youth whose parents had forcibly removed them from COG; and from the anxiety generated when young converts suddenly dropped out of sight and ceased communicating with their families.

FREECOG was at first reluctant, for fear of "spreading itself too thin," to become involved with families who had begun contacting it, seeking information on sons and daughters in numerous other marginal religious groups. By then in the heyday of its recruitment/visibility-seeking activities, the UM was becoming noticed and prominent among these "other" groups. In the next two years, however, pressures to expand FREECOG's scope and the range of groups about which it was concerned culminated in what quickly became the major anticult organization in the western United States: the Citizens Freedom Foundation. Like other anticult groups that were emerging about the same time or that were to follow, CFF saw as its dual-purpose the charge to aggressively expose (i.e., publicize) the "deceptive fund-raising and recruitment activities" of those groups pejoratively labeled cults and to locate/recover "lost" family members in any way possible.

The following two years (1974-1976) witnessed a rapid increase in the number of similar anticult groups. Many surfaced independently and spontaneously across the country on an ad hoc basis, sometimes existing briefly and then dissolving, other times merging into larger groups and coalitions. This coalescing process, the products of which more closely resembled networks of communications than formal organizations, resulted in a number of anticult groups with such patently expressive names as The Spiritual Counterfeits Project (Berkeley, California), Citizens Engaged in Reuniting Families (Scarsdale, New York), Love Our Children (Omaha, Nebraska), Return to Personal Choice (San Diego, California), and Committee Engaged in Freeing Minds (Arlington, Texas).[5]

The latter group, CEFM, become the national coordinating body for all major anticult organizations in February 1976, following public hearings on the UM in Washington, D.C., chaired by Senator Robert Dole in response to a petition campaign (orchestrated by anticultists in and around the state of Kansas) producing 14,000 signatures (CEFM, I-II, 1976a). The hearings offered anticult spokesmen (over 400 attended at their own expense) an opportunity to voice their concerns over UM activities to congressmen, various federal agency officials, and the press. They produced a major reaffirmation of commitment to the ACM's goals and heightened its sense of solidarity. Faced with what they perceived to be an increasing measure, the ACM sought first of all to organize itself more "tightly" into a national coalition, of which CEFM was the first interim body. By March 1, 1977, the six largest national ACM organizations agreed to merge into a national coalition organization entitled The International Foundation for Individual Freedom which obtained the status of an Internal Revenue Service tax-exempt 501(6)(3) educational trust.

IFIF as a coalition did not solve all organizational problems. Many of the literally dozens of small and large ACM groups and chapters were reluctant to immediately dissolve their identities and local organizational structures into IFIF, and coordination of finances was a stubborn obstacle. Despite its promise IFIF did not solve all of the organizational problems. However, it did allow the ACM to attack the UM on a national level and to use its limited personnel and resources more effectively. By the summer of 1977, five months later, a compromise arrangement was enacted: the continental United States was divided into eight regions, each to have a volunteer director who assembled mailing lists, kept abreast of legal/media/cult activities in the given region, and served as liason between the regional and national (IFIF) levels.

Along with the ACM's succession of attempts at national reorganization was the focusing of its efforts on the most visible, powerful, and therefore the most symbolically significant cult in order to establish legal (and other) precedents for attacking cult groups in generál (Personal Interviews, 1976; CEFM, 1976a). This target group was, of course, the UM, specifically the Unification Church of America (though the anticultists treated all other aspects of the UM as merely fronts for the UC). This strategy was predicated on the assumption that if the ACM could effectively counteract the UM in some critical way, e.g., securing revocation of its tax-exempt status, prohibiting its fund-raising activities, or publically discrediting its intentions, similar battles could be successfully waged against other marginal religions. This strategy also emerged from the fact that ACM leaders were disproportionately family members of UM recruits.

THE ANTICULT MOVEMENT IDEOLOGY

The ACM originated in the basic motives of parents to recover their offspring from what they perceived to be pernicious pseudoreligions. Their specific early actions in pursuit of this goal therefore preceded any well-developed ideological rationalization of these actions. Just as the organizational structure of the ACM emerged over a period of several years from small, ad hoc groups into a more integrated network of organizations, likewise their ideology also was an emergent phenomenon, the product of inputs from a variety of sources. The formulation of a convincing, articulate rationale for their actions was vital for achieving visibility, legitimacy, and financial/membership growth. The existence of this ideological resource permitted the ACM members to portray marginal religions as a public threat and thereby cloak their private interests with the mantle of civic responsibility. For some time in the early-to-mid seventies the ACM was relatively successful in promulgating this ideology, and the latter was sufficiently alarming and pervasive across a range of institutions to markedly obstruct the UM's rapid mobilization.

The pivotal component of the ACM's countermovement ideology was a set of beliefs which we have referred to elsewhere as the "deprogramming rationale" (Shupe, Spielmann, and Stigall, 1977a, 1977b). This rationale posited all unconventional religious groups such as Transcendental Meditation, Hare Krishna, the Worldwide Church of God (as it operated under Herbert and Garner Ted Armstrong), Scientology, and, of course, the "targeted" Unification Church to be fraudulent and exploitive pseudoreligions existing solely for the personal, economic, and/or political aggrandizement of their leaders. It was a viewpoint fueled by parents who demonstrated an unmistakable desperation to "rescue" young adults who in their view had been beguiled and manipulated into abandoning conventional lifestyles and careers in exchange for servitude to would-be messiahs. The men and women who sincerely promulgated it saw themselves as patriotic, conscientious Americans reluctantly undertaking an unpleasant but necessary task that had defaulted to ordinary citizens such as themselves. Thus, one ACM leader stated:

> Sometime in our life we may find ourselves in a position that requires of us certain judgements and positive actions that we may be poorly equipped and unqualified to make and yet we are mandated by circumstances to function in that position [CFF, 1976a: 1].

This ACM ideology alternated between, in its mildest forms, assumptions often based on honest misunderstandings of religiocultural differences mixed with superficial knowledge of social psychology, and, at its worst, undisguised ethnocentrism and intolerance. In the latter vein it spoke stereotypically of cults, the "cult problem," and "cult techniques of recruitment." As Ted Patrick, archetypal deprogrammer, brusquely commented in his apologetic account of his creation of the "deprogramming process" (Patrick and Dulack, 1976: 11): "Not a brown penny's difference between any of 'em." The crude "know-nothingism" explicit in such core assumptions about the uniformity of cults' means to recruit and maintain religious commitment tended to blot out the distinctive theologies and lifestyles of separate religions and resulted in sweeping generalizations that frequently broke down logically under rigorous examination. Thus, specific allegations concerning the UM were extended to other religious groups as well.

Over time the ACM sought to develop a more sophisticated ideology by drawing upon available social science knowledge as frequently served up by sympathetic professionals with medical/psychological training or in related fields. Such interpretations, with all the legitimate trappings of scientific precision, had a powerful explanatory value for anxious families unable otherwise to account for their offsprings' bizarre behaviors and seemingly incomprehensible severing of links with mainstream American society. They also functioned to increase the ACM's public credibility.

Where there existed a range of consensus about the deprogramming rationale both within and between the various groups in the ACM, the following four points represent those aspects of the ideology most widely accepted and promoted within the movement about cults, particularly the UM:

(1) *The UM and other groups were regarded as pseudoreligions which only adopted a religious guise to enjoy their tax-exempt privileges; they were in reality profit-making ventures operated for the most part by ego-manic charlatans* (e.g., CFF, 1976b: 1). This was perhaps the most persistent theme running through the ACM's newsletters, other publications, and communications. For example, one prominent ACM leader directed the following invective toward cults in general and the UM in particular:

> Tens of thousands of our youth are being manipulated by leaders of cults for personal power and wealth. . . . Cult leaders have tremendous wealth available for their purposes. They take all of the personal resources of the member victim and then use those members to solicit millions from the public—all tax-free under the exemptions allowed religious organizations. The money is re-invested in business to earn more for the leader's personal luxury [CEFM, 1976b: 1].

(2) *The youth who become involved in the UM did not join through a true conversion process but rather were victims of overwhelming processes that destroyed free will by seduction, manipulation, and/or deception.* Fairly standard accounts were given by apostates and investigative journalists of the UM Oakland Family's deliberately orchestrated recruitment efforts which involved affectively powerful workshops. These, coupled with the Oakland Family's reluctance to identify its association with the UM, were grist for the mill when critics claimed that persons were dishonestly introduced to the UM and subtly coerced into joining. The ACM's recognition of the emotional, rather than cognitive, emphasis in much of the Oakland Family's recruitment techniques (such as love-bombing, the group hug, and other means of breaking down inhibitions) were generalized to all branches of the UM. Few if any young persons, maintained the ACM, had ever been genuinely converted. Rather, as West

(1975: 1) maintained: "Most of the cults whose members are subject to deprogramming were actually brainwashed rather than converted in the first place." An ACM activist who was also a psychiatric social worker, also contended that UM members were not exercising their free will, saying: "Their free will has been given up to the whims of their leaders by the isolation, lack of sleep, sexual acts, poor eating and the sophistication of the psychological manipulations of the leaders . . ." (Merritt, 1975:3).

Conversant with the psychological literature on brainwashing published shortly after the Korean war (e.g., Lifton, 1963, 1957; Hunter, 1962, 1953; Sargent, 1957, Meerloo, 1956), ACM spokesmen claimed that the UM and other groups employed methods of indoctrination which they termed mind control and mental manipulation similar to those used by communist thought reformers on Korean and Vietnam prisoners of war. Such factors as strategically induced fatigue, inadequate nutrition, arousal of guilt and denial of adequate time to rationally evaluate claims, and the mesmerizing repetition of chants, cheers, and songs resulted in "pseudo-conversion." The latter was described as "unthinking participation in group activities, a schedule designed to deprive followers of sleep, and a technique for short-circuiting reason through a conditioned reflex which is reinforced by group interaction" (West, 1975: 2). The Oriental origins of many of these new religions lent support to these assumptions.

(3) *Young members' UM-imposed or "programmed" behavior, aside from its heretical repugnance, was considered both physically and mentally deleterious to them as well as socially injurious to such American institutions as the family, Judaic-Christian (i.e., "legitimate") religion, and democracy.* In early 1978 the president of The Personal Freedom Foundation in Baltimore, Maryland noted in a personal communication to one of the authors that "young people are being duped, exploited, and physically and psychologically damaged. I deplore the interference with creativity, growth and God-given potential." This view was typical among ACM adherents, many of whom had suddenly found their adult children manifesting total disinterest in what formerly had been conventionally approved and (from the parents' points of view) promising, rewarding career/lifestyle trajectories. In fact, by the mid-1970s there had even developed a standard list of physical signs or "stigmata" in the ACM folklore that "Moonies" were alleged to manifest, such as a fixed, permanent smile ("with the mouth only"), glassy eyes and dialated pupils, hunched frames and gaunt faces, "Moonie odor" (presumably due to neglect of daily hygiene in slavish pursuit of the restoration), "Moonie rash" (alleged to result from a vitamin A deficiency in diet), general debilitation, hyperactivity, and so forth (see Shupe and Bromley, 1978).

These stigmata were offered as evidence that youth had experienced concrete, observable changes (for the worse) at the hands of the UM.

Social institutions were also alleged to be threatened by the existence of the UM. Moon's substitution of he and his wife as True Parents for members' "physical parents," as well as his characterization of the latter's objections to UM involvement as satanic, separated families. His opulent surroundings and personal wealth resulting from UM enterprises "abused" the delicately maintained tax privileges of all religions in America. Moreover, UM apostates' claims that he at one time ordered attractive female UM members to lobby in Washington, D.C. in congressmen's offices on behalf of South Korean military aid (CEFM, 1976a), as well as his authoritarian pronouncements on the need to overhaul American democracy, gave many an uneasy sense that the UM was politically subversive if not in deed then most certainly in intent.

(4) Finally, *the victims of programming were deemed incapable of simply "walking away" from UM encapsulation. Their free will having been removed, the only hope was to "deprogram" them, usually against their UM-imposed will.* As Wilson (1973: 226) observed, social movements often gain their public image and general reputation through specific tactical behaviors arousing public attention. This was never truer for any movement than for the ACM. Despite the fact that the bulk of the ACM's efforts and resources went to underwrite conventional, legal, and noncontroversial techniques of influencing public and official opinions (such as media advertising and lobbying), the ACM's deprogramming tactic of abducting and, under coercive siege-like confinement (in motels, basements, and the like), conducting lengthy sessions of argumentation, cajoling, and downright "brow-beating," won it an ineradicable identity as "the deprogramming movement."[6] Coercive deprogramming was justified for ACM members by the previous three points. Coercive deprogrammings, they argued, did not involve questions of freedom of religion or the First Amendment. UM membership involved only pseudoconversion. *Real* freedom of religion, said ACM spokesmen, involved the freedom to rationally and freely select one's faith. The presumed conditions of proselytization and indoctrination that operated in such contexts as the UM Oakland Family (generalized to the entire UM) disqualified pseudoconversion from constitutional protection. While some members did not condone coercive deprogrammings and none seemed to consider them in any way pleasant, many members sincerely perceived them to be the only remaining alternative, particularly as the complexities and slow pace of legal avenues became apparent.

Thus, the ACM ideology which characterized marginal religions as exploitive, manipulative, personally and socially deleterious, and encapsulating, once generally accepted provided the ACM with a powerful weapon with which to combat the UM. It was utilized strategically in two ways: first, direct action in the form of spectacular coercive deprogrammings; and second, as a vehicle for discrediting the UM in the eyes of the public which otherwise had no personal stake in the controversy.

DEPROGRAMMING AND CONFLICT

Given that the ACM's primary goal was the rescue of youth from pseudoreligions, and that an ideology emerged which attributed to the latter methods of manipulative mind-control, the most logical and direct tactic for dealing with "the problem" was to remove, by force if necessary, these youth. This tactic, of course, became known as deprogramming. While deprogrammings constituted only a tiny fraction of all ACM activities, because of the sensational family drama associated with them they came to identify the ACM in the public mind.

Ted Patrick was only the best known deprogrammer, in part through his own narcissistic account of his exploits (Patrick and Dulack, 1976). In a period of several years he had either "trained" or inspired a number of others, many of whom had themselves once been members of the UM and then deprogrammed. Operating across the continental United States and not loathe to exercise their new "profession" on a wide range of nonconventional religious adherents (including such groups as the Old Catholic Church or even on individuals who simply ceased to participate in their families' traditional faiths), it was not long until what began as a rough-and-tumble, ad hoc attempt to remove persons from what others perceived as threatening situations began to develop critical dimensions of harassment inhibiting the UM's mobilization efforts. The real threat of "Moonies" being abducted and subjected (from their perspective) to brutal, satanic torture put them on the defensive. This threat caused a pervading atmosphere of distrust, or (at the very least) of wariness, between youth and their families. It produced reluctance to always comply with the law, as in instances where UM members had to give their names to local authorities in order to receive solicitation permits, knowing well the often "cozy" relations between such persons and local ACM activists. Deprogramming also attacked the morale of UM members. It was understandably disheartening for members to hear of former coworkers and friends condemning them and the UM's goals, to read of their idealistic motives called into question and their venerated leader slandered. Moreover, to the extent that deprogrammings were successful these served as major symbolic defeats for the UM in that they buttressed the credibility of the deprogramming model and "proved" that this extremist tactic worked, restoring children to their parents.

Deprogramming as a tactic produced mixed success, as some deprogrammed UM members renounced their faith and joined the ACM while others endured one or more deprogrammings only to return to the movement at the first opportunity. The combination of successes and failures, claims and counterclaims, produced considerable confusion among those whom the ACM sought to influence. However, the coercive type of deprogrammings, while always a minority of such actions, caused an increasing amount of public and legal controversy. This backlash was sporadic at first while public awareness and indignation at deprogrammings were relatively low. Patrick was literally in and out of courts in 1972 and 1973, successfully defending his tactics against the occasional angry members of the UM and other groups who escaped deprogrammings and later brought suit. Gradually public awareness grew that instances of coercion frequently involved individuals who were legally adults, and civil libertarians came to the defense of the UM in the name of religious freedom. Various deprogrammers, as members of the legal profession themselves or with the cooperation of such persons, then attempted to add a certain measure of legitimacy to their activities by locating their activities within the provisions of existing "temporary conservatorship" laws. (These laws were originally designed for those emergency situations when senile or otherwise irresponsible adults might squander savings, make decisions, and so forth that would prove irreparably injurious. Ordinary conservatorship proceedings required legal counsel for the person accused of incompetency. However, a judge might, at his or her discretion, issue a temporary conservatorship for limited periods, i.e., thirty days, if convinced by relatives or friends of the accused that lengthy procedures would not prevent injury from occurring.)

By late 1976 the ACM's direct-action tactics had produced considerable opposition as the number of suits and complaints of members of various religions mounted. All of these complaints recounted essentially the same elements of coercion and brow-beating (or worse), and the hoary issue of constitutional guarantees of religious freedom were raised. In early 1977, the American Civil Liberties Union in cooperation with the Alliance for the Preservation of Religious Liberty, sponsored a conference on "Religious Deprogramming" and asserted:

> This hostile assault on freedom of association and religious liberty represents one of the most serious challenges to civil liberties today. Please be alert to kidnapping and deprogramming efforts in your area and to the use of legal processes to aid these activities. Be prepared to intervene in court or to provide testimony where appropriate [Prichard, 1977; see also ACLU, 1977].

A number of prestigious lawyers were enlisted by the ACLU to give advice in such cases; several were also employed by the UM to defend its members in deprogramming suits.

Other conferences were held to consider the practice of deprogramming and its civil liberties implications, and articles reviewing the same began to appear in increasing frequency, almost all taking a liberal and scathingly critical position. Referring to deprogramming as "spiritual gang-rape," the National Council of Churches' Dean Kelley (1977: 32) wrote that "It should be prosecuted, not just as any other kidnapping, undertaken for mercenary motives would be, but even more vigorously, since it strikes at the most precious and vulnerable portion of the victim's life, religious convictions and commitments."

The failure of possessing temporary conservatorship writs to lend legal support to deprogrammings, the willingness of groups like the UM and others to cooperate (through APRL and the ACLU) in protecting their common civil liberties, and the increasing frequency of the UM (predominant among other groups) to defend its interests in court significantly tarnished the ACM's public image and, by late 1978, had all but relegated deprogramming to the historical infamy of witch-pricking and similar repressive practices which enjoyed brief but sensational popularity. By late 1978 even the Freedom of Thought Foundation's notorious deprogramming ranch at Tucson, Arizona had closed down under the burden of law suits and criticism. This is not to say that deprogrammings had disappeared by 1978. Indeed, the authors were personally acquainted with more than one such abortive abduction/reconversion attempt during our fieldwork and writing. However, toward the end of the decade the ACM was unmistakably on the defensive and deprogrammings had noticeably declined in number.

GAINING VISIBILITY

Attaining visibility became for ACM groups the primary tactic for achieving their goals for two reasons: first, the direct-action approach was expensive, evoked enormous controversy, and produced mixed results; and second, gaining visibility for the ACM ideology (and correspondingly exposing the UM and its ideology) would contribute to the weakening of the UM (*and* indirectly help recover youth). Stimulating public awareness of marginal religions was intended to prevent the "unwary" from lending support to the UM or from being recruited, arouse public and official indignation to the point of evoking acts of repression, and mobilize both financial and manpower resources to serve the first two purposes. Creating visibility for the ACM's claims also served both symbolic and expressive functions for frustrated families who in many cases had little idea of where their children were or who had unsuccessfully deprogrammed their young persons and had the latter return to the UM. Thus, for example, the president of the Citizens Freedom Foundation disassociated himself from the deprogramming tactic per se and emphasized CFF's "educational/ informative" goals vis-à-vis the public (CFF, 1974).

From mid-1973 on, the ACM was effectively able to slant media coverage of the UM and similar religious groups. ACM newsletters and correspondence conveyed information to members on the most effective means of producing visibility-producing tactics. Some of the more articulate spokesmen produced church sermons, public lectures, or magazine articles that outlined the "cult menace" and the ACM's counterideology. Whenever possible, professionals (such as social workers, clergymen, and social/behavioral scientists) and civil leaders were requested to endorse the ACM's ideology and were included in public forums for their obvious legitimating contributions. (Often such forums, with panels of outraged but otherwise conventional parents and credible "experts," functioned as media events when they attracted the press.) ACM spokesmen eagerly solicited the attention of newspaper reporters and local television/radio talk-shows. When Ted Patrick, archdeprogrammer, appeared on the nationally syndicated Phil Donahue Show in 1973, ACM leaders could and did approach local talk-show hosts with offers to present similar discussions. The electronic media were often amenable to a topic that had so many sensational elements of tragedy, drama, and conspiracy. Soon both ABC and NBC produced documentaries that focused heavily on the recruitment and fund-raising practices of the UM, largely relying on the accounts of disgruntled ex-members directed their way by the ACM. In such ways as these the ACM was successful in promoting the dissemination of its own ideology, as illustrated by the case of NBC's 1975 clearly unsympathetic documentary on the UM when a CFF newsletter urged ACM members to "Write to express your appreciation for the service to the public NBC contributed" (CFF, 1975).

Whenever the media carried stories or programs which could be interpreted as favorable to groups such as the UM, protest was immediately marshalled. When Edmund Gravely, staff member of the New York *Times* and alleged member of the New Testament Missionary Fellowship (a cult, according to the ACM), wrote an article critical of deprogramming, a flyer went out to ACM members that included names and addresses of the *Times'* editor and assistant national editor, urging: "Please contact The New York Times and ask that OUR side of the story be told in their newspaper. Comment about the unfairness of a newspaper to allow a cultist to write his biased views" (IFFET,SW, 1978). Likewise, in 1978 when the popular "Lou Grant Show" television series (about an investigative newspaper editor) featured a sympathetic story about a youth who joined the Hare Krishna movement against the wishes of his parents, the call went out in ACM newsletters across the nation for members to write letters of protest to the CBS network, the program's producer, and one of the series' prime sponsors, the Prudential Insurance Company of America. An ongoing effort was also conducted to direct letters and petitions to the succession of judges and district attorneys prosecuting Ted Patrick for his numerous abortive deprogrammings. Finally, other campaigns were continually underway, such as one to encourage the Parent Teachers Association at local, regional, and national levels to adopt a "Pseudo-Religious Cults" resolution, another to pressure congressmen into voting a citation of contempt against an UM official who refused to testify fully to the Fraser Committee's congressional investigation into allegations of South Korean influence buying in Washington, D.C. (see below), and one for ACM members to counterprotest Moon's 1976 Yankee Stadium rally outside on the streets with posters, placards, and picketlines. At one point, in protest of Ted Patrick's 1976 imprisonment, several ACM leaders even considered the move of having every parent and ex-cult member across the nation simultaneously turn themselves into authorities for "unlawful imprisonment" as a symbolic gesture to show solidarity with Patrick (CEFM, 1976b).

In all of these campaigns apostates from the UM were dramatic witnesses for ACM allegations. It was these individuals who had experienced first-hand life in the UM and who credibly recounted atrocity stories about its manipulative, exploitive character. Such emotionally charged testimonies provided the basis for the ACM's creation of media events and gained them so much of what they desperately needed, operating as they did on volunteer help and shoe-string budgets: free media attention.

Other Institutional Reactions

RELIGIOUS

As we saw in Chapter 6, Moon's whirlwind Day of Hope tours in the early 1970s generated sporadic, isolated protests by fundamentalist Christian groups. However, these few demonstrations were fomented largely by persons and organizations themselves outside mainline American Christianity, and to those who observed the occasional disturbances which broke

out at Moon's public speeches it all probably appeared as curious, internecine squabbling between pre- and postmillenial sects.

Toward the middle of the decade, however, the character of this
religious opposition began to change, shifting from the preoccupation of
only marginal fundamentalist groups to a relatively significant priority of
many conventional groups. Aside from the spate of unabashedly evangelical Christian (and hence unavoidably critical) monographs of the UM that
appeared within a fairly brief period (e.g., Yamamoto, 1977, 1976; Hefley,
1977; Enroth, 1977; Bjornstad, 1976), specific actions of various mainstream Christian denominations began to coalesce into a pattern of organized, coordinated opposition. Chapter 6 recounted how, by 1974, clergymen and their professional/denominational associations across the nation
spread the word and organized resistance in advance of Moon's tours,
alerting citizens from the pulpit as well as the media about his "false"
messiahship. From that time on, there were few champions of the UM's
right to coexist among the members of the otherwise closed community of
American religious pluralism.

For example, during the summer, 1976, the National Council of
Churches' multidenominational Commission on Faith and Order criticized
Moon and the UM, and in July of that year the New York City Council of
Churches (composed of over 1,700 member-churches) rejected the UC's
membership application despite the latter's intense lobbying efforts. (Subsequent attempts by the UC to have the courts reverse this decision and
legitimate its bid for membership failed.) The American Jewish Committee
(through its National Director of Interreligious Affairs), the County Coordinator of the Office of Communication in the Catholic Archdiocese of
New York, and representatives of the National Council of Churches of
Christ at a joint meeting in January, 1977 condemned Moon's UM as
"anti-democratic, anti-Jewish, and in direct conflict with basic Christian
teachings" (Amsterdam News, New York, January 1, 1977). Rabbi James
Rudin, national official of the American Jewish Committee, claimed to
have counted more than 125 examples of blatant antisemitism in *The
Divine Principle* (e.g., The Catholic News, New York, January 6, 1977).
More than one denomination attempted to come to grips with the cult
threat. For example, the Lutheran Campus Ministry Programs printed a
collection of brochures entitled *The Cults: A Resource Packet* (LCMP,
1977) which included such topics as how to distinguish cults from legitimate religions, who typically joins the former, descriptions of each groups,
and how to combat them. The fundamentalist Spiritual Counterfeits
Project in Berkeley, California, staffed by ex-cult members, was another
source of anti-UM pamphlets and tracts. Finally, clergymen were pre-

dominantly represented in the ranks of anticult spokesmen: Rabbi Maurice
Davis (Citizens Engaged in Reuniting Families), George Swope (a Baptist
minister, also of CERF), Rabbi James Rudin, and Father Kent Burtner, to
name several of the more outspoken.

GOVERNMENTAL

At the state and federal levels there were two broad types of responses
to the UM which we shall call expressive and instrumental actions. The few
instrumental actions taken against the UM included the Immigration and
Naturalization Service in 1974 refusing to admit 583 Korean and Japanese
members whose primary activities were to be fund-raising (and secondarily
proselytizing) as part of the UM's "missionary program" (Uhlmann, 1976)
and apprehending/deporting forty German IOWC team members with
expired visas after a long cross-country search (Salt Lake City Tribune,
Utah, April 10, 1974). In 1976 the Internal Revenue Service also conducted extensive investigations of the Unification Church in conjuction
with its petition for tax-exempt status. Ultimately, such status was granted
to the church, sharply limiting further governmental control of surveil-
lance of the movement.

Expressive actions at both levels involved legislative hearings, resolutions, and investigative committee formations, the main consequences of
which was to provide public forum for the expressions of indignation and
outrage by ACM spokesmen and sympathizers. There were legislative
hearings and investigations related to the UM and other marginal religious
groups in states such as Texas, New York, and Vermont. Perhaps the best
publicized, however, was the investigation conducted by the House Subcommittee on International Organizations, chaired by Congressman
Donald Fraser (see U.S. Government, 1978). One of the committee's tasks
was to uncover the details of alleged Korean influence buying in Washington, D.C. Over a two and one-half year period, the committee took special
pains to investigate and highlight any possible links between UM leadership
and "Koreagate." When the final report was released to the public in late
fall, 1978, little substantive evidence beyond allegations that the UM
might have been guilty of tax and banking law improprieties as well as
circumventing arms control/import regulations came to light. Hard evidence was not forthcoming, and the perennial call for further investigation
by the federal bureaucracy diluted much of the crisis flavor so necessary to
sustain public or congressional interest. However, in the interim the UM
was constantly under attack through allegations of conspiracy, bribery,
and other crimes. In sum, the effect of these actions was to generate

widespread suspicion of the UM, publically discredit the movement, and allow a source of tension release for its irate opponents.

At the local level there were efforts to disrupt UM activities which were carried out through the use of zoning ordinances and building codes and through denying solicitation permits. The latter was clearly the most significant tactic from both the UM's and local communities' points of view. Under such regulations UM fund-raisers were treated as subject to ordinances which had been originally designed to control peddlers and solicitors. Often UM fund-raisers were refused solicitation permits outright; were arrested, fined, or jailed for violations of such laws; or were required to comply with time-consuming, restrictive authorization procedures. Because community tolerance and the rules governing solicitation varied enormously among municipalities, this tactic was for some time relatively effective. As community leaders were well aware, cutting off the movement's financial resource base ipso facto made the locale unattractive to UM members, and they would invariably move on. But not infrequently UM members would simply ignore or circumvent local regulations in the belief that their civil rights were being violated. Such surreptitious fund-raising, however, only served to exacerbate community hostility.

MEDIA

As Chapter 6 discussed, the American media initially formed a neutral-to-positive image of the UM as simply an evangelistic, nondenominational Christian group. This image did not last long. The UM's deliberately staged media events and a succession of sensational, emotionally charged themes related by ACM opponents (ranging from a depiction of tragically separated families to a portrayal of Moon as a sinister Pied Piper) turned the media sour on UM activities. From the early 1970s until the backlash against deprogrammings began in 1976, media coverage of the UM tended to present it as either a bizarre but laughable minority (recall the headlines on the UM's mass marriages in Chapter 6), or, when prompted by ACM spokesmen, as a malevolent foreign conspiracy. Major television network documentaries, which presumably sought objective evidence, also tended toward this stereotypical style of presentation. Pot-boiler magazine articles in such unlikely places as *Good Housekeeping* and *McCalls* were equally vitriolic, recounting the pious recantations and horror stories of UM apostates designed to outrage the typical middle-class reader.

Newspaper versions of these stories, with such lurid titles as "I was Moon's Programmed Robot" and "'I was Slave . . . Zombie,' Returned Son Relates," reiterated a standard set of "atrocities" to which UM members had allegedly been made victims (see Bromley, Shupe, and

Ventimiglia, 1979). Predominant among these was the individual's loss of freedom and accompanying exploitation by UM leaders. Specific atrocities attributed to the movement included *physical* (e.g., deprivations of nutrition, rest, safety, and freedom of movement), *psychological* (e.g., threats to ego security and attenuation of creativity and independent choice), *economic* (e.g., being encouraged to deceive outsiders for money and then contributing all personal wealth to the movement), *associative* (e.g., limiting relationships to celibate fellow members and breaking off all but fund-raising/proselytizing contacts with outsiders, including families), *political-legal* (e.g., improper political lobbying and threats of conspiracy), and *general cultural* (e.g., Moon's messianic claims and grandiose style).

The constraints on the press (e.g., limited time and resources for independent investigations, difficulties in verifying an informant's reliability, and reliance on national and international wire services for news), the importance of the "spectacular" in marketing news and the persistent agitation of ACM members, made it almost inevitable that local stories with sufficient sensational appeal and superficial validation would be published and then disseminated throughout the United States. For example, on numerous occasions "revelations" concerning the Oakland Family's Booneville recruitment farm (treated in the press as representative of the entire UM) were picked up by the national wire services and widely reprinted throughout the country in countless local newspapers.

SCIENTIFIC/ACADEMIC

It is a safe generalization that, with the exceptions of Lofland (1966) and a few East Asian area specialists, the American scientific/intellectual community remained unaware of the UM's existence until the early 1970s. By the end of the decade the reverse was true. Many academics learned of Moon from his attempts to court scientific interest and prestige through his staging of annual International Conferences on the Unity of Science. Founded by Moon and lavishly sponsored by the UM's International Cultural Foundation, this conference series was ostensibly aimed at restoring dialogue among specialized scientific disciplines in the hopes of constructing permanent unity of science and ethical values. These initially were well attended and coordinated by luminaries from all academic disciplines. But once Koreagate, the Fraser Committee's allegations, and the possibility of the Korean Central Intelligence Agency's entanglements with UM activities became public issues criticisms arose that Moon was coopting participants and literally buying legitimacy by underwriting the series (e.g., Horowitz, 1977; SGR, 1975). As a result, some scientists declined invitations and refused to participate in the conferences while others withdrew when the UM's sponsorship became known to them; still others defended the quality and aims of the conferences, regardless of the source of sponsorship. Amidst this minor furor that touched all academic disciplines, the ACM annually attempted to obtain the list of conference participants and engaged in letter-writing campaigns to dissuade them from attending.

After the mid-1970s, however, professionals in general had a much different association with the UM. Primarily social and behavioral scientists, journalists, and theologians, they took the UM itself as an object of study and thus helped to interpret it to the public. This activity manifested itself either through monographs (e.g., Lofland, 1977; Enroth, 1977; Sontag, 1977) and journal articles (e.g., Robbins et al., 1976) or in special sessions of professional organizations' regional and national conferences. For example, such groups as the Society for the Scientific Study of Religion, the American Sociological Association, and the American Psychiatric Association considered in formal papers and panel discussions a range of topics related to the UM, such as religious freedom, deprogramming, and UM recruitment/socialization techniques. These scientific products varied widely in their sophistication and perspectives. Some scientists used their professional credentials to directly discredit the UM as well as other religious groups by vindicating (frequently from clinical observations or mere speculation) the brainwashing argument. Their papers were circulated within the ACM and often they were invited as plenary speakers at ACM gatherings and forums (e.g., Galanter et al., 1978; Grossman, 1978; Marks, 1978; Kaplan, 1978; Clark, 1976). This is not to say that papers and findings emphasizing the opposite, i.e., that cult members were not victims of any insidious mental manipulations, were nonexistent but rather that these latter (e.g., Underleider and Wellisch, 1978a, 1978b) received less notice.

Conclusions

SUMMARY

In this chapter we described how those internal strategies most effective for the UM in mobilizing resources were also the ones that evoked the most outrage and social reaction. The very nature and content of its theological innovations were condemned as heresy; its paninstitutional style of organization and broad definition of religion that caused it to disregard "arbitrary" institutional boundaries generated suspicion as to its motives and intentions; its adoption of systematic, high-pressure recruitment/socialization methods, so vital in view of its timetable for restoration, branded it in the eyes of outsiders as manipulative; and its full-time fund-raising tactics, with their occasional elements of deception, became regarded as exploitive of both local charitable markets as well as of the young fund-raising members themselves. These features, when contrasted with the UM's public protestations that it was a religion and its willingness to enjoy the tax-exempt privileges of religion, caused consternation to both public officials and to the angry families of idealistic youth who had joined the movement. In particular, the latter had great difficulty in gaining leverage to redress grievances against the UM and similar groups, mainly because of the UM's legal status as a religion. As a consequence, in 1971 a "boot-strap" vigilanteeism began in the form of the ACM. Local groups of zealous families who were dedicated to rescuing sons and daughters from cults and in discrediting the latter began to proliferate over the next several years. In the course of their expansion and consolidation their leaders developed an ideology to justify their concern and occasional abduction of offspring from cults. This ideology, based on a behavioral science model of sensory deprivation and radical personality/attitude change, emphasized that cults such as the UM brainwashed or programmed youth and therefore that such youth must be forcibly removed from the cultic group and deprogrammed. In time the UM became the ACM's primary target, not in little part because of its long sought public visibility. Through persistent lobbying and publicity-seeking activities of its own, the ACM was able to muster support for its drive against the UM from a variety of other institutions, notably the mainstream religious, governmental, scientific/academic, and various media. These latter efforts, in turn, by the mid-1970s began to tell on the mobilization and image-making activities of the UM.

IMPLICATIONS

The internal mobilization strategies of world-transforming movements inevitably entail social deviance over which conflict with the larger society arises. This deviance is primarily ideological and organizational. The ideology by its vary nature defines the contemporary social order as corrupt and calls for radical restructuring of the society. Thus, sacred cultural symbols that legitimate and sustain the status quo are directly challenged and impugned. The social organization of a world-transforming movement engenders conflict because (1) it draws upon an apathetic or even hostile society for many of the resources it needs (e.g., money and members), (2) the movement's communal organization, in order to maintain high levels of commitment, removes individuals from former lifestyles and presents

them with a new set of roles that clash with conventional expectations as
they segregate movement members, and (3) members correspondingly may
feel limited obligation to conform to the norms and institutionally prescribed boundaries of what they perceive to be a corrupted, discredited
system. The more successful the movement is in implementing its mobilization strategies, hence the more perceived instances of deviance that are
generated, then accordingly the more intense the conflict with larger
society is likely to be.

When world-transforming movements do become involved in larger
societal conflict, they are likely to have few if any allies (i.e., they have
low legitimacy). This is true not only because there are no major groups
within society that have greater vested interests in the movement's vaguely
defined utopia than in the status quo system but also because in complex
societies institutions are specialized and possess clear boundaries, the latter
which are ignored or "trespassed" by the paninstitutional world-transforming movement. Therefore, it is often only those groups that are
committed to promoting "due process" and similar principles (e.g., courts,
civil libertarians) which defend the world-transforming movement. By
contrast, the interests of certain institutions are likely to be directly
threatened in some way (e.g., the UM's challenge to orthodox Christianity)
and/or the institution may be in a poor strategic position to protect its
interests (e.g., the initial lack of organization of individual American
families versus the constitutionally protected legal status of the UM as a
religion). *The degree of threat experienced by the larger society varies
directly with the size of the discontinuity between the values and lifestyle
of the movement and society. The less movement members' behavior is
interpretable in terms of conventional, shared symbol systems, the more
threatening that behavior is perceived to be.*

Lacking supporters and defenders in larger society, the world-transforming movement becomes vulnerable to formal and informal social
repression. If groups arrayed against the movement have sufficient power
and legitimacy in their own right, they may undertake their own direct
actions as a countermovement (as in the ACM's self-styled ad hoc deprogrammings). Otherwise, such groups may seek to enlist the aid of legitimate institutions which do have social control mechanisms at their
disposal (e.g., ACM families lobbying for governmental investigations and
regulations of cults and their many letter-writing/petition campaigns to
influence media treatment of the same).

If power is to be brought to bear against the world-transforming
movement effectively, it must be perceived as legitimate. Such legitimacy
is most easily attached to repression which reacts to the movement's

violation of norms for which a social control apparatus already exists, this apparatus being deemed to represent "the public interest" (e.g., in the UM's case, the criminal code, immigration laws, and federal tax regulations). When such apparatuses do not exist (such as the absence of recognized ecclesiastical courts to pronounce heresy), *or* when official action on violations does not occur, *or* when sanctions which might appear to be disproportionately severe relative to actual violations are being sought, then some rationale must be constructed to justify social repression. In essence, the countermovement creates an ideology which seeks to cloak its own interests with the mantle of public concern and portrays the world-transforming movement's organization and activities as destructive and threatening to the society in general. *In the same way that the ideology of the world-transforming movement reflects the kind of relationships that members wish to sustain with one another, the ideology of the countermovement reflects the kind of control relationships that it wishes to have vis-à-vis the movement. Thus, the greater the sense of threat that the countermovement can impart to society at large, and the greater the countermovement's relative power and legitimacy, the more likely will the labels attached to a world-transforming movement and its members be such as to justify actions that are unilateral and noncontestable* (for example, the ACM's portrayal of UM members as brainwashed automatons, an image which justified temporary conservatorships and deprogrammings).

NOTES

1. Wallis (1975: 104) observed a similar paninstitutional orientation in Scientology: "The boundaries between church business, science, and to a lesser extent psychotherapy are relatively clearly drawn. Scientology infringed these boundaries.... Since it behaved as a business as well as a religion ... many argued that its religious claim must be purely 'a front,' and Scientology 'a con.' "

2. Despite pointed denials to the authors by UM leaders, such lobbying appears to have occurred during the mid-1970s, though with little demonstrable success. Much of the evidence came from apostates who in official and quasi-official forums gave quite detailed accounts of their participation in lobbying efforts to the point of providing specific names of congressmen and "Moonies" assigned to their offices as well as daily "report" forms on which all contacts were to be recorded (see CEFM, 1976a; U.S. Government, 1978: 342-343).

3. For more complete historical and organizational descriptions of the anticult movement, see Shupe, Spielmann, and Stigall (1977a, 1977b).

4. The mistaken view that all anticult activities began with, and were under the coordination of, archdeprogrammer Ted Patrick has been sometimes promulgated by

the press and even the anticultists' opponents such as the Alliance for the Preservation of Religious Liberty (APRL) and the American Civil Liberties Union (see APRL, 1977). This is, in part, a function of the relative paucity of historical research into the ACM's origins and in part also a function of Patrick's own blatantly self-serving account of his deprogramming activities in his popular book *Let Our Children Go!* (Patrick and Dulack, 1976).

5. A definitive list of *all* such groups would be enormously difficult to construct due to the fluid nature of the ACM. New groups continually arise, working independently (and with often scant publicity) for an indefinite period or soon after formation changing their names as they merge with older groups (see Shupe, Spielmann, and Stigall, 1977b).

6. Within the ACM a range of activities, from the most coercive extreme to simply "talking a youth out of the cult" via telephone or noncoercive face-to-face debate, were all referred to by the single term deprogramming, as if it were a monolithic practice.

Chapter 9

THE UM COUNTERATTACK

By 1976 the UM clearly was on the defensive: deprogrammings and associated conservatorships were at their apex, recruitment and fundraising had become more difficult and media coverage had become almost exclusively negative. In contrast to the salad days of the early 1970s, the UM suddenly found its mobilization stymied. Beginning in 1977, therefore, the UM initiated a broadly based campaign to counteract the growing societal negativity, knowing that if the conflict continued to broaden and intensify the movement's capacity to promote its most basic goals and values would be increasingly jeopardized.

The solution that the UM chose to contain this conflict with the larger society and reverse its public image was a blend of accommodation and confrontation, with a strong emphasis on the former. Confrontation was sharply restricted to an assertion of its legal rights while a variety of new efforts at accommodation emerged during 1977 and 1978. Since by 1979 many of these accommodationist efforts had been underway for only a short time, the UM's long-term commitment to them and the response of the larger society were difficult for us to assess with confidence. However, all available signs indicated a quickening pace of accommodation and adoption of a deliberately lower, less controversial profile.

It is important to note that the accommodationist strategy that became so visible and prominent in UM activities by 1977 was not entirely new; in fact, it had been a fundamental part of its stance toward larger American society since Moon's first tour in 1972. For example, the UM had solicited the approval and association of notable public figures during its tours and rallies and attempted to pass as a merely evangelistic Christian movement. When faced with the deportation of a large number of German IOWC members by the Immigration and Naturalization Service in the early 1970s, the UM took great pains to assemble letters expressing support from respected citizens across the country in a volume entitled *As Others See Us* (Jones, 1974). The difference between these earlier activities and those of 1977-1978 was the latter campaign was part of a planned, concerted effort to woo public opinion and regain the initiative at a time when the movement was under sharp attack. The UM's blend of confrontation and accommodation took three distinguishable forms: (1) assertion of legal rights, (2) a public relations campaign to upgrade its image, and (3) internal organizational changes that modified some of its controversial practices. In each case the more seriously the UM perceived its interests or survival to be threatened, the greater its willingness to utilize confrontation tactics.

Assertion of Legal Rights

COUNTERING DEPROGRAMMINGS

The greatest single threat to the UM was deprogramming of its members through the use of either physical abduction or conservatorship laws. While coercive deprogrammings never constituted the primary ACM tactic by which to separate individuals from the UM, the potential threat was enormous. They created a pervasive sense of insecurity for individuals (particularly when tacitly or openly supported by the police and courts), produced a siege mentality in the movement as a whole, necessitated constant secrecy and movement of members to avoid detection, and prevented members from freely contacting their families or friends outside the movement. Even more importantly, successful deprogrammings undermined the UM's internal solidarity and external image. If presumably deeply committed converts could simply be talked out of their faith in a few hours, members had to wonder about the depth of their fellows' commitment. The ACM of course seized upon such events as evidence that coercive, manipulative mind control rather than voluntary conversion lay behind UM membership. For its part the UM spotlighted the more physical or violent aspects of deprogramming both to discredit deprogrammers and to undermine the impression of superficial commitments.

There were some major problems in combatting deprogramming. One of the most delicate issues was that the members' parents usually were integrally involved in deprogramming; indeed professional deprogrammers took great pains to implicate parents fully. Criminal prosecution or civil suits raised the specter of seeing one's parents incarcerated or financially ruined. While there were some instances in which intergenerational hostility was sufficiently great (either prior to or as a result of deprogramming) to support legal action, this frequently was not the case. Second, deprogramming could be attacked legally only when it was conducted forcibly and when it was unsuccessful, conditions which often did not exist. Finally, while the UM could protest abrogation of their religious rights, the ACM could with equal eloquence condemn destruction of family ties. Regardless of legal rights, then, combatting deprogramming was a delicate matter.

While many UM members who were subjected to deprogramming through abduction or conservatorships resisted these procedures through noncooperation or physical escape, the UM's primary means of combatting deprogramming was through seeking relief in the courts. In these cases individual UM members (rather than the movement itself) brought charges against the deprogrammers and/or parents, and legal fees were paid by the UM. As long as UM members brought suit as individuals the Unification Church (or other UM organizations) were not directly involved in the proceedings. The individual member could initiate criminal proceedings on charges such as false imprisonment, assault, or kidnapping. Members could also bring a civil suit seeking a permanent injunction against interference in his or her religious beliefs and associations, compensatory damages, or punitive damages on the basis of charges such as physical injury, mental and emotional distress, financial loss, damage to reputation, interference with constitutional rights of due process, freedom of religion, freedom of speech, freedom of travel and association, and the right to counsel.

By 1978 the UM had been extremely successful in reducing the number of coercive deprogrammings through physical abduction or conservatorships although many parents continued to pressure their sons or daughters to terminate affiliation with the UM. The ACM's direct action strategy had been undercut, and the ACM concentrated the majority of its efforts toward public education, continuing legislative investigations of UM political activities, and revoking the tax-exempt status of UM organizations. The UM's success was not surprising in light of the fact that virtually all of the individuals forcibly deprogrammed were legally adults, criminal statutes as well as civil and constitutional rights were violated, and, in the case of the awarding of temporary conservatorships, proper legal procedure was contravened or disregarded to provide the "color of law" for illicit actions. Deprogrammers were literally besieged with suits totaling tens of millions of dollars, and the symbolic leader of deprogramming activity, Ted Patrick, was jailed on several occasions for his participation in these activities. The UM concentrated most of its legal attack on the deprogrammers directly because their actions were so clearly in violation of the law and because UM members had no qualms about prosecuting these individuals to the full extent of the law. Even if cases had proven more contestable, the mere cost of defending themselves against these legal actions became prohibitive to deprogrammers who could not hope to match the UM's financial resources or legal talent. In the face of impending incarceration, protracted legal proceedings, and financial ruin the viability of these tactics for both deprogrammers and parents plummeted rapidly.

The decisiveness of the UM's victories in the courts with respect to coercive deprogrammings and conservatorships is illustrated by the cases of Wendy Helander and the "Faithful Five." After having been abducted and deprogrammed several times, Wendy Helander brought suit against Ted Patrick, his assistants, and her parents. In a decision against Patrick et al., awarding her $5,000 in damages, the Judge made reference to "crude, callous, brow-beating tactics . . . which smack more of a fictional television melodrama than a real life incident" (e.g., during the ordeal, Patrick "labeled her a vegetable, a dog, a bitch, and maintained that she was out of her mind" as well as accusing her of being a prostitute for Moon—see Helander v. Patrick et al., 1976.) In the nationally reported trial of the UM's "San Francisco Five," a group of parents sought conservatorship custody of their five respective adult offspring. After protracted hearings and an initial decision awarding custody of the UM members to their parents, the decision was reversed in favor of the defendants. Although four of the five eventually defected within a short time anyway, the UM achieved a significant legal precedent—conservatorship laws were clearly not meant to legitimate coercive deprogrammings.

DEFENDING THE RIGHT TO FUND-RAISE

A second major conflict the UM faced revolved around its fund-raising practices. Street solicitation was the financial lifeblood of the movement and had been ideologically justified as a means of fostering members' spiritual growth. For both of these reasons fund-raising activities were a vital concern to the UM. For their part local communities had a legitimate interest in regulating both charitable and commercial solicitation. Transient peddlers, fradulent "charitable" organizations and extralocal organizations which drained the limited pool of charitable contribution dollars posed a real problem for the public at large and competing legitimate local charities. Thus, most communities had passed ordinances regulating solicitation by, for example, requiring applications be filed with municipal officials and permits be issued mandating that solicitors wear identification badges, limiting times and places at which solicitations could be conducted, requiring that bonds be posted, and demanding disclosure of certain financial records by the parent organization.

When the UM became a highly visible center of controversy in 1974 and its media coverage became increasingly negative, UM members found that local communities (which most frequently encountered the UM in the course of its fund-raising/proselytization activities) increasingly sought to block UM solicitation activities. Local officials reflecting public hostility toward the UM correctly observed that if fund-raising activities were obstructed UM members quickly moved on to "greener" pastures. The simplest means of controlling UM fund-raising was through existing ordinances regulating solicitation. From the UM's perspective not only did such laws violate their Constitutional rights but even good faith efforts to comply with these laws were problematic because the innumerable local ordinance variations, their vagueness, their broad discretionary powers, and the potential interminable procedural delays made obstruction of UM fund-raising relatively easy in the hands of suspicious or hostile local officials.

The UM combatted restrictions on its fund-raising activities by contesting the ordinances in court on the basis of their unconstitutionality. Within a relatively short time the UM had amassed an impressive string of legal victories which rapidly reduced harassment of UM fund-raising teams by local municipal officials. The legal and constitutional issues were clearly drawn. As one federal judge stated in his ruling in favor of the UM,

It is a well established law that distribution of literature and solicitation of funds to support religious organizations are well within the protection of the First Amendment. . . . The loss of First Amendment freedoms, even for minimal periods of time, unquestionably constitutes irreparable injury (The Kansas City Times, Kansas City, Missouri, April 15, 1978).

Despite the fact that the UM consistently won such cases, municipal officials were likely to obstruct fund-raising activities until legal action was threatened. In order to avoid the prospect of countless suits against every local government, which would arouse continuing negative media coverage and involve substantial commitments of UM members' time and energy, the UM adopted a strategy of suing one municipality in an area as an example to its neighbors. If the municipality did not acquiesce it was threatened with suit for punitive or compensatory damages as well as legal fees incurred. As one UM spokesman stated in an interview with us about one such suit: "We've got a complaint prepared against Columbia [Tennessee] . . . and the punitive damages will probably be upped somewhat. The church doesn't want to go to court every time with every town. We want to show them we mean business" (Personal Interviews, 1978). In general once the locality agreed to "reasonable" solicitation requirements the UM simply dropped the suit in order to avoid producing further ill will. The UM did not contest ordinances with provisions limiting the hours during which solicitations could be conducted, prohibiting blocking of streets, requiring solicitors to conform to the policies of their own organization, and requiring solicitors to wear identification badges. These types of regulations were viewed as reasonable and presumably applied to all organizational solicitations.

OTHER SUITS

The UM sought to gain a state charter for the Unification Theological Seminary as early as April 1975. Lacking this the seminary could not receive accreditation by professional associations, grant degrees or credits acceptable at other schools, apply for some types of educational loans, obtain study visas for foreign students, or make its faculty eligible for some pension plans. Thus, the seminary had a substantial stake in gaining accreditation, and its opponents could impose significant sanctions merely by denying it. After a number of site visits by State Education Department staff that recommended approval of the application but repeated deferral of any decision by the New York Board of Regents and a resolution from the New York State Legislature opposing approval, the seminary undertook legal action. Suits were filed in 1977 to compel the Regents to render a decision and to enable seminary representatives to attend closed hearings on the application. In February 1978 by a unanimous vote the Regents denied the application, and an appeal of that decision was immediately initiated by the seminary.

In spring 1978 the UM undertook a series of lawsuits against the publishers and authors of various books and articles which, in its opinon, served to "ridicule and defame the church in such a way as to deprive it of present and potential membership and contributions" (New York Times, May 8, 1978). Thus, fifteen million dollar suit was lodged against E. P. Dutton and Ted Patrick for the latter's coauthored pot-boiler, *Let Our Children Go!,* while Harper & Row and authoress Dusty Sklar were sued for four million dollars on account of unfavorable comparisons between the UM's recruitment tactics and those of the pre-World War II Nazi movement in her book, *Gods and Beasts: The Nazis and the Occult.*[1] In May 1978 the UM took on the giant of the American Press, the *New York Times,* over a pair of "exposé" articles based on an admittedly erroneous, "unevaluated" American Central Intelligence Agency report claiming among other things that the Korean Central Intelligence Agency had founded the Korean Unification Church in the early 1960s. Besides the ten million dollar suit, protesting UM members by the hundreds marched in downtown Manhattan in front of the New York Times Building.

This latter case in particular illustrated the limited protection against libel and innuendo provided the UM through the courts. Reports such as the above CIA one, with anonymous authors, were leaked to the press. The press in turn reported the "allegations" contained there, and these reports were then picked up and repeated as fact by foreign news services. The UM had no recourse to defend itself against such circuitous rumor-generation except through occasional suits; hence a congressman with legal immunity or an anonymous, unsympathetic bureaucrat could provide the fuel for further attacks on the UM.

Upgrading the UM Image: Frontier '78

The idea for a concentrated public relations campaign to upgrade the UM's public image had been "in the air" for some time among the movement's leaders following the successful 1977 Unity of Science Conference in San Francisco. Preparations for it took shape shortly after God's Day (January 1) 1978 when Neil Salonen met with national and state directors and then issued a directive to announce Frontier '78. Frontier '78 consisted of a series of waves or tours of publicity teams that canvassed key cities across the country and that repeatedly contacted influential civic, political, and religious leaders. Each team consisted of seven advance members, staffed largely by the UM's "Capitol Hill ministry," and coordinated, respectively, by leaders Neil Salonen, Dr. William Bergman, and Dan Fefferman. The advance teams arranged press conferences, media interviews (particularly on radio and television talk shows), guest lectureships at local colleges, and appointments with public officials for each of the three coordinators on a fairly hectic schedule. On the first two-and-one-half month tour in early 1978, for example, each team leader visited cities in an average of seventeen states; by fall 1978 there had been three such tours (with a fourth planned), all meeting fairly favorable public response according to UM informants and press descriptions.

A number of themes were conveyed in the PR teams' contacts with leaders and media in the various cities: contrition for past mistakes, continuing to pass, self-portrayal as persecuted underdog, self-depiction as maturing, and rationalizing deviant activities.

CONTRITION FOR PAST MISTAKES

On a number of occasions UM leaders frankly acknowledged that the organization and its members had committed normative violations, thus stealing much of the thunder from their critics. For example, Neil Salonen met with the Southern Nevada Better Business Bureau and discussed means to "rectify and overcome past mistakes" (Las Vegas Sun, Las Vegas, Nevada, March 22, 1978). Throughout the tour UM spokesmen sought to reassure those who interviewed them that such mistakes were not likely to recur in the future. Thus, Dan Fefferman affirmed: "Some members of the church have not abided by the [prescribed] procedures. We want to know who these people are so we can straighten them out" (Columbus Evening Dispatch, Columbus, Ohio, February 11, 1978). He added that UM members were now required to wear name-tags and clearly represent themselves as such.

CONTINUING TO PASS

Despite the numerous problems that the UM had encountered in past attempts to represent itself as Christian, UM spokesmen continued to reaffirm this theme. For instance, Dan Fefferman stated that "The church generally follows Christian beliefs with a few deviations such as Cain and Abel representing the struggle between communism and democracy" (The Cincinnati Post, Cincinnati, Ohio, February 16, 1978).[2]

SELF-PORTRAYAL AS UNDERDOG

In our own interviews with UM leaders they made frequent reference to themselves as the "underdog" in their controversies and explicitly compared themselves to other persecuted religious minorities in American history (e.g., Irish-Catholics, Mormons, and the like). Fefferman drew upon this imagery in an interview in Columbus, Ohio when he told reporters that he wished "to clarify what he called distorted information about the church reported by the media" (Columbus Evening Dispatch, Columbus, Ohio, February 11, 1978). In this context UM spokesmen frequently impugned the motives of their accusers, such as Fefferman's statement that "Fraser is interested in building his political future and

Rev. Moon is merely a good headline" (Minnesota Daily, Minneapolis, Minnesota, May 12, 1978).

SELF-DEPICTION AS MATURING

UM leaders made frequent reference to the rapid growth and maturation of the movement. For example, Salonen talked of the UM's plans to expand the seminary into a four-year liberal arts college (The Denver Post, Denver, Colorado, May 2, 1978). Fefferman was even more graphic in his imagery, saying "The Unification Church is entering its adolescence, moving out of its infancy." He went on to add that the "Moonies are maturing into a church which may be like any other church in the city" (The Seattle Daily Times, Seattle, Washington, February 23, 1978). UM spokesmen also observed that they were reaching out to different kinds of people such as older adults and people in professional life (Personal Interviews, 1978).

RATIONALIZING DEVIANT ACTIVITIES

While acknowledging past errors, UM spokesmen always presented these as the products of individual errors in judgment rather than as systematic features of the organization. Thus, Fefferman claimed: "Members of the church misrepresented themselves because they were 'overzealous' and wanted to spread the word about the church no matter how it was done" (Columbus Evening Dispatch, Columbus, Ohio, February 11, 1978). Earlier on the tour Fefferman explained: "Deception in fund-raising did occur with some frequency in the period from 1972 to 1974. . . . The early converts felt the Kingdom of God was at hand any day, and this caused some people to do things the church now regrets" [Note the implied retreat from millenarian expectations—Eds.] (The Hartford Courant, Hartford, Connecticut, January 22, 1978).

Organizational Changes

Although the organizational changes introduced in 1977 and 1978 hardly allayed all the fears, suspicions, and objections of UM opponents, they did hold the promise of lowering the level of conflict in the future. Foremost among these innovations were the beginnings of new means of fund-raising and recruitment. With respect to fund-raising, the UM, fully cognizant of the widespread hostility generated by sidewalk solicitation and the vulnerability of this technique, began acquiring a diverse array of business enterprises that would support the movement and its members by selling socially valued goods and services (e.g., fishing industries, news-paper, ginseng tea distributor, janitorial service company). With respect to proselytization and recruitment beginning in 1978 there was a turn toward what the UM termed "home ministries." Under this concept (as of summer, 1978 operating on an experimental basis in New York City) individual UM members took up residence in assigned neighborhoods, attempted to develop close relationships with other area residents and, through these, sought to live exemplary lifestyles and interest others in becoming part of the movement. One additional, if minor, consession concerning recruitment was one the UM's Oakland Family made to dis-traught parents of lost new recruits. They offered to supply information on the youths' whereabouts and to facilitate communication with the latter through a neutral party.

Two examples of lifestyle rapproachment were the establishment of engagements prior to marriage and the reconciliation of youth to their families of orientation. While members apparently had always had some degree of choice in the determination of their marriage partner, the decision frequently was consummated after a single meeting. In the fall of 1978 members for the first time tentatively agreed upon marriage partners but then enjoyed a period of reflection, including a UM-style "engagement party," during which the individuals could become better acquainted before making a final commitment. The other lifestyle shift was symbo-lized by Moon's designation of 1978 as the "year of reconciliation." Individual members were encouraged to reestablish communication and ongoing relationships with their families, visits home for birthdays, holi-days and other important occasions were arranged. Family members in turn were invited to visit the members when feasible. For example, the seminary held a conventional graduation ceremony which allowed for the participation of "proud families." Further, a UM member with a graduate degree in social work was assigned the role of liason and counselor for anxious parents as a means of reducing suspicion and friction.

Conclusions

SUMMARY

As this chapter chronicled, by the mid-1970s the UM had moved to an unmistakably defensive stance. Media coverage was preponderantly nega-tive when not undisguisedly derisive. This bad press had the effect of damaging the movement's fund-raising and recruitment efforts. Depro-grammings were attempted fairly frequently and under the color of law provided by temporary conservatorship statutes. Such deprogrammings, when successful, struck a blow to membership morale, and in any event their persistent possibility contributed to the tension between many members and their families. Faced with this hostile situation, the UM had few alternatives for action. Both morally and pragmatically, the movement could not act coercively against its enemies, nor, in view of its dependence on larger society for members and money, could it feasibly retreat to some remote but safer locale. Therefore, its strategy was a blend of accommodation and selective confrontation. It began to accommodate by modifying many of its controversial practices (e.g., substituting industrial income for fund-raising, providing more conventional career opportunities for older members, and promoting reconciliation with parents) and presenting a less radical public image in its public relations (e.g., as in the Frontier '78 campaign). When necessary it was not loathe to seek legal redress against what it interpreted as unjust detractors and clear threats. On a broad range of issues, from its constitutional right to publically solicit donations to charges of libel, the UM became involved in lawsuits that, through their victories, became potent deterrents to attacks on the movement.

IMPLICATIONS

In the introductory chapter we argued that one of the major determinants of social movement organizational structure (in addition to amount and type of change) is strategy for implementing change. In addition to the preference for voluntary over involuntary relationships, a strategy of persuasion is fostered to the extent that there is a threat of sanctions if coercion is used, that force and/or violence is/are inconsistent with the movement's ideology, and that strong links exist between the movement and the society. *We would argue that once a basic strategy has been adopted it would be reflected in the organizational structure in such a way as to create strong pressure for continued implementation of the strategy even in the face of sanctions from the larger society. Indeed, to abandon the movement's primary strategy is tantamount to fundamental restructuring of the movement.*

In the case of movements which adopt persuasion as a strategy, for example, the ideology is based on metaphors which idealize perfectly benevolent relationships (e.g., the UM's emphasis on family, love and fall or loss of natural loving relationships). Recruitment involves a voluntary self-selection process by the individual, a process which is then reinforced by strong positive instrumental, affective and moral attachments within the group. Not only is recruitment based on loving relationships with potential converts, but benevolence and selflessness become major criteria for status within the group (e.g., basing status on heartistic qualities and winning spiritual children through such qualities in the UM). For reasons previously discussed, world-transforming movements relying on a strategy of persuasion typically become dependent on donations and contributions as a means of generating financial resources. Solicitation of charitable funds requires mutually held values between donor and solicitor (or at least the perception of these by both) and, in addition, this solicitation process comes to take on significance within the movement (seen not only in the UM's definition of members' exchange of token gifts such as pins or flags for money as a mutual acknowledgement of God but also in the UM's definition of fund-raising capacity as indicative of a member's capacity to love others). Finally, visibility and legitimacy for the movement are sought through such techniques as revival-style meetings and coopting of luminaries which are premised on voluntary participation. At the same time such persuasive activities have a substantial impact on in-group solidarity (e.g., the UM's definition of such events as the series of nationwide tours as signs of spiritual success).

Even when confronted with social repression (as described in detail in the preceding chapter), then, movements which have adopted a strategy of persuasion are likely to move in the direction of accommodation rather than conflict. What confrontation does occur is likely to be restrained so as to create an image of "self-defense." There is, of course, some point at which societal repression may make accommodation untenable, and the movement may alter its basic strategy. However, the cost of strategy shift is exceedingly high. Even to retreat in order to escape conflict would be to forego its transformative goals as well as the round of life dedicated to their achievement. Thus, we would contend that continuity in strategy is not determined simply by member attitudes and value preferences but by the organizational exigencies created by the initial adoption of a strategy. Continuity is likely to be maintained even at the cost of muting controversial aspects of the ideology and altering organizational activities.

NOTES

1. It appeared that only the most aggredious cases of "slander" were to be attacked. Thus, as a national UM legal advisor explained to us, the journalistic book *All Gods Children* (Stoner and Parke, 1977), while short on praise for the UM, nevertheless was the thoughtful product of research that had included efforts to obtain the "Moonies' " side of the story (albeit with conclusions unpalatable to the UM), and its authors/publisher were not sued.

2. This is not to suggest that the UM representatives were necessarily duplicitous in claiming to be "Christian." Indeed, UM theology claims that to accept *The Divine Principle* is to become *completely* and *truly* Christian. However, there is no doubt that UM spokesmen knew what *their own* claims to be Christian, and the label "Christian" in the minds of outsiders, meant, respectively, and the difference therein.

Chapter 10

THE UM AS A WORLD-TRANSFORMING MOVEMENT

SUMMARY

In the previous nine chapters we examined a contemporary world-transforming movement at a relatively early stage of development that adopted a strategy of persuasion to reach its sweeping goals, namely the American Unificationist Movement of the Rev. Sun Myung Moon. The resource mobilization perspective was utilized as a heuristic device for presenting and analyzing our data because the psychological reductionism characteristic of the motivational model obscures the organizational aspects of social movements. By rejecting an a priori assumption of strong grievances motivating affiliation with a world-transforming movement that would restrict analysis to that level of inquiry, the resource mobilization perspective opens up the possibility of a variety of links between member and movement, focuses attention on the organizational aspect of social movements, and emphasizes the ongoing exchange between movement and society. In adopting a resource mobilization perspective we attempted to identify the UM as a particular type of movement in order that the mobilization process could be linked to specific organizational characteristics. In doing so we noted that the world-transforming movement as we described it constituted an ideal type in the sense that no such movement had every fully achieved its goals. The most appropriate research objective that we could establish, therefore, was to examine how this specific type of movement mobilized resources in pursuit of its goals; that is, what types of resources are central to such a movement, and how are they mobilized? Thus, we examined six critical dimensions affecting this mobilization process: environmental conduciveness, movement ideology, leadership and organization, visibility and legitimacy, organizational commitment, and the societal reaction to deviance.

Beginning with Moon's boyhood vision of Jesus Christ in pre-World War II Korea, we traced the formation of expansion of the UM in that country. Moon underwent various experiences and privations during the Korea war period, and his movement, despite official government persecution and public disapproval, grew in the late 1950s and early 1960s. During that time it developed two crucial features: a Biblically based eclectic, systematic ideology that linked problems of human estrangement, theodicy, and international political conflict; and an organization which successfully merged the necessary bureaucratic structures with charismatic leadership by clearly separating Moon's prophetic functions from more mundane administrative ones. By 1959, when Moon assigned the first missionaries to the United States, the UM was already a burgeoning movement with increasing legitimacy and economic/political connections in South Korean society.

Our review of the two decades during which the UM was active in American society argued that environmental conditions can be more or less supportive or nonsupportive of a movement's goals. The 1960s did provide the requisite pool of young, relatively unattached members for a number of social movements due to a number of structural features of American society (such as the deferral of formal adulthood into the early twenties, large numbers of youth in a lengthened educational process concentrated in urban clusters, and a positive ethos of experimentation with alternative lifestyles and philosophies). Yet, as we and others have argued, early in this period there existed a reservoir of faith in the legitimacy of national purposes and institutions—a belief in America's civil religion—that directed expectations toward secular (i.e., socioeconomic and political) solutions to major problems. When that legitimacy began to erode, the reaction was both militant and secular. The UM, with its millenarian theology, increased its membership base only incrementally during this decade in stark contrast to the explosive growth of the early 1970s. Thus, this sudden expansion of the UM in the 1970s must be placed in the context of a societal resurgence of religion, much of it outside the domain of mainstream American churches. The erosion of confidence in secular solutions and the accommodation of established churches to secular society certainly encouraged this extramural revival of religiosity.

A movement's ideology is an emergent phenomenon and is gradually altered (within limits) to maximize its appeal to a particular target group and cultural environment. This was shown in the UM's ideological extensions when it was transplanted into the United States, both in its East Coast mainstream theological form and in the West Coast Oakland Family's humanistic variation. In the first instance the ideology's prediction of imminent change was modified, and a new important role for American in world restoration was created. American members were confronted with the awesome challenge of morally uniting the country, finding themselves caught up in far-flung travels, numerous adventures, and possibly rewarding careers in an expanding movement. In the second instance certain themes of the original Korean-produced theology were translated into humanistic, countercultural terms more palatable to the youth of the San Francisco-Berkeley area. In both cases the emergent, open-ended quality of the UM's ideology strengthened its ability to adapt to a new cultural environment and attract members.

Moon's transfer of his personal ministry to the United States in late 1971 was of signal importance for the American UM. Acting in terms of his own already established charismatic tradition, Moon's presence served as a unifying force in leading the American UM out of decentralized, economically weak obscurity. His personal example of dedication and his grandiose fiery exhortations provided powerful motivators for members. As the movement pushed on and achieved visibility, his hob-nobbing with influential American leaders (or at least the appearance of it) and the continuous emergence of apocryphal tales about his exploits in the United States confirmed his unique status for members. More importantly, Moon's arrival contributed both directly and indirectly to significant organizational changes in the UM. It was Moon's critical redefinition of UM membership from part-time to full-time which reorganized such members into easily assembled mobile units that could be deployed for any number of purposes, and it was his arrival that lent the impetus to such factors as the serendipitous discovery of how to accumulate vast sums of money with only a small corps of dedicated followers and the employing of more systematic recruitment and socialization techniques that turned the UM's fortunes around. With these resources mobilized the UM was able to initiate a wide range of projects such as the movement's numerous publications, its expanding industries, and its growing international missions. Correspondingly, the sheer number of organizational positions and career opportunities, staff and executive, also grew. That the latter did not result in a crystallized bureaucracy was due in part to Moon's direct insistence that members develop minimal entrenched interests in particular roles and positions. Further, the requisites of a communal lifestyle, the bedrock organizational principle of the movement, militated against the development of bureaucracy. In part, also, it was due to the persistence of strains toward factionalism not completely obviated by Moon's reorganization of the movement. Indeed, as we argued in our description of the leadership and operations of the West Coast's Oakland Family, some factionalism was permitted to exist for its pragmatic value in recruitment and training for the larger movement.

As a world-transforming movement the UM sought to garner visibility in order to achieve mass support and at the same time secure the appearance of legitimacy in order to make its message credible to potential converts. Our account of how the UM attempted to attain both resources simultaneously included a discussion of a number of specific tactics that it employed: passing as an evangelistic Christian group and publically deemphasizing Moon's messianic potential, coopting the association of luminaries by inviting their participation in UM functions or by soliciting ceremonial endorsements, and creating spectacular media events that attracted free coverage by news media. The UM experienced image problems somewhat sooner than might otherwise have been the case precisely because it courted the media so assiduously in order to disseminate its message. These problems flowed from more than simply Moon's inability to speak English and the cryptic content of his speeches themselves. Once the media began to probe for details (often at the instigation of the UM's growing opposition) beyond simply what the UM itself was willing to provide, legitimacy began to erode fairly quickly and the publicity obtained often was distinctly unfavorable. When dissemination of the UM's message was no longer under the movement's control and it was laid out before the public in unsympathetic terms, the limitations of a persuasion strategy became excruciatingly apparent.

The UM was perhaps best known for stories told of its systematic attempts to engender instrumental, affective, and moral commitment among members. From its first "street" encounters with self-selected individuals through recruitment and initial socialization to the gradual development of permanent, long-term membership, a variety of techniques were used to build commitment on all three levels. The UM required sacrifices of former relationships, career plans, and lifestyles, beginning first as simply a brief "trial" period during a weekend workshop and culminating in a radical disengagement from all of these when an individual joined the consuming communal lifestyle of the movement's groups. Continual sacrifices, such as fasts and self-imposed ascetic resolutions (setting conditions) as well as the growing responsibilities of each individual also contributed to the continual sense of investment and instrumental commitment to the movement. Affective commitment resulted from the ideologically based emphasis on love and relating to other persons openly and altruistically (i.e., heartistically) beginning in the emotionally high-pressure workshop situations of initial socialization and continuing in the numerous activities which required interdependent efforts. The UM also generated moral commitment by gradually transforming individuals' indentities beginning during their first encounters with the movement in workshops when they were provided with appropriate role-model testimonies and affirmations of such transformations. Other deliberate practices, such as the confessions before marriage or the more commonly encountered introspective reconstructions of biographies which members freely gave during their witnessing and in interviews, encouraged this type of commitment. There were, however, limitations on the amount of commitment actually generated. Members could successfully pursue their roles in the group with a modicum of religious belief or commitment to the movement's larger goals. Indeed, a given sample of members could reveal a wide range of belief sophistication and commitment to the restoration per se, and the nature of many group activities made the amount of any individual's commitment problematic.

Finally, in the process of mobilizing resources a world-transforming movement engages in a continuous exchange with the larger society to be transformed, and conflict is an inevitable outcome of such contacts. The UM, because it had originally presented itself as a church in the orthodox Christian tradition, found its first conflict with the most traditional elements of established Christianity (particularly fundamentalist churches) and the first accusations against it involved theological heresy. The conflict quickly spread, however, as the organizational style of the UM created friction with other institutions. The UM's incursions into the political, economic, and educational arenas led to accusations of misrepresentation and illicit activity. Most established institutions used their symbolic and instrumental sanctioning power, formally or informally, to discredit the UM and obstruct its activities. While the opposition was far from monolithic, social control was exerted relatively effectively in large measure because the UM had few powerful allies. Only civil libertarians consistently defended the movement and then only its rights as a religious entity. It was the family institution, through coalitions of individual family units, that reacted most hostilely to the UM. As their sons and daughters were recruited to a stigmatized movement, parents felt the "loss" in a personal and direct way. They responded by creating vigilante-style organizations which initiated direct action (e.g., deprogrammings) to "free" their offspring and launched a nationwide drive to enlist the aid of other more powerful institutions in battling cults. Although sympathetic leaders of established institutions were able to provide anticultists with limited assistance, the parents were ultimately forced to rely primarily on their access to the media in order to discredit the UM symbolically. These efforts were effective, however, given the UM's need for legitimacy, and by the mid-1970s the UM's image was severely tarnished and its ability to mobilize several critical resources had been markedly reduced. As a result, in the late 1970s the UM began to counterattack with a new public image that it vigorously promoted and with legal procedures to discourage what it considered to be the more serious of its enemies' manuevers. The former image involved a certain amount of accommodation in its public statements and internal practices; the latter entailed a number of lawsuits designed to harrass or block those who themselves had been engaged in harrassing the movement. After a short time it is our distinct impression that this counterattack had begun to have an effect.

IMPLICATIONS

In the remainder of this chapter we shall discuss some of the broader implications of our findings which seem to us to be both conclusions and preliminary observations for future investigations of social movements. Specifically, we are concerned with the concept of mobilization which Oberschall (1973: 102) defined as gaining control over resources. We would argue that from an organizational standpoint mobilization involves creating congruence among organizational characteristics and managing conflicts which arise from the contrasting internal and external consequences of the mobilization process. Finally, we shall offer some observations on the goals of mobilization by world-transforming movements.

Congruence and Mobilization Effectiveness. As we observed in our introduction, success is an ambiguous benchmark for investigators of world-transforming movements. Strictly speaking, no such movements have ever achieved success if the latter is defined solely in terms of total, global transformation. However, it is clear that such movements do distribute themselves along a continuum of effectiveness in surviving and prospering in their social environments. We would argue that the critical factor determining this *internal* effectiveness is the relative *congruence* of a world-transforming movement's techniques of resource mobilization (in particular fund-raising, membership recruitment, and generating visibility/ legitimacy) with both its ideology and its communal lifestyle. *A world-transforming movement can mobilize more effectively when its generic characteristics are consistent with one another and with the world-transformative type (i.e., they are congruent).*

Congruent techniques of fund-raising, for example, must permit members to actualize key metaphoric values of the ideology (e.g., UM fund-raising was defined as both a means of building spiritual strength and as an index of members' heartistic qualities) while in pursuit of financial resources. At the same time, to have maximum internal effectiveness these fund-raising techniques should preserve and strengthen the communal lifestyle by permitting full-time collective efforts of members that reinforce solidarity and interdependence (e.g., the UM's expansion of street solicitation practices, particularly in communally organized MFT teams that insulated individuals from the corrupt world by their rapid geographical mobility and sharply limited ritualized interaction with potential donors). In this way meeting needs for financial resources becomes consistent with and supportive of those generic characteristics of a world-transforming movement's ideology and communal organization which we delineated earlier. Likewise, congruence in recruitment activities is created to the extent that these can be given ideological significance (e.g., UM members seeking spiritual children through whom they could recapitulate God's loving relationship to all persons) and linked to maintenance of the communal lifestyle (e.g., OWC witnessing teams which operated as full-time, communal units much like MFTs). Finally, congruent techniques of mobilizing visibility and legitimacy would involve full-time efforts by members who are communally organized and supported to carry forth the movement's message (e.g., the series of Moon's speaking tours throughout the early 1970s which required full-time commitment to movement activities) and manifest ideological significance (such as the various stops on Moon's tours which were regarded by members as providential events in the world restoration process).

Indeed, our data demonstrate the importance of congruence in the effective mobilization of a movement over time. A comparison of the UM during the 1960s and the 1970s reveals a relative lack of congruence among the movement's characteristics in the former period. As Chapter 2 detailed, while members lived communally they worked outside the communal group at separate jobs and careers. Full-time fund-raising, recruitment-socialization, and efforts to stimulate visibility therefore were impossible, and activities in those separate spheres were poorly integrated with one another and with the ideology. What mobilization did occur was extremely limited in its fruits, and as a result the movement expanded at a tortuously slow rate, remained financially precarious, and was all but invisible. The "turnaround" in the 1970s was in part a consequence of several factors that produced greater congruence, principally: Moon's redefinition of the membership role to require full-time commitment to the communal group, a series of ideologically legitimated projects to create visibility and legitimacy and occupy members' full energies, and the serendipitous discovery of full-time street soliciting as a lucrative and ideologically compatible resource mobilization technique.

If congruence increases organizational effectiveness, the question remains: How is the congruence achieved? Our data suggest that ideas are created and adjusted to legitimate organizational structures and activities that promote stability and effective mobilization. That is, changes in ideology tend to follow and reflect organizational developments. In various chapters throughout the book we presented illustrations of this process. For example, the original date established for world restoration was postponed in order to retain the crisis atmosphere in the movement. The serendipitously discovered fund-raising tactic of street solicitation was endowed with theological significance *after* it proved so strikingly successful. Likewise, recruitment of new members became defined as a measure of spirituality. Finally, as we argued in Chapter 5, apocryphal tales were constructed to attribute to Moon the kinds of charismatic personal qualities which legitimated the authority relationships and personal sacrifices so important to communal groups. This is not to say that ideas have no impact on organization or only secondary importance. The creation of charimsa, for example, does most certainly produce behavioral changes in the individual to whom it is attributed. However, we would have to conclude that ideas can be more accurately seen as the products rather than the causes of social relationships.

Mobilization as Conflict Management. We would argue that from an organizational perspective one aspect of mobilization defined as gaining control translates into "managing conflicts" which emerge in large measure from the contrasting internal and external consequences of the mobilization process itself. These conflicts constitute literal dilemmas in the sense that while the conflict may be managed in some fashion it cannot be completely resolved. Among the dilemmas related to conflicting internal and external consequences of the mobilization process for world-transforming movements are the following:

Ideology. All world-transforming movements construct metaphors in terms of which an analysis and critique of human history and a vision of the future is presented. A critique of the present evil, corrupt, or unnatural world is requisite to explain the source of humanity's problems and to justify the scope of change for which the movement calls; a vision of the future is requisite because the principles of the new order fly in the face of present realities as individuals know and experience them. While *internally* the ideology constitutes a shared interpretive framework which provides an ultimate justification for members' personal commitment to the movement and therefore promotes solidarity, *externally* it is typically regarded as threatening and heretical to outsiders. In fact basic points of difference between the movement's ideology and conventional cultural assumptions often become the bases for attacking the movement. Thus, the ultimate source of legitimation and meaning *internally* becomes a primary source of mistrust and antagonism *externally*. Similarly, changes in the ideology which *internally* are useful in adjusting it to new environments or events within the movement itself prompt charges of credulity and opportunism *externally*.

Leadership. Charismatic leadership is an important organizational characteristic which we stressed in our introductory discussion of world-transforming movements. Members' acknowledgement of the charismatic leader both as an ideal or model to be emulated and as as an inspiring example whose own sufferings and trials members must recapitulate (even if only symbolically) in order to attain those personal qualities idealized by the movement serves an important function in sustaining their commitment. However, the hierarchical authority relationships which emanate from the creation of charisma by members as well as the apocryphal tales through which members express their leader's idealized, larger-than-life qualities appear alarming to outsiders who have not experienced the powerful confirmatory experiences of faith within the group. Thus, what is a focal point for group striving and solidarity *internally* becomes simultaneously a focal point of alarm and suspicion *externally*.

Fund-Raising. Because it is unlikely that a fledgling world-transforming movement will be able to offer a service or product which would provide sufficient revenues to underwrite rapid large-scale growth, it must turn to the society which is to be the target of change for donations. Soliciting funds from larger society provides a ready source of revenues and still allows members to devote their full energies to the movement; however, the larger society resents contributions to causes toward which it is apathetic or opposed. Indeed, the more the movement's purposes are known the less likely the movement is to obtain donations, and subsequently there is a gravitation toward some use of deception and/or high pressure tactics in order to elicit contributions. Such tactics are, of course, met by efforts to expose the movement's tactics and restrict its fundraising activities. Thus, an organizational innovation which increased congruence and efficiency *internally* had the effect of mustering substantial opposition to the movement *externally*.

Recruitment/Socialization. As in fund-raising, the process of producing new members for the movement involves drawing on larger society for its pool of potential recruits. We argued in Chapter 7 that this process is most efficiently accomplished by exposing recruits to a communal lifestyle under specific circumstances. The communal lifestyle of a world-transforming movement requires total involvement in the group, insulation from the outside world, the assuming of diffuse roles and a selfless orientation toward group tasks; these characteristics of the recruitment/ socialization process are important in engendering the high level of commitment needed to sustain the group. However, separating individuals (temporarily or permanently) from family members, former acquaintances, conventional careers, and marriage and family formation, particularly in pursuit of what is perceived to be a "false" cause, evokes hostility from the larger society. The latter may merely regard movement members as lost or throwing away their lives, or, in the extreme case, consider them duped, manipulated, or coerced. Thus, engendering commitment, perhaps the most basic resource of a world-transforming movement, *internally* evokes outrage and repression *externally*.

Visibility/Legitimacy. For a number of reasons which we presented in Part II of this book, a world-transforming movement pursues the related goals of visibility and legitimacy simultaneously. In part these flow out of adopting a persuasion strategy. In part also, like proselytization and fund-raising, vigorous pursuit of visibility and legitimacy serves to build the movement while simultaneously involving existing members full-time in the movement's activities. In addition, achieving visibility and legitimacy may substitute for producing structural change in society. However, in curvilinear fashion the more aggressively a movement seeks visibility and legitimacy the more likely legitimacy is to be lost ultimately (although negative publicity and notoriety may continue unabated indefinitely). This occurs because the movement faces a fundamental dilemma in that the more it reveals the full content of its ideology the more likely it is to be met with charges of heresy. Yet, to reveal initially only part of the message prevents the movement from emphasizing those qualities which differentiate it from conventional groups *and* increases the possibility that the movement will later be charged with duplicity when more controversial aspects of the ideology do become known. Thus, the very act of disseminating its ideology, which is crucial to the movement's sense of purpose and uniqueness *internally*, has the effect of reducing its legitimacy, a crucial resource on which the strategy of persuasion depends, *externally*.

Bureaucra⊔c/Communal Organization. Certain other dilemmas are related *solely* to a world-transforming movement's *internal* mobilization processes. Perhaps the most salient termed the "dilemmas of institutionalization" accompanying a movement's survival and growth over time. While our case study illustrated this process in an accelerated form, at one time or another all world-transforming movements which do not pass into extinction must deal with it. If the movement is to continue to pursue its ambitious goals, then pressures to mobilize resources more efficiently will eventually have to be reconciled, however imperfectly, with the spirit and function of the communal group. Thus, the communal organization, which is the source of the intense commitment requisite to sustain a world-transforming movement, clashes directly with bureaucratic organization, the means by which the growth and development of the movement crucial to achieving its transformative goals can most effectively be directed.

The Objectives of of Resource Mobilization. Social movements frequently are judged in terms of their formally designated goals or rhetorical statements about the meaning of their activities and programs. However, we would argue that whatever these goals are proclaimed to be, once a social movement organization has been established its primary concern becomes its own survival. Two implications follow from this observation. First, practically speaking, this means that the movement focuses its energies upon and accommodates itself to those groups upon which it relies most for mobilization of crucial resources. In the case of world-transforming movements like the UM, which rely on persuasion as a strategy and which expect to play a major role in producing social change, the movement's membership base is its most important source of support. Members are volunteers who commit all of their time, energy, and personal resources to the movement and who mobilize the key resources (i.e., new members, money, visibility/legitimacy) that insure the movement's survival and growth. (As Chapter 7 pointed out, the intense commitment fostered in a communal setting is the most fundamental resource upon which the movement draws.) Beyond its immediate membership the next greatest effort is focused on those groups in the larger society that have the greatest potential to facilitate or inhibit the movement's mobilization (e.g., the UM placed great emphasis on influencing political, intellectual, and religious leaders as well as the media). Individual members of the larger society who hold no relevance to the organization's survival and/or development are accorded relatively low priority (except as they show high potential for becoming part of the former two groups), the movement's universalistic rhetoric notwithstanding.

254 "MOONIES" IN AMERICA

It might be argued that in small movements lacking visibility, members and adequate finances that these priorities simply reflect their extremely limited resource base. However, we would contend that growth of the movement does not alter these priorities. As the movement expands in size the cost of maintaining it increases. There is a limited demand for whatever "commodity" (e.g., message, product, or service) that the movement offers. Following this market/exchange analogy, there are two possible avenues of movement expansion. The first avenue is to attempt to exploit fully the limited "market" to which the movement addresses itself. However, the cost of reaching additional "consumers" increases as those most readily available are contacted first and succeeding consumers are more difficult and expensive to reach. For example, there is presumably a limit to the number of charitable dollars available to "Christian Youth Groups." As the proportion of available dollars obtained by the movement increases, the amount of time, energy, and personnel required to gather the rest also increases. (This was also evident in Chapter 6 as the UM was forced to spend larger and larger sums of money to attract smaller audiences as the movement began to exhuast its "audience appeal" in major metropolitan centers and moved on to smaller, more remote communities.) Second, the movement may seek to broaden the market to which it appeals, but this implies offering more, or a greater diversity of, "commodities." To do this then entails greater expense as well as the potential danger of drifting away from its unique appeal for its original consumers. In sum, despite growth in the aggregate size of movement resources, the cost of operation increases in roughly corresponding fashion. This means that growth does not usually entail "surplus" resources and hence the vast majority of resources continues to be directed to those groups which ensure organizational survival and development.

Second, what appears to be "transformative activity" in the sense of creating a social order based on utopian principles can be better understood as "revolutionary activity" in the sense of increasing organizational power with the objective of replacing one regime with another. The fact that at some point the movement might choose accommodation rather than pursuing hegemony does not obviate this point as the movement is simply accepting a less dominant power position. (This is an organizational analysis and is not to suggest that transformative fervor does not exist or that such sentiments do not sometimes provide an impetus for various organizational activities. Certainly the movement mobilizes discontent; further, preexisting discontent often is created or accentuated within the movement. As individuals participate in communal groups both personally experiencing the confirmatory evidence that the idealized lifestyle is in fact possible and suffering the indifference or apathy of larger society, fervor may well increase. Still, individuals' transformative fervor does not adequately account for organizational activity and policy.) As we have already noted, even at an early stage of development the movement's primary emphasis is on gaining organizational resources. As the chapters in Part II of this book illustrated, during the early 1970s the UM directed virtually all of its efforts to establishing communal solidarity, recruiting, fund-raising, and gaining visibility/legitimacy. The few additional activities the movement undertook were aimed almost exclusively at influencing decision makers as a means of building political support. Ostensibly civic projects (e.g., local beautification, antipornography demonstrations, support for human rights) were largely designed either to increase internal solidarity or to improve the group's public image, both of which were related to building organizational strength.

Later activities of world-transforming movements reveal the same pattern. Once a movement has proceeded beyond the stage of cult/communalism and began to implement bureaucratic principles, the type and scale of organizational activity change but the pragmatic objectives remain building organizational power and stability. The search for more reliable sources of income (e.g., the UM's preference for movement-owned businesses over street solicitation), more stable recruitment base (e.g., the UM's gradual movement toward forming families and rearing children), viable careers within the movement (e.g., the UM's establishment of the seminary, newspaper and fishing industry) all reflect changing organizational exigencies. These needs in turn are largely a function of the movement's larger size, the changing social class, mean age and so forth of its membership, and the larger fixed expenses incurred as a result of its investments and expansions. Indeed, the very act of creating bureaucratic organization undermines the communal solidarity on which the lifestyle envisioned in the transformative ideology is predicated. Communal organization by its very nature assumes a small group and limited formal structure. Attempting to generalize this model and institutionalize it on a macrobasis inevitably destroys its very essence. Thus, there is an inescapable irony in the fact that the necessary process of moving from communal to bureaucratic organization shifts a world-transforming movement's goals from "transformative" to "revolutionary" and in doing so proves ultimately self-defeating to the movement's original inspiration.

CONCLUDING REMARKS

What the future holds for the UM is difficult to project. Some observers (e.g., Lofland, 1977: Epilogue) have suggested that faced with continuing

harassment it will retreat into relatively self-sustaining communities; others
see it becoming just another denomination, with the Mormons being the
most commonly cited analogue. In our personal interviews during 1978
with the American UM's highest leaders they themselves suggested the
latter parallel. The UM itself has evoked the accommodationist imagery in
public statements, and its efforts along those lines between 1976 and 1978
give some credence to that hypothesis. However, there are numerous
factors which will operate to influence future directions of the movement,
the impact of which we have little ability to foresee. For example, the
climate of the times may change sufficiently to reduce the UM's attractiveness to the young and either dramatically reduce its size and vitality or
alter the age composition of its membership substantially. Further, there
continue to be strains toward factionalism in the movement. How cohesive
the UM will be once Moon has turned over the mantle of leadership to
some as of yet undisclosed successor remains an open question. Finally,
the movement's ability to achieve status as a conventional religion, even if
it desires to do so, is problematic. Events such as the tragic deaths of over
900 cultists in Jonestown, Guyana at the end of 1978 and public suspicion
of UM members as potential suicidal zealots dramatically demonstrated
the vulnerability of new religious groups to contemporary events in which
they are neither directly involved nor which they control.

   In ending this book we have one personal note to offer. That the UM
could be analyzed and understood by organizational concepts, whatever
the latters' limitations in the eyes of partisans for and against the movement, should come as no major surprise to social scientists, but it may be
of some potential significance to legislators and policy makers who continue to be bombarded with citizens' demands to investigate, restrict, or
even outlaw cults such as the UM because of their alleged "seductive,"
"menacing," or "mysterious" powers. Between the champions of civil
liberties and innovative religions in one camp, and exasperated, angry
parents and ex-cult members in the other, intense, sometimes ugly confrontations have occurred and will likely persist indefinitely. It is a conflict
that has been contained at times only by the restraining arm of the law
and one that has been rife with all the stereotyping and hysterical atrocity
stories normally associated with the worst of wartime propaganda. As
researchers we have had the opportunity to establish contacts, friendships,
and confidences in both camps, "Moonie" and anticultist. In many cases
we have tested the validity of numerous allegations against each side only
to find them severely wanting. For the sake of those on both sides whom
we count as friends, and for ourselves as citizens, we will be pleased at
whatever moderation this volume is able to introduce into an already
fierce and sometimes tragic debate.

REFERENCES

Aberle, D. (1966) The Peyote Religion Among the Navaho. Chicago: Aldine.

Allan, V. (1975) "Korean evangelist buys in Booneville." The Press Democrat. Santa Rosa, California (August 29).

American Civil Liberties Union [ACLU] (1977) "Memorandum RE: Kidnapping people from religious groups." February 16. New York: ACLU Church-State Committee.

Alliance for the Preservation of Religious Liberty [APRL] (1977) Deprogramming: Documenting the Issue. New York: APRL.

Ayella, M. (1975) "An analysis of current conversion practices of followers of Reverend Sun Myung Moon." (unpublished manuscript)

Barker, E. (1978) "Living the Divine Principle: inside the Reverend Sun Myung Moon's Unification Church in Britain." Archives de Sciences Sociales des Religions 45/1(Janvier-Mars): 75-93.

Basham, T. (1973) "West: Rev. Moon." Performance (October 26-November 1): 4ff.

Bell, D. (1976) The Cultural Contradictions of Capitalism. New York: Basic Books.

Bellah, R.N. (1976) "New religious consciousness and the crisis in modernity," pp. 333-352 in C.Y. Glock and R.N. Bellah (eds.) The New Religious Consciousness. Berkeley: University of California Press.

——— (1967) "Civil religion in America." Daedalus 96(Winter): 1-21.

Berton, P. (1965) The Comfortable Pew. New York: J.B. Lippincott.

Bjornstad, J. (1976) The Moon is Not the Son. Minneapolis, MN: Bethany Fellowship.

Bromley, D.G. and A.D. Shupe, Jr. (1979) " 'Just a few years seem like a lifetime': A role theory approach to participation in religious movements," forthcoming in Louis Kriesberg (ed.) Research in Social Movements, Conflict, and Change Greenwich, CT: JAI Press.

Bromley, D.G. and A.D. Shupe, Jr. (1980) "Evolving foci in participant observation: research as an emergent process" in W. Shaffer, A. Turowetz and R. Stebbins (eds.) The Social Experience of Field Work. New York: St. Martins Press (forthcoming).

Bromley, D.G., A.D. Shupe, Jr., and J.C. Ventimiglia (1979) "The role of ancedotal atrocities in the social construction of evil," forthcoming in J.T. Richardson (ed.) The Deprogramming Controversy: Sociological, Psychological, Legal, and Historical Perspectives.

California (1974) Registration Form, Registry of Charitable Trusts. Sacramento, California: Office of the Attorney General.

––– (1973) Periodic Report to the Attorney General of California. Sacramento, California: Registry of Charitable Trusts.

––– (1972) Registration Form, Registry of Charitable Trusts. Sacramento, California: Office of the Attorney General.

Citizens Freedom Foundation [CFF] (1976a) News 3(January). Chula Vista, CA.

––– (1976b) News 3(February-March). Chula Vista, CA.

––– (1975) News 2(May). Chula Vista, CA.

Citizens Freedom Foundation [CFF] (1974) News 1(November). Chula Vista, California.

Clark, J.G. (1976) "Investigating the effects of some religious cults on the health welfare of their converts." (Testimony of John G. Clark, Jr., M.D., to the Special Investigating Committee of the Vermont Senate) Arlington, TX: National Ad Hoc Committee Engaged in Freeing Minds.

Coser, L. (1974) Greedy Institutions. New York: Free Press.

Cox, H. (1977) Turning East. New York: Charles Scribners.

Dornbusch, S.M. (1955) "The military academy as an assimilating institution." Social Forces 33(May): 316-321.

Ellwood, Jr., R.S. (1974) The Eagle and the Rising Sun. Philadelphia, PA: Westminster Press.

Enroth, R.M. (1977) Youth, Brainwashing and the Extremist Cults. Kentwood, MI: Zondervan.

Etzioni, A. (1961) A Comparative Analysis of Complex Organizations. New York: Free Press.

Flacks, R. (1971) Youth and Social Change. Chicago: Markham.

Friedenberg, E. (1965) Coming of Age in America. New York: Random House.

Galanter, M., R. Robkin, J. Rabkin, and A. Deutch (1978) "The 'Moonies,' a psychological study: Conversion and membership in the Unification Church." Paper presented at the annual meeting of the American Psychiatric Association. Atlanta, GA.

Gamson, W.A. (1975) The Strategy of Social Protest. Homewood, IL: Dorsey.

Glock, C.Y. (1976) "Consciousness among contemporary youth: An interpretation," pp 353-366 in C.Y. Glock and R.N. Bellah (eds.) The New Religious Consciousness. Berkeley: University of California Press.

Glock, C.Y. and R.N. Bellah [eds.] (1976) The New Religious Consciousness. Berkeley: University of California Press.

Glock, C.Y. and R. Stark (1965) Religion and Society in Tension. Chicago: Rand McNally.

Goodman, P. (1960) Growing Up Absurd. New York: Random House.

Grossman, J.C. (1978) "The cult victim: A forensic case of competency." Paper presented at the annual meeting of the Philadephia Society of Clinical Psychologists. Philadelphia, PA.

Hadden, J.K. (1970) The Gathering Storm in the Churches. Garden City, NY: Doubleday.

Heenan, E.F. [ed.] (1973) Mystery, Magic and Miracle: Religion in a Post-Aquarian Age. Englewood Cliffs, NJ: Prentice-Hall.

Hefley, J.C. (1977) The Youth Nappers. Wheaton, IL: SP Publications.

Helander, W.J. v. T. Patrick, Jr. et al. (1976) "Memorandum of decision in re Helander vs. Patrick, Jr." Superior Court, Fairfield, New York. September 8, 1976. No. 15-90-62.

Hine, V. (1974) "The deprivation and disorganization theories of social movements," pp. 646-661 in I.I. Zaketsky and M.P. Leone (eds.) Religious Movements in Contemporary America. Princeton, NJ: Princeton University Press.

Hodges, S. and M.D. Bryant (1978) Exploring Unification Thought. New York: The Edwin Mellen Press.

Holy Spirit Association for the Unification of World Christianity [HSA-UWC] (1977) Divine Principle. Condensed Version. Washington, D.C.

——— (1977) "The Unification Church national policy on fundraising." Revised, March 3. New York: HSA-UWC.

——— (1976) "An interview with Reverend Sun Myung Moon." (Reprinted from Newsweek International, June 14, 1976).

——— (1973) Divine Principle. Original English-language edition. Washington, D.C.

Horowitz, I.L. (1977) "Science, sin, and sponsorship." The Atlantic Monthly 239(March): 98-102.

Hunter, E. (1953) Brainwashing in Red China: The Calculated Destruction of Men's Minds. New York: Vanguard.

Hunter, E. (1962) Brainwashing: From Pavlov to Powers. New York: Bookmailer.

Individual Freedom Foundation [IFF] (1978) News. February 16. Pittsburgh, PA.

Individual Freedom Foundation Educational Trust, Southwest [IFFET, SW] (1978) Regional Memo. January. Dallas, TX.

International Reeducation Foundation [IRF] (1969) Prospectus for the Establishment of the International Re-Education Foundation. San Francisco: Unification Church.

Jonas, H. (1963) The Gnostic Religion. Boston: Beacon Press.

Jones, W.F. [ed.] (1974) As Others See Us. Washington, D.C.: The Holy Spirit Association for the Unification of World Christianity.

Kanter, R.M. (1972a) Commitment and Community. Cambridge, MA: Harvard University Press.

——— (1972b) "Commitment and the internal organization of millennial movements." American Behavioral Scientist 16(November/December): 219-243.

Kaplan, H. and Mrs. H. Kaplan (1978) "Our experience with a cult." Paper presented at the annual meeting of the Philadelphia Society of Clinical Psychologists. Philadelphia, PA.

Kelley, D. (1972) Why Conservative Churches Are Growing. New York: Harper & Row.

Kelley, D.M. (1977) "Deprogramming and religious liberty." The Civil Liberties Review 4(July/August): 32-33.

Kenniston, K. (1971) Youth and Dissent: The Rise of a New Opposition. New York: Harcourt Brace Jovanovich.

——— (1965) The Uncommitted: Alienated Youth in American Society. New York: Dell.

Killian, L. (1965) "Social movements," pp. 426-455 in R. Faris (ed.) Handbook of Modern Sociology. Chicago: Rand McNally.

Kim, B. (1976) "Conversion and faith maintenance: The case of the Unification Church of Rev. Sun Myung Moon." Paper presented at the annual meeting of the Society for the Scientific Study of Religion. Philadelphia, PA.

Kim, D. S. C. (1977) Day of Hope. vols. 1 and 2. New York: Unification Church.

Kim, Y.O. (1975) Unification Theology and Christian Thought. New York: Golden Gate.

Kornhauser, W. (1962) "Social bases of political commitment: A study of liberals and radicals," pp. 321-339 in A.M. Rose (ed.) Human Behavior and Social Processes. Boston: Houghton Mifflin.

Lifton, R.J. (1963) Thought Reform and the Psychology of Totalism. New York: W.W. Norton.

——— (1957) "Thought reform of Chinese intellectuals: A psychiatric evaluation." Journal of Social Issues 13: 5-20.

Lofland, J. (1977) Doomsday Cult. (enlarged edition). New York: Irvington.

——— (1966) Doomsday Cult. Englewood Cliffs, NJ: Prentice-Hall.

Lutheran Campus Ministries Program [LCMP] (1977) The Cults: A Resource Packet. Chicago: Lutheran Council in the USA.

Lynch, F.R. (1977) "Field research and future history: problems posed for ethnographic sociologists by the 'Doomsday Cult' making good." American Sociologist 12: 80-88.

McCarthy, J. and M.N. Zald (1977) "Resource mobilization in social movements: A partial theory." American Journal of Sociology 82(May): 1212-1239.

——— (1974) "Tactical considerations in social movement organizations." Paper presented at the annual meeting of the American Sociological Association. Montreal, Canada.

McFarland, H.N. (1967) The Rush Hour of the Gods. New York: MacMillan.

McHugh, P. (1966) "Social disintegration as a requisite of resocialization." Social Forces 44(March): 355-362.

Marks, E.S. (1978) " 'Religious' cults use brainwashing." Paper presented at the annual meeting of the Philadelphia Society of Clinical Psychologists. Philadelphia, PA.

Marks, J.D. (1974) "Shadows on Rev. Moon's beams." Chicago Tribune.

Master Speaks [MS-416] (1974) "Parents day, 1974." Jackson, Mississippi: HSA-UWC.

——— [MS-314] (1973) "God's day midnight address." January 1. Tarrytown, New York: Unification Church.

——— [MS-300] (1972) "Opening of the training session." Washington, D.C.: HSA-UWC.

——— [MS-7] (1971a) "History of the Unification Church." December 27-29. Parts I-III. Washington, D.C.: HSA-UWC.

——— [MS-7] (1971b) "How God is pursuing His restoration providence." December 22. Washington, D.C.: HSA-UWC.

——— [MS-7] (1971c) "Divine providence and the turning point of history." Washington, D.C.: HSA-UWC.

——— [MS-7] (1971d) "What the Unification Church is trying to solve after taking the responsibility of Jesus on earth." December 26. Washington, D.C.: HSA-UWC.

——— [MS-7] (1965) "On Bible interpretation." Washington, D.C.: Unfication Church.

——— [MS-1] (1965) "On the Lord of the Second Advent." Parts 1 and 3. Washington, D.C.: Unification Church.

Matza, D. (1961) "Subterranean traditions of youth." The Annals 338(November): 103-118.

Mead, S. (1975) The Nation with the Soul of a Church. New York: Harper Forum Books.

Meerloo, J. (1956) The Rape of the Mind. New York: World.

Merritt, J. (1975) "Open letter." Lincoln, MA: Return to Personal Choice, Inc. (pamphlet)

Mills, C.W. (1959) The Sociological Imagination. New York: Grove.

Moon, S.M. (1976) "America and God's Will." Speech delivered at the Washington Monument Rally, September 18, 1976.

——— (1974) "God's hope for America," pp. 39-67 in Bo Hi Park (ed.) Christianity in Crisis: New Hope. New York: HSA-UWC.

——— (1973) "America in God's providence," pp. 59-66 in R. Salonen (ed.) New Hope: Twelve Talks by Sun Myung Moon. New York: HSA-UWC.

Moos, F. (1967) "Leadership and organization in the Olive Tree movement." The New Religions of Korea (Transactions of the Royal Asiatic Society, Korea Branch) 43: 11-27.

Neal, A.A. (1970) "Conflict and the functional equivalence of social movements." Sociological Focus 3(Spring): 3-12.

Needleman, J. (1972) The New Religions. New York: Pocketbooks.

Oberschall, A. (1973) Social Conflict and Social Movements. Englewood Cliffs, NJ: Prentice-Hall.

O'Dea, Thomas (1961) "Five dilemmas in the institutionalization of religion." Journal for the Scientific Study of Religion 1(October): 30-39.

Patrick, T. and T. Dulack (1976) Let Our Children Go! New York: E.P. Dutton.

Prichard, A. (1977) "Response to kidnapping and deprogramming efforts." (American Civil Liberties Union Memo to the ACLU Affiliates). New York.

Reich, C. (1970) The Greening of Ameica. New York: Random House.

Richardson, J.T. (1974) "The Jesus movement: An assessment." Listening: Journal of Religion and Culture 9(Autumn): 20-42.

Robbins, T., D. Anthony, and M. Doucas, and T. Curtis (1976) "The last civil religion: Reverend Moon and the Unification Church." Sociological Analysis 37(Summer): 111-125.

Robbins, T., D. Anthony, and J. Richardson (1978) "Theory and research on today's 'new religions'." Sociological Analysis 39(2): 95-122.

Roberts, J. (1978) "Happiness ginseng from earth-conquering Moonies." Far Eastern Economic Review (June 23): 58-60.

Ross, A. (1976) "We wish you a Merry Moonmas?" The Berkeley Barb. Berkeley, California.

Salonen, N.A. (1976) "A statement by Neil Albert Salonen, President, Unification Church of America." January 12. New York: HSA-UWC.

Sargent, W. (1957) Battle for the Mind. New York: Doubleday.

Segger, J. and P. Kuntz (1972) "Conversion: evaluation of a step-like process for problem-solving." Review of Religious Research 13(Spring): 178-184.

SGR (1975) Science and Government Report 5(August 1): 1ff.

Shupe, Jr., A.D. and D.G. Bromley (1978) "Some continuities in American religion: witches, moonies, and accusations of evil." Paper presented at the annual meeting of the Association for the Scientific Study of Religion, Southwest.

Shupe, Jr., A.D. and D.G. Bromley (1979) "Walking a tightrope: participant observation among groups in conflict." unpublished manuscript)

Shupe, Jr., A.D., R. Spielmann, and S. Stigall (1977a) "Deprogramming and the emerging American anti-cult movement." Paper presented at the annual meeting of the Society for the Scientific Study of Religion.

——— (1977b) "Deprogramming: The new exorcism." American Behavioral Scientist 20: 941-956.

Smelser, N. (1962) Theory of Collective Behavior. New York: Free Press.

Sontag, F. (1977) Sun Myung Moon and the Unification Church. Nashville, TN: Abingdon.

Sorensen, T.C. (1966) Kennedy. New York: Bantam Books.

Stoner, C. and J.A. Parke (1977) All God's Children. Radnor, PA: Chilton.

Sudo, K. (1975) The 120-Day Training Manual. Belvedere, NY: HSA-UWC.

Syn-duk, D. (1967) "Korea's Tong-Il movement." The New Religions of Korea (Transactions of the Royal Asiatic Society, Korea Branch) 43: 167-180.

Taylor, D. (1978) "The social organization of recruitment in the Unification Church." Master's thesis, University of Montana.

Thomsen, H. (1963) The New Religions of Japan. Rutland, VT: Charles E. Tuttle.

Turner, R.H. (1970) "Determinants of social movement strategies," pp. 146-164 in T. Shibutani (ed.) Human Nature and Collective Behavior. Englewood Cliffs, NJ: Prentice-Hall.

Uhlmann, M.M. (1976) Letter of Michael M. Uhlmann, assistant attorney general, to Honorable Robert Dole, Senator. February 17 (copy provided in personal correspondence with authors).

Ungerleider, J.T. and D.K. Wellisch (1978a) "Coercive persuasion (brainwashing), religious cults, and deprogramming: A study of the phenomena." Paper presented at the annual meeting of the American Psychiatric Association. Atlanta, GA.

––– (1978b) "Cultism, thought control and deprogramming–observations on a phenomenon." Unpublished manuscript.

U.S. Government (1978) Investigation of Korean-American Relations. Report of the Subcommittee on International Organizations of the Committee on International Relations, U.S. House of Representatives. Washington, D.C.: U.S. Government Printing Office.

Wallis, R. (1978) "The rebirth of the gods?" Reprinted inaugural lecture delivered before the Queen's University of Belfast, Northern Ireland.

––– (1975) "Societal reaction to scientology: a study in the sociology of deviant religion," pp. 86-116 in R. Wallis (ed.) Sectarianism: Analyses of Religious Sects. London: Peter Owen.

Warder, M.Y. (1978) Another Watchdog. New York: News World Communications.

Wattenberg, B.J. (1976) The Real America. New York: G.P. Putnam's.

Weber, M. (1964) The Theory of Social and Economic Organization. New York: Free Press.

Welles, C. (1976) "The eclipse of Sun Myung Moon." New York Magazine (September 27): 33-38.

West, W. (1975) "In defense of deprogramming." Arlington, Texas: International Foundation for Individual Freedom.

Wilson, B.R. (1959) "An analysis of sect development." American Sociological Review 24(February): 3-15.

Wilson, J. (1978) Religion in American Society, The Effective Presence. Englewood Cliffs, NJ: Prentice-Hall.

––– (1973) Introduction to Social Movements. New York: Basic Books.

Wuthnow, R. (1978) Experimentation in American Religion. Berkeley: University of California Press.

––– (1976) "The new religions in social context," pp. 267-293 in C.Y. Glock and R.N. Bellah (eds.) The New Religious Consciousness. Berkeley: University of California Press.

Yamamoto, J.I. (1977) The Puppet Master. Downers Grove, IL: InterVarsity Press.

Yamamoto, J.I. (1976) The Moon Doctrine. Downers Grove, IL: InterVarsity Press.

Yankelovitch, D. (1974) The New Morality: A Profile of American Youth in the 70's. New York: McGraw-Hill.

Zald, M.N. and R. Ash (1973) "Social movement organizations: Growth, decay, and change," pp. 80-101 in R.R. Evans (ed.) Social Movements: A Reader and Source Book. Chicago: Rand McNally.

Zald, M.N. and M.A. Berger (1978) "Social movements in organizations: coup d'etat, insurgency, and mass movements." American Journal of Sociology 83(January): 823-861.

Zygmunt, J.F. (1972) "Movements and motives: Some unresolved issues in the psychology of social movements." Human Relations 25(November): 449-487.

INDEX

ABOUT THE AUTHORS

David G. Bromley received his Ph.D. in 1971 from Duke University, specializing in political and urban sociology. After serving on the faculty of the University of Virginia for six years he moved to the University of Texas at Arlington where he is currently an associate professor of sociology. His primary research interests are in the areas of social movements, deviance, and political and urban sociology. Professor Bromley has authored numerous articles which have appeared in journals such as *Journal of Health and Social Behavior, Phi Delta Kappan, Social Forces, Society,* and *The Canadian Review of Sociology and Anthropology.* He also coedited *White Racism and Black Americans.*

Anson D. Shupe, Jr. received his Ph.D. in 1975 from Indiana University, specializing in comparative political sociology. After teaching one year at Alfred University he moved to the University of Texas at Arlington where he is currently associate professor of sociology. His primary research interests are in the areas of social movements, sociology of religion, and political sociology. Professor Shupe has authored numerous articles which have appeared in such journals as *Social Forces, The Journal for the Scientific Study of Religion, Comparative Political Studies,* and *The Journal of Communications.* He is currently engaged in long-range study of social movements and societal response with coauthor David Bromley.